American Girls and Global Responsibility

American Girls and Global Responsibility

A New Relation to the World during the Early Cold War

JENNIFER HELGREN

RUTGERS UNIVERSITY PRESS

NEW BRUNSWICK, CAMDEN, AND NEWARK, NEW JERSEY, AND LONDON

Library of Congress Cataloging-in-Publication Data
Names: Helgren, Jennifer, 1972– author.
Title: American girls and global responsibility : a new relation to
the world during the early Cold War / Jennifer Helgren.
Description: New Brunswick, New Jersey : Rutgers University Press,
[2017] | Includes bibliographical references and index.
Identifiers: LCCN 2016025800| ISBN 9780813575797 (cloth) | ISBN
9780813575810 (ePub) | ISBN 9780813575827 (PDF)
Subjects: LCSH: Teenage girls—Political activity—United States—History—20th
century. | Youth—Political activity—United States—History—20th century. | Girls—
United States—Societies and clubs—History—20th century. | Sex role—Political
aspects—United States—History—20th century. | Responsibility—Political aspects—
United States—History—20th century. | Citizenship—United States—History—
20th century. | Internationalism—Social aspects—United States—History—20th
century. | Cold War—Social aspects—United States—History. | United States—Foreign
relations—1945–1953. | United States—Foreign relations—1953–1961. | BISAC: SOCIAL
SCIENCE / Women's Studies. | HISTORY / United States / 20th Century. | POLITICAL
SCIENCE / Public Policy / Cultural Policy. | SOCIAL SCIENCE / Children's Studies.
Classification: LCC HQ798 .H437 2017 | DDC 320.40835—dc23
LC record available at https://lccn.loc.gov/2016025800

A British Cataloging-in-Publication record for this
book is available from the British Library.

♾ The paper used in this publication meets the requirements
of the American National Standard for Information Sciences—
Permanence of Paper for Printed Library Materials, ANSI Z39.48-1992.

www.rutgersuniversitypress.org

Manufactured in the United States of America

CONTENTS

American Girls and Global Responsibility

Introduction

"Encouraging Friendships between the Girls of All Nations"

Teenagers, especially teenage girls, have often been regarded as frivolous. Few have considered them worthy of weighty issues such as citizenship and international diplomacy. Teenage girls have begged to differ. In 1947, a Missouri girl offended by the way the popular girls' magazine *Seventeen* depicted her peers wrote to the editors to complain: "You say your stories depict typical teen-agers. If so, heaven help us! You make us sound like heathenish creatures with no thought beyond boys and clothes. Actually, we're interested in the world crisis, international relations, labor situations, racial and religious tolerance and political affairs, and many of our hen parties are spent in discussing these very things."[1] *American Girls and Global Responsibility* takes the Missouri teen seriously and argues that a new internationalist citizenship role for girls took root in the United States in the years following World War II in girls' organizations such as the Camp Fire Girls, the Girl Scouts, and the Y-Teens of the Young Women's Christian Association (YWCA); in schools; and in magazines like *Seventeen*.

This book examines the post–World War II lessons about world friendship and peace that appeared in mainstream girls' organizations as educators and youth leaders sought to reduce conflict in the atomic age and contribute to an image of the United States as a benevolent global leader. Despite the association with frivolity, adults did identify girls with the work of building international friendships. President Harry S. Truman congratulated the Camp Fire Girls on their fortieth anniversary in 1950, calling on girls to play a broader role in advancing world friendship. "The task of stimulating international goodwill does not fall to adults alone," he declared. "The vigor and inspiration of young people who will face tomorrow's problems are also required."[2]

Youth organizations, schools, and media had already initiated the foreign aid, pen pal exchanges, and education about the United Nations that Truman invited. The 1945 Camp Fire project, "Make Democracy Mine," emphasized intercultural and international understanding. The Girl Scouts of the USA dedicated their first anniversary celebration after the war to "world citizenship" and asked girls and leaders to "build world friendship and peace" through specific projects to rehabilitate war-torn areas.[3] Schoolchildren and youth organization members wrote to pen pals, participated in "sister-school" and "sister-club" affiliations, and read about the United Nations and girls in other parts of the world in *Seventeen* and youth organization periodicals. As one historian writes, no mainstream "school or club program was complete without at least one United Nations or world-affairs event."[4]

Adults urged young people to learn about and actively shape the postwar world they were inheriting, and many young people in the 1940s and 1950s took this charge seriously. As Truman's words show, youth internationalism—the awareness of the interconnectedness of people globally, knowledge of different cultures, duty to those beyond national borders, and international cooperation—carried broad adult support, from the president of the United States to youth organizers and many in between. As part of the nation's newfound global leadership, adults taught girls and boys about U.S. strength and privilege and the duty of the country's young people to foster world friendship. Internationalist youth culture, mainstream U.S. educational goals, and the U.S. government converged to create and market the internationalist girl citizen.

Part of the growing exploration of the ways that Cold War politics and American culture were intertwined in the 1940s and 1950s, this book sheds new light on how age and gender work together to form categories of citizenship and their intersection with foreign diplomacy. Girls' studies has examined the gender contradictions of the postwar period, illuminating how girls were pulled between traditional claims of the family and eventual marriage as embodied in the feminine mystique and the lure of careers, consumer culture, and their peer culture's claims to teen independence.[5] Scholars, however, are just beginning to explore the ways that foreign relations have been the province of children and youth.[6] In peace studies, research acknowledges youth involvement in nonviolent action and peace education programs and extends the field's simplistic model in which boys figure as perpetrators of violence and girls appear as its victims.[7] Important studies by historians Naoko Shibusawa and Sara Fieldston focus on familial metaphors as well as children's images of dependence to show how "pre existing ideologies about gender and maturity" play a role in foreign relations. Such images "made it easier [for Americans] to humanize the Japanese" after World War II and offer benevolent aid to a dependent in need of guidance. Child sponsorship offered a family-like relationship through which ordinary Americans sought to foster international friendship and secure world peace.[8]

Although young people—especially girls—have rarely had direct access to formal political channels for peace building, *American Girls and Global Responsibility* contextualizes indirect pathways—pen pal correspondence, learning about girls in other countries, and sending "party kits" and magazines along with reconstruction supplies—through which girls added their voices to those shaping local and global peace. Tammy M. Proctor's, Marcia Chatelain's, and Mary Rothschild's studies of Girl Scouts and Girl Guides have begun to chart this history, revealing the uneven results of travel and exchange to produce mutual understanding.[9]

This book revises the periodization of youth internationalism. A reemergence of internationalism, especially among young people in the United States, is commonly associated with John F. Kennedy's appeal "Ask not what your country can do for you, ask what you can do for your country" and with the establishment of the Peace Corps in 1961.[10] Recent scholarship on Cold War childhoods also argues that, in the late 1950s and early 1960s, a new Cold War kid, "an activist for the promotion of government-led peace around the world," appeared along with the establishment of Dwight D. Eisenhower's People-to-People and Kennedy's Peace Corps.[11] Although this periodization may be accurate for schools and boys' organizations, girls' organizations had continued all along to offer unique spaces for the articulation of a world citizenship based on personal relationships, even if only by post. They did so despite anticommunists and isolationists, who coupled internationalism with subversive politics and attacked the Girl Scouts and Y-Teens directly. Rather than disappear, internationalism was modified and absorbed into the People-to-People campaign and the Peace Corps. Many girls embraced the broadened citizenship role that internationalism offered them, casting aside negative portrayals of frivolous teen culture.

Girls' institutions and agencies incorporated the human rights ideals outlined in the Four Freedoms of the Atlantic Charter and the United Nations Charter and, fearful of a third world war, cultivated an international ethic that promoted U.S. moral authority abroad and helped to legitimize U.S. power. Girls' institutions acted both alone and sometimes in collaboration with the Department of State and United States Information Agency and through military connections abroad. Just as State Department officials sent jazz musicians abroad as "ambassadors" to promote a favorable, antiracist vision of American democracy to counter Soviet propaganda, education boards, authors of juvenile literature, youth organizations, and girls' media, all of which played a role in socializing American children, promoted international contacts that favored

American aims abroad.[12] They helped shape a girls' political culture, a shared outlook fashioned by the generational experiences that situated girls as peace builders in relation to national and global power relations.[13]

International friendships responded to the needs of postwar reconstruction as well as to the Cold War confrontation with the Soviet Union. Nations rebuilt more than physical infrastructure in the postwar period. They also remade the "intangible social, emotional, and cultural infrastructure," renegotiating meanings, relationships, and structures of power.[14] Many Americans, influenced by the pragmatic experimentation of the New Deal, assumed that multilateral agencies would extend the New Deal's vision of security and economic stability to rebuild Europe, Asia, and the developing world.[15] Indeed, girl-centered agencies such as the YWCA, Girl Scouts, and Camp Fire Girls and even *Seventeen* magazine informed girls about multinational organizations and the status of all these. Youth organizations serving as consultants to the United Nations furthered the identification of girls with multilateral structures. The ideas of multinational organizations also provided language and experiences that encouraged an expanded definition of peace as involving not only the cessation of war but also cooperation, tolerance, and human rights principles that reflected the goals of women in progressive and social justice movements.

Youth organizations also served U.S. interests by offering a benign image of American power during the Cold War as the United States extended its influence in the world. Following World War II, the United States sought to reestablish international trade markets and to exert its influence within multilateral institutions and military alliances. Although youth organizations did not control these larger goals, as idealized American boys and girls, Boy Scouts and Girl Scouts offered service to the world, and girls especially symbolized the potential to connect through friendship for peace. In addition, Cold War tensions and the uncertain outcomes of liberation movements around the world gave youth organizations added reason to promote internationalism and world friendship even as they made it harder to do so. The dissolution in the postwar 1940s of independent youth organizations within newly communist countries limited internationalist aspirations to interactions with U.S. Cold War allies. Then, too, as British and French colonies, many with Scouting programs, sought independence, the language of international friendship was hard to maintain.[16]

Sources for Studying Girls' Institutions

Documents from the Girl Scouts, the Camp Fire Girls, and the YWCA Y-Teens, and such literature for girls as *Seventeen* magazine make up the most significant research sources for this book. It relies as well on textbooks and education resources, especially those pertaining to the San Francisco Unified School

District's postwar intercultural program and the White House Conferences on Children and Youth.

Not only have youth organizations archived the voices of young people and the central projects that adults formulated to train young citizens, but these organizations, as sex-segregated institutions, also offer a window into the way that girls and adults understood gendered citizenship. Therefore the multitude of youth organization publications, including handbooks, magazines for girls and leaders, plays, and pageants are the focus of research, as are internal memos and meeting records. Although adult prescriptions tell us a great deal about how girlhood was perceived, I have analyzed, whenever possible, girls' essays, stories, plays, letters, and poems printed in youth magazines, as well as scrapbooks, pen pal letters, and oral histories that reveal girls' experiences with internationalism.

These sources are especially pertinent because the postwar period saw the growth of girls' organizations, and Americans identified them with training for middle-class democratic citizenship. In the 1950s, experts and teenagers alike believed that youth clubs and organizations gave young people, who joined clubs at rates as high as 78 percent by some estimates, a sense of belonging and purpose that girded them for the adult world.[17] The number of Girl Scouts doubled after the war to top two million by 1953 and nearly four million by 1959. Membership in the smaller Camp Fire Girls also more than doubled between 1943 and 1963, reaching a membership of nearly half a million girls. The various groups' constituencies—nearly 20 percent of American girls were involved with girls' organizations in 1950—indicate how critical the groups were to shaping twentieth-century concepts of girlhood.[18]

The major twentieth-century national girls' organizations, and also the Boy Scouts, were established in the 1910s as part of a middle-class effort to protect and cultivate adolescents in an extended period of childhood.[19] These organizations served as an important bridge between the home and the public school and a place where young people could experiment with semisupervised adventure, service, and friendship. These organizations saw young people as agents, "citizens in the moment," and not merely as future citizens to be molded.[20]

Central to their missions was gender-specific training for modern, industrial, mass society. The Boy Scouts, established first in England in 1907 by Robert Baden-Powell, arrived in the United States in 1910 and, like its British counterpart, sought to protect boys from the erosive effects of overcivilization through "robust masculinity associated with the vigorous pursuit of an 'outdoor life.'" In the United States, two rival organizations, the Camp Fire Girls and the Girl Scouts, grew out of various attempts to establish a corollary for girls. Although the Girl Scouts bore the name of Baden-Powell's organization, and its founder, Juliette Gordon Low, was a close friend of the British Boy Scout founder, the American Boy Scout organizers favored the Camp Fire Girls, which they had formed in collaboration with female educators to more deliberately develop "feminine instincts and tendencies."[21]

In England many girls simply adopted *Scouting for Boys*, Robert Baden-Powell's 1908 Scouting manual, as their own. Baden-Powell soon determined that a separate institution for girls was necessary, and Agnes Baden-Powell, his sister, wrote the 1912 *Handbook for Girl Guides, or How Girls Can Help Build the Empire.* When Low started her Girl Scouts in 1912, with the likeness in name and retaining many of the badges and language of *Scouting for Boys*, American Boy Scout officials resisted her attempt to create an equal and similar organization.[22] In the United States, both organizations taught girls traditional women's roles but supplemented them with appealing outdoor adventure and civic opportunities. The Girl Scouts differed in that women designed and controlled the program, whereas Camp Fire did not have its first female director until 1944.

The YWCA USA formed in 1906, when predecessor organizations on college campuses agreed to merge to form a larger, more efficient, and more influential organization for liberal Christian ideals. It was connected to an international YWCA movement. The national YWCA soon established a girls' organization, the Girl Reserves, which was renamed Y-Teens after World War II. Like the secular Girl Scouts and Camp Fire Girls, Y-Reserves trained girls for future leadership and worked to instill wholesome values. The YWCA's explicitly Christian mission, however, meant that international Christian fellowship was stressed more than patriotism and that its social gospel dedication to "social justice and community empowerment" was international as well as local.[23]

Like the YWCA, the Girl Scouts was connected to a broader international Scouting movement. Although the Camp Fire Girls also had clubs in twenty-four countries and U.S. territories by 1923, its outreach beyond the United States and a small network of leaders and friends abroad was always small. Scouting and Guiding, however, quickly spread throughout the British Empire. In the British context, "imperial adventure" was an antidote to overcivilization for boys and important for girls, who learned to act as "comrades" and "companions" to male imperial citizens and as "moral guardians of the home."[24]

The Scouting, Guiding, and Camp Fire movements spread rapidly during World War I as a result of young people's contributions to the war efforts. In addition, following on the devastation of World War I, the thinking of Robert Baden-Powell and Scout and Guide leaders evolved from the "defensive imperialism of the prewar period" toward committed internationalism. The boys' World Organization of the Scout Movement, made up of over thirty countries, and the World Association of Girl Guides and Girl Scouts (WAGGGS), beginning with fifteen nations, were both established in the 1920s and represented the new commitment. Both emphasized League of Nations ideals, global belonging, openness and inclusiveness, and the maintenance of peace. Still British and American leaders dominated the early world movement and "egalitarian sisterhood was far from a reality in Guiding" in the 1920s. Nonetheless, aspirational goals of world sisterhood and training girls to "produc[e] universal peace and happiness" were important shifts in the self-representation and recruitment of Girl Scouts and Guides.[25]

Still, a "conflict of values" persisted in Scouting's model of citizenship education, since loyalty to one's own community and nation remained important in national branches of Scouting, and nationalism and local customs were often "incompatible with the sense of international fraternity or the principle of non-discrimination."[26] The Girl Scouts strove for balance, but the Boy Scouts in the United States leaned more definitely toward patriotic training. The world organization of Boy Scouts received mention in *Boys' Life*, the magazine for American Boy Scouts, and was introduced in the U.S. Boy Scout manual, but the proportion of material focused on the international movement as compared with national patriotism was decidedly less. The Boy Scouts of America also paid far less attention to their international movement than did the Girl Scouts of the USA.

Although boys' organizations, especially the dominant Boy Scouts of America, promoted "world brotherhood," they emphasized duties to the nation-state. The Boy Scouts of America saw itself as a character-building organization rather than one geared to military preparedness, but there were "cadet corps" at the local club level. Nationally, it "aggressively appropriated symbols of American nationalism, superimposing the American eagle on the international Scout badge, securing the U.S. President as honorary president, attiring Boy Scouts in uniforms so like the U.S. Army's that Congress had to provide exemption from laws against civilians aping the military."[27] The Boy Scouts advised its members that "Scouting carries friendship across all sorts of boundaries, across mountains, continents and oceans, across boundaries of race and religion," but it socialized boys to the norms of masculine nationalism and groomed them to be political leaders and potential warriors if war should come.[28]

The Girl Scouts' international connections produced transnational efforts to create peace and international friendship in the interwar period. WAGGGS, established in 1928, aimed "through cooperation to promote unity of purpose and common understanding in the fundamental principles of Girl Guiding and Girl Scouting throughout the world, and to encourage friendships between the girls of all nations." It provided an international network that shared ideas about Scouting, exchange services, and several international retreat sites.[29] Internationalism, then, was a core identity early in the Scouting movement for girls.

But they were also born of colonial histories and so represented those pasts. The Girl Scouts and Girl Guides were inclusive, but internationally and within nations, the norm was to accommodate national racial laws and customs, and girls usually organized in separate groups in colonial areas.[30] In British-controlled India, for example, Girl Guides were at first all the children of settlers, but by 1916 Indian girls were included in sometimes segregated and sometimes mixed groups. Colonial values, however, shaped the Guiding experience, and Guide texts emphasized the value of camp experiences to "teach Indian girls western standards of discipline and hygiene" and emancipate them from the supposed backward customs of their own cultures. Missing from these texts was information about the dispossession of the Indian land on which Guide camps were constructed. In these ways Girl Guides, even in their transnational ideal-ism, were implicated in the histories of colonialism.[31]

In the United States, youth movements also promoted racial and nationalist assumptions about citizenship, appropriating American Indian culture to sup-port nationalistic histories of American progress that masked contestation and conquest. In the Camp Fire Girls, girls dressed in Indian-like ceremonial gowns and chose Indian-sounding names in what was thought to be a reenactment of the timeless primitive feminine qualities of care for the hearth and home. At the same time, the organization recruited new members among Native American girls at boarding schools, who were then taught modern American norms of feminine decorum.[32]

In addition to youth organizations, gender-specific literature directed at girls burgeoned in the postwar period, material that also fostered international-ist youth culture and marketed the international girl citizen. With its first issue in 1944, *Seventeen* magazine, founded by Helen Valentine as a service magazine for girls, joined the *American Girl*, the Girl Scouts' monthly periodical, with a clear mission to articulate girls' roles in democracy as well as to entertain. *Seventeen* is an important source for historians of girlhood because of its broad readership as well as for the magazine's interesting mix of civic training and consumer culture. In 1945, content on service and citizenship was almost always more than 35 percent of the magazine.[33] It quickly became an important force in teenage girls' lives with over eight hundred thousand copies sold in January 1946 and topping one million monthly sales in 1961. The readership was far broader as girls shared copies with siblings and friends.

Valentine used the magazine to sponsor progressive ideals for its first six years but was pushed out by publisher Walter Annenberg, who shifted the con-tent to include more fashion, recipes, and dating advice.[34] Although the maga-zine carried less political content over time, it regularly featured articles during the immediate postwar years and through the 1950s and 1960s by professors like Michigan State University's Thomas G. Osgood and renowned journal-ists like Dickey Meyer (Chapelle). Its book review section covered politically sophisticated texts such as *One World or None* and *All the King's Men*. Its pages featured citizenship training for the postwar world. Although these lessons gave way in the 1950s to more stereotypical articles about teen culture, the internationalist girl citizen continued to appear alongside fashion and beauty advice throughout the 1950s.

Seventeen's readers were much like the girls who joined girls' organizations. Its advertising surveys in 1945 and 1947 indicated that the average *Seventeen* reader was sixteen years old, attended public high school, lived in a town or a city, and was middle to upper class. Her father could afford college for her, but she learned responsibility and participated in consumer culture with her own babysitting jobs and allowance. Articles and images presented a white middle-class girlhood, but girls from multiple racial groups wrote letters to the editor.[35]

Fiction for girls, including short stories in the *American Girl* and *Seventeen* and book series like Cherry Ames, The Bobbsey Twins, and Nancy Drew, entertained even as it opened girls' imaginations to choices and opportunities in travel, careers, and adventure.[36] Fiction for young readers grew increasingly gendered. Despite a girls' culture "seemingly centered on love, doll play, relationships, hairdressing, and grooming," girls' "magazines, movies, music, and television produced a female culture that cultivated a highly self-conscious sense of girls' importance. Girls learned they were members of a new, privileged generation whose destiny was more open and exciting than that of their mothers."[37] In *Seventeen*, especially, internationalism was treated as an important feature of an engaged girl citizen.

The International Girls' World

American girls' new relation to the world emerged in the context of the tensions of the Cold War. With the detonation of atomic bombs over Hiroshima and Nagasaki in August 1945 and with the rise of the United States as a global power, scientists, philosophers, educators, and cultural critics talked about the future in absolute terms. There would be "one world" characterized by international cooperation, international control of atomic science, "brotherhood," and peace, or there would be "none."[38] The one-world theme found broad support in U.S. schools and youth agencies as adults sought to equip young people for adulthood in a world that many adults and young people believed had been transformed.

By the late 1940s, fears of international communist domination dimmed the hopes for one world, as did the failure of the United Nations to produce an agreement on the international control of atomic weapons, the Soviet Union's detonation of its own atomic bomb, the communist revolution in China, and the outbreak of the Korean War and the United States–led UN military response. Indeed most Cold War scholarship, recognizing the existence of a window of

opportunity in the mid-1940s, regards grand hopes for international cooperation as collapsing into the Cold War. Some mark the window's closing in March
1946 with Winston Churchill's declaration that an "Iron Curtain" had descended
across Europe. Many educators and pundits shifted attention to civil defense,
self-reliance, and securing democracy at home.[39]

Educating children and teenagers about internationalism remained important, however, to how Americans viewed themselves in relation to the world.
Americans understood the day-to-day basis of global power relations in two
overlapping ways. One emphasized containment, and with it a defensive posture against the Soviet Union, virulent internal anticommunism, and the arms
race. The other, a "global imaginary of integration," borrowed from Wilsonian
internationalism to promote the ideals of reciprocal exchange and understanding as the basis for American expansion. Although its goal was integrated markets, it "generated an inclusive rather than a policing energy."[40]

Cold War internationalism combined these two strands, and popular writers and intellectuals worked through the press and educational institutions
to show Americans the significance of assuming international responsibility
given that the integration of the free world through alliances and economic
exchanges depended upon American support.[41] Although insecurity prompted
the domestic containment of girls, emphasizing their prepubescent innocence
and idealizing their protection and insulation within the family and traditional
gender roles, girlhood also provided a space for the articulation of the goals of
the global imaginary of integration. Meanwhile boys' organizations adopted the
symbols of militarization and containment.[42]

In addition, Americans were more cosmopolitan in outlook and experience in the 1940s and 1950s than the previous generation had been. Veterans
who had traveled and experienced international relationships and new cultures during the war returned with cosmopolitan outlooks that further shifted
U.S. public opinion to accommodate multilateralism.[43] In 1956, the government
estimated that two million Americans, half military, were living and traveling
abroad, a number that reflected the expansion of tourism, international business, and military bases. The Girl Scouts' Troops on Foreign Soil, American Girl
Scouts living abroad, grew tenfold from 1950 through 1958 through the increase
in military installations around the world and the growth of American business
abroad.[44] The number of American organizations concerned with international
affairs also grew. "More than five thousand separate *national* organizations in
the United States," journalist William Harlan Hale reported, "ranging from
Women United for the United Nations and the Children's Plea for Peace to the
General Motors Corporation and the [American Federation of Labor-Congress
of Industrial Organizations]," were in some way engaged with international
affairs. The primary impetus, he believed, was the recognition that isolation

was not an option and that with wealth and power came responsibility.[45] The desire to make the world friendlier and the economic wherewithal to do so made the new relation of girls to the world possible.

International student exchanges, which focused primarily on college students, similarly increased at midcentury, boosted by government support and collaborations with private agencies. U.S. students abroad and carefully chosen student visitors from foreign countries were expected to diffuse information about the United States and to legitimize the nation as a global power through positive descriptions.[46] Girls' institutions played a similar role for a younger age group.

The changing roles of women also made the expanding citizen responsibilities of girls possible. Both world wars produced surges in women's employment followed by a reduction in their employment numbers that never fully returned them to prewar lows. American women saw their involvement in government services, the armed services, and munitions production and other war industries as evidence of their patriotic commitments. Although anxieties at the end of the war about jobs for returning veterans and the effect of women's work on their ability to nurture and raise children and provide a satisfactory home life to husbands resulted in policies geared toward returning women to domestic roles, wartime activities for women and girls continued during the Cold War in civil defense organizing but also found new focus in voluntary work that included girls' citizenship training.[47]

Girlhood and the Postwar Age Cohort

This book focuses on girls from the ages of ten to seventeen, because this was the group that educators, youth leaders, and girls' magazine editors most often targeted for international activities. Age, much like gender, affects how people identify themselves and how societies conceptualize citizens' privileges and responsibilities. Definitions of childhood and girlhood fluctuate over time and across regions, cultures, and religions, and distinct postwar concepts of childhood were as crucial to the construction of the international girl citizen as was the expansion of women's service. Political and civic leaders articulated their ideas about the nation-state and political ideologies through their programs for children as they tried to mold a new generation to fit what they saw as the social and political demands of the time. In addition, advertisers developed distinct marketing to attract teenagers that also prescribed social roles.[48]

Nearly sixty-five million Americans were born between 1928 and 1950—individuals who were children and teenagers at the dawn of the atomic age. The younger ones grew up in a world with the United Nations and with the United States as an economic and military superpower. These children learned, as the popular Macmillan textbook *History of a Free People* explained, that unprecedented forces had "thrust" the United States into world leadership and that the American people were now "[willing] to take on world-wide responsibility."[49] These schoolchildren grew up with "idealistic—and propagandistic" lessons in school and from the media that depicted the United States as strong, prosperous, benevolent, and egalitarian. They reflected "ideological certainty about what the United States ought to be." Along with patriotism came school lessons that taught about American democracy and the "[eradication of] hate and other antidemocratic tendencies."[50]

Within this generation, several age cohorts took shape with unique concerns related to the bomb. Michael Scheibach calls the Americans born between 1928 and 1942 the "atomic generation." They experienced Hiroshima as school-age children and teens. They not only heard the emphasis on democracy and freedom but also absorbed the immediacy of creating peaceful solutions to the challenge of nuclear weapons. Girls born between 1928 and 1931, high school aged in 1945 and therefore socially and politically aware, heard about the optimism of the philosophers, scientists, and world leaders who anticipated that a world federation would establish peace. Those born between 1932 and 1937 approached or reached adolescence as the Cold War was intensifying, and their high school years were marked by the Korean War and civil defense campaigns. For those born after 1938, the Cold War was an established fact. This "sixties generation," those too young to remember Hiroshima but exposed to atomic narratives and civil defense drills in school, was later associated with antimilitarism, antiracism, and the desire for decolonization, ideas prominent in many of the cultural spaces children occupied in the 1950s.[51]

Postwar adults had contradictory views of adolescents. On the one hand, they saw young people as malleable, without prejudice, and uniquely capable of creating a peaceful future.[52] Their view of adolescents, on the other hand, sensationalized maladjustment—delinquency, materialism, self-centeredness, and excessive conformity. Officials in the Federal Bureau of Investigation (FBI) and Children's Bureau, youth organization leaders, and educators battled juvenile delinquency in the 1950s as acts of violence and other misbehaviors appeared to increase among teenagers of all classes. Although boys were regarded as much more likely to be maladjusted, girls, too, drew much attention for their desire to "date, dance, and drink," although youth authors and *Seventeen* regularly maintained a wholesome picture of the teenage girl as an "innocent bobbysoxer" who avoided such temptations.[53] Parents and other adults saw youth organizations as one means for channeling the anxieties and irresponsible behaviors of young people toward global friendship as well as leadership, service, spirituality, and personality adjustment within the group setting.

Adults articulated young people's social roles in terms of gender. Girls were assumed to mirror women's supposed predisposition toward peace and nurture even as they were associated with a child-specific malleability through which adults sought to shape the future. Girlhood in the context of internationalism was, moreover, associated with a freedom from prejudice that made learning about others a probable means for cultivating world understanding. To be a proper wholesome girl was to develop tolerance and understanding. Although boys were also thought to be plastic and less prejudiced than adults, boyhood was associated with toughness over close affection and self-reliance over interdependence.

Although mainstream organizations, schools, and girls' literature began to expose and challenge racial, religious, and national prejudice, girls' organizations such as the Girl Scouts and the Camp Fire Girls and even Y-Teens, where the internationalist message was strong, had a predominantly white, middle-class membership. These organizations' ideals and agendas coexisted with deep class and racial barriers to equal participation. The typical international-ist girl citizen of the 1940s and 1950s was usually white and middle class, but she challenged her prejudices. The incorporation of multicultural images and rhetorical commitments to intercultural tolerance were important, nascent changes that provided mainstream support for the civil rights movement in the 1950s and 1960s, but there remained multiple girlhoods in American society. Girls' relationships in the 1940s and 1950s, therefore, were simultaneously depicted as spaces for the exploration of fashion, boys, and dating as well as for mirroring and adding a human face to international alliances and tolerance. The global girl was not exclusive but she importantly answered Cold War concerns.

A Female Responsibility to the World

The new girl citizen borrowed from historic forms of U.S. femininity, especially Progressive Era models of maternal feminism that broadened women's roles on the basis of service to family, to carve out responsibilities in cultivating international friendships. Personal connections and nurturing relationships emerged as part of the role of girls as international citizens. As World War II drew to a close, girls' organizations in the United States reevaluated their programs and determined that girls needed a new relationship to national and international politics. The new girl citizens embraced a feminine association with service and nurture but extended these duties to the world, where they meshed with U.S. foreign policy aims. The Camp Fire Girls' postwar program, for example, recognized "profound changes in [girls'] personal and social lives in the postwar world," especially the need for "training for democratic living."[54]

Girls' organizations developed programs and addressed in their publications methods to help their young members combat prejudice within the United States, foster world friendship, and reshape the postwar world on the American democratic model, as well as learn to establish a happy home. They extended the feminine form of service to family and community, to the nation and the world. In the words of the 1956 address of Camp Fire's director of field operations, Lou B. Paine, "Home will always be the center of woman's life, but it is not her circumference. Women have come to realize that the walls of her home must expand to include the community, that the fences around communities must expand to include the whole world."[55] Activity categories in girls' organization guidebooks reflected the concentric circles of responsibility assigned to girls. The Camp Fire Girls' manual mapped girls' widening circles of civic responsibility. These began with "Myself" and extended to "My Family, My Camp Fire Group and Other Friends, My School, My Religion, My Community, My State and Country," and ended with "Our World."[56]

Girls' organizations benefited from the internationalist ethos that followed World War II and sought to establish a larger "culture of peace" that included mutual understanding, tolerance, antiracism, services for health and safety, and security from want and fear.[57] It reflected the interwar cultural gifts movement and its emphasis on cultural diversity and tolerance as an American asset appropriate to women's social and political networks.[58] Girls' institutions incorporated progressive women's language and political strategies as well as their capacious definitions of peace and security.

Girls' new relation to the world rested on essentialized feminine characteristics. Members of the Women's International League for Peace and Freedom (WILPF) and the Women's Peace Party had in the 1910s and 1920s regularly incorporated maternal metaphors and the life-giving and nurturing associations of motherhood to support their political activities. National WILPF head Anna Garlin Spencer spoke "in the name of womanhood" to argue that newly enfranchised women had a duty to sustain life through the support of a range of social welfare reforms in education, labor conditions, and the safety of women and children, all initiatives she insisted were continually threatened by men's propensity for going to war.[59]

During the Cold War, the maternal role gained a new significance, since women and families were thought to be on the front line of the atomic age. When strontium 90, a by-product of nuclear testing, appeared in the milk that mothers served to children at the breakfast table, groups like Women Strike for Peace adeptly marshaled traditionalist maternal rhetoric for the goal of nuclear disarmament.[60]

Although mainstream Cold War girls' institutions were not radical, they absorbed and articulated a definition of security much broader than national defense. Indeed they demonstrated the reach of more radical women's groups and the ongoing efforts of feminists to define security in terms of health, social welfare, and freedom from sexualized violence rather than masculine military protection. As recent scholarship illustrates, women's work to establish peace, which employed a broad definition that included social justice and security as well as feminist, labor, and antiracism goals, continued in progressive women's networks throughout the mid-twentieth century, despite the period's reactionary red scare.[61]

The global girl citizen, however, was not supposed to be a mother. Instead, girls between nine and eighteen were idealized as adolescent children with emerging heterosexual desires. The global girl citizen tapped into notions of female friendship that offered an alternative to maternalism for entry into the wider world. Friendship extended the "private" loyalties of women and girls beyond the walls of the home and family and claimed for them access to civil society. Although friendship has historically been seen as the province of men, as women's friendships were ignored, viewed as sexually suspect, or trivialized, women have had charge of nurturing human relationships and forming social networks outside the home. Through gifts and calling, women built alliances within communities and extended their claims to civil society. Not only did women use friendships to enter into the realm of international politics, but they also used familial metaphors to solidify their international friendships, referring to friends as *sisters* and *mothers*.[62]

Moreover, it is possible that political marginalization led some women to lean toward extending loyalties beyond the nation to humankind and asked girls to do the same. Until 1931, some American-born women lost their American citizenship upon marriage to foreign men. Unequal access to education and the means to earn a living persisted long into the twentieth century. As Virginia Woolf put it in *Three Guineas*: "As a woman, I have no country. As a woman I want no country. As a woman my country is the whole world." The more precarious relationship of girls and women to the nation-state made them in some ways more likely global citizens. Although mutual friendship of this sort had the potential to weaken nationalism as it produced a set of responsibilities beyond the family and country when one's loyalty was to friend rather than country, girls' institutions generally supported international efforts as a form of "intimate diplomacy" that boosted Cold War policymakers' aims.[63]

Girls' international friendship provided a vehicle for sharing the American way of life abroad and securing allies.[64] Truman picked up on the importance of personal friendships in statements he made to the three largest youth organizations in 1946. To boys and girls, he underscored the importance of "fostering good-will, understanding, and respect through continued [international]

cooperation." To the Girl Scouts, he remarked particularly on their work "cultivating personal understanding between peoples and governments as a means of
developing international friendship and good will."[65]

Although girls' roles broadened as a result of their contributions to and
awareness of the international arena, preexisting patriarchal gender patterns
supporting U.S. global economic and military power framed the discourse on
girls as citizens. The Scouts rested much less of its attention on building boys'
personal relationships. Much as Girl Scouting and Guiding emphasized the individual connections of girls to each other, Scouting for boys urged them to think
of each other in egalitarian but ultimately abstract ways as a universal brotherhood.[66] Gendered concepts such as the need to protect women (and children)
and the idealizations of tough masculinity promoted and maintained a militarized postwar culture within boys' organizations.[67] Girls were granted the
chance to be the representatives of peace.

The difference can be seen in the coverage of the United Nations in *Boys'
Life* in early 1949. At a time when the *Camp Fire Girl Bulletin* announced the
Declaration of Human Rights, the Boy Scouts of America commemorated
the launching of its "Strengthen the Arm of Liberty" campaign to "buttress the
entire organization and enable it more fully to serve the nation in its endeav-
ors for a free post-war world." The February cover featured Boy Scouts in uniform holding the flags of various UN member nations, but the article inside
told the story of a refugee boy from an unnamed communist country where
he heard of the United States on Voice of America broadcasts and now reveled
in American individual freedoms. His story served to reprimand the native-
born Scouts. "Guys, like you," the article regretted, discovered that "the newly
arrived boy knew more about the Statue of Liberty, its history and its presentation to this country, and what it symbolizes than all the rest of the Troop combined." The Boy Scouts' magazine turned such stories of international interest
into a glorification of U.S. exceptionalism.[68]

The Boy Scouts groomed boys to be potential warriors if peace should
fail. Boys were also more often groomed for national leadership, whereas girls
received instructions that subsumed international action in the language of
personal relationships, consumption, and service to families.

American Girls and Global Responsibility seeks not to idealize youth organizations of the past. Indeed, although girls' roles broadened as a result of their contributions to and awareness of the international arena, the model of females as
mothers and nurturers failed to confront the warrior-nurturer dichotomy that
supports militaristic values. Still, that girls and their organizations regularly used
the term *brotherhood* to describe international friendship showed not only the
nomenclature of the time and the linguistic exclusion of females but also girls'

insistence that they participate in creating brotherhood and that it include them. Girls meant to include themselves in the international human family when they used the word.

American Girls and Global Responsibility presents a multifaceted and complex portrait of the significance of the new concept of girl internationalist in the postwar United States. Chapter 1 sets the stage by introducing the main concerns of the atomic age and probing the gendered discourse on youth citizenship as it emerged in the postwar era. Although both boys and girls expressed fear about living in the atomic age and both were thought to be vital to the future security of the nation, girls were understood to have a new responsibility. No longer could they limit their service to the home but would need to build connections in the world. UN-related projects were a key way that girls learned about international cooperation, and girls' organizations offered its multilateral structure as a model for girls' own ties to others around the world. In the process girls were exposed to the human rights language of the international organization and were encouraged to apply its lessons at home. Although girls' organizations such as the Camp Fire Girls, the Girl Scouts, and other institutions that challenged intolerance failed to consistently behave according to their own stated ideals, the goal of combating prejudice at home worked together with internationalism to open horizons and encourage broadminded thinking about the diverse peoples of the world. Building tolerance and support for the United Nations in girls' organizations contributed to U.S. moral authority, a necessary ingredient for strengthening U.S. cultural, economic, and even military power in the Cold War era.

Chapter 2 examines the pen pal and relief package projects that were undertaken by youth organizations and schools in the immediate postwar years. It contextualizes girls' writings and sending of relief packages and gifts in the international power politics of the postwar period. Girls' letters sent abroad and the packages that went to war-ravaged Europe and Japan and to the developing world were in the same spirit as the Marshall Plan in that they were intended to provide both relief and an increase in foreign consumer desire. They fit with U.S. foreign policy, as they constituted a vision of benevolent power that the U.S. government hoped to cultivate at home and abroad. In the post–World War II period, educators and youth leaders around the world encouraged pen pal friendships as a way of reducing conflict and strengthening peace. In gendered and age-specific ways, girls' pen pal friendships were imagined as peacekeeping ventures. Pen pal relationships could open young people to new cultures and new ways of thinking. They could also accentuate asymmetrical relationships as the nation's resources and power led some U.S. girls to view the American democratic capitalism as a superior model for the world.

Although girls' organizations cautioned against creating an image of materialism in pen pal letters, youth literature and media were often unabashedly consumerist.

In Chapter 3, the exploration of prejudice extends to the postwar reconciliations with Japan and Germany. Youth media and literature, educators, and youth organizers reimagined the dehumanizing stereotypes of enemies. Japan was reimagined as a tourist destination of "fairyland gardens and richly ornamented Buddhist temples."[69] The U.S. press used feminized and infantilized images of former enemies that helped neutralize those figures. Indeed, U.S. girls and boys also encountered neutralized images of former enemies in schoolbooks and in magazines. Reports that German and Japanese gender roles were becoming more like those in the United States fed an ideal of progress along a U.S. capitalist-democratic model. Girls participated in the process of reimagining enemies. In this way, they not only served as symbols of potential peace but also articulated visions of their nations through pen pal letters and letters-to-the-editor sections of girls' magazines. American girls projected an image that was both benign and expansionist, and Japanese girls emphasized a peaceful Japan moving toward democracy.

Chapter 4 analyzes the consumerism that attended the role of girl citizens in the postwar era. Youth media such as *Seventeen* and youth organizations taught girls to buy curios and fashions from abroad to demonstrate their developing international commitment and their growing worldliness. Girls learned that females were the primary consumers in their families and that universal consumer values connected girls and women around the world. They also learned to judge other nations' progress by the degree to which adolescents could participate in a consumer economy. The consumer message, at the same time, sparked unease among those youth leaders who worried about materialism and social justice.

Chapter 5 investigates the politicization of girls' organizations in the 1950s as anticommunist forces grew more vocal in the United States. Anticommunists regularly targeted organizations supporting "world citizenship," civil rights, and peace as un-American, and right-wing conservatives sought to curtail the influence of youth organizations that supported internationalism and civil rights. When organizations asserted a world citizenship duty for girls, such groups were susceptible to the attacks of McCarthyites. Although the forces of resistance to and the limits of the internationalist model are addressed throughout the book, this chapter focuses specifically on conservative anticommunist attacks on youth organizations' internationalist ideals. The chapter explores why the attacks occurred and how youth organizations moderated their internationalist approaches in response. The chapter contends that anticommunism limited the efficacy of the internationalist vision in girls' organizations but ultimately failed to undermine its popularity among them and, more broadly, among mainstream Americans. An epilogue concludes this volume by highlighting girls' continuing international role in and beyond the 1950s. Girls' organizations tied their efforts more directly to federal projects like People-to-People and the Peace Corps, but American global actions became more contested within the United States and the popularity of girls' organizations' began to decrease.

In the United States, youth organizations and educators articulated a role for girls as global ambassadors of world friendship, which emphasized alliance building and reconciliation. Pen pals, foreign relief packages, lessons about the United Nations, and international products and fantasy tours constituted key components of girls' contributions to world politics and a new concept of girl citizenry.

1

"What Kind of World Do You Want?"

Preparing Girls for Peace and Tolerance in the Atomic Age

In 1948, a girl from Altona, Illinois, wrote a letter to *Seventeen* magazine that called for political action to deal with her fears: "Everyone talks about another war. They talk about an atom bomb with all kinds of bacteria in it." Rather than succumbing to despair, she wanted her peers to "think of all the suffering and disaster that we could prevent by spreading tolerance and brotherly love. . . . I'm willing to do all I can to help. I'm sure many of my fellow teenagers are. Couldn't we get some sort of national organization started in our schools to preserve peace?" The editor's response, typical of those from girls' magazines and organizations, pointed her to an article in the same issue about joining United Nations Youth, thus giving girls specific direction to act on their internationalist impulses, one part of preparing girls for peace and tolerance in the atomic age.[1]

After World War II, concern about the atomic bomb shaped the approaches of child experts and educators to both child rearing and education. In children's cultural spaces, images and information about the bomb were constant reminders of a possible World War III, one presented as far more destructive than any war that had come before.

Girls' organizations and media committed themselves to training their members as global citizens. Such institutions took girls more seriously than in earlier generations, treating them as world citizens and training them to play a role on the international stage. They provided them with information about atomic energy's dangers, but by also offering information about its potential for good, tried to instill hope for the future. They told girls ways they could take part in keeping themselves and the world safe; these included engaging in civil defense drills, supporting the United Nations, and increasing their inter-cultural awareness.

Although girls shared much with their male peers, girlhood was treated as a special space for the cultivation of relational solutions to global conflict. Broad training in internationalism, new leadership skills, a healthy personality, and, above all, teachings about democracy and the United Nations would help the internationalist girl citizen triumph over the dual threats of atomic war and the spread of communism. Girls themselves reflected this duality, and their creative and expository writing captured not only their pervasive fear of the bomb's destructive powers, of catastrophe and death, but also the hope that this threat to humankind might be countered through international understanding, world federation, and love.

Child Experts and the Atomic Age

Girls needed a new relation to the world because, child experts believed, they faced unprecedented stresses growing up. As Dorothy Baruch, a psychologist who specialized in juvenile delinquency, put it, "Ever since the bursting of the fearful bomb in Hiroshima, we have known that our children are facing an age different from any previous age."[2] Children and adolescents seemed prone to maladjustment, juvenile delinquency, fatalism, and inadequate self-identity formation. Citing Anna Freud's studies of evacuated British children in World War II, psychologists saw prolonged exposure to uncertainty and fear as one root of long-term psychological maladjustment. Fears and the lack of hope inherent in the inability to envision the future disrupted the psychological well-being of children and youth and threatened the very way of life Americans sought to protect.[3]

To many experts, juvenile delinquency appeared as potentially dangerous as communism or the bomb itself. As *Senior Scholastic* warned its readers, their generation's delinquent behaviors threatened to undermine the nation from within even as atomic war threatened it from without.[4] Children's Bureau reports indicate that along with other social disruptions such as the rise in crime and familial breakdown, there were marked increases in juvenile delinquency during the war, followed by a slight decline in the late 1940s, with rates again climbing after 1949. Media tended to blame permissive child-rearing practices for the perceived uptick in vandalism, shoplifting, truancy, drug and alcohol use, resistance to authority, and sexual promiscuity.[5] Many child experts, however, believed that getting to the root of delinquency and other maladjustments required addressing anxieties associated with the atomic age.

Although the degree to which atomic fears shaped daily behavior remains controversial, Gallup polls in the first decade of the Cold War showed that most

Americans (at some points as many as 70 percent) thought they would see another world war in their lifetimes, one with "a new level of horror and destruction."[6] Children also worried. Months before North Korean forces crossed into South Korea, a twelve-year-old African American Girl Scout in Seattle wrote to the president, "I hope no Americans won't have to go to war again. . . . I keep praying and saying, 'Peace on earth good will to men.'"[7] Although one canvass showed that people under thirty were slightly more optimistic than older adults, polls of young people revealed marked apprehension.[8] Regional and national surveys recorded that young people believed that their chief problem was the "draft and threat of war" (followed by "finding the right girl or boy" and family, school, and job-related concerns).[9] In the early 1960s, prior to the Cuban missile crisis, psychologist Sybil K. Escalona's research showed widespread knowledge and fear among ten- to seventeen-year-olds. In response to Escalona's open-ended questions about the future, 70 percent of the children surveyed spontaneously mentioned war or peace. One fourteen-year-old expected "either complete peace or total destruction."[10]

Training adolescents to engage and act offered some reason for hope. Baruch advocated "emotional education" in schools using clubs and youth organizations to foster cohesiveness; offer leadership opportunities; and inculcate a sense of belonging, confidence, and individuality.[11]

These were the basic selling points of 1950s citizen-building youth organizations. Escalona found that young people who worked alongside adults in activities that those young people and adults hoped would ensure peace formed strong personal identities in relation to their work, thereby escaping fatalism or delinquency.[12] Child psychiatrist Milton Schwebel proposed that "opportunities to participate in the social act of protecting one's community and achieving peace" might have a "therapeutic" effect.[13] Indeed, the educators who brought civil defense training into their schools and classrooms had embraced the activities as a way to offer a plan of action and a sense of security to students and parents.[14] Knowledge about atomic science, foreign diplomacy, and the effects of atomic blasts, although likely to produce more initial anxiety, might lessen youthful denial and apathy if channels were provided for constructive action.[15] Camp Fire publications argued that it was not helpful to shelter children entirely from the problems of the world. It would be more constructive to give them ways to be "a part of a constructive force."[16]

Among educators, a broad consensus developed that young people needed authoritative information to produce a matter-of-fact attitude about the new reality of atomic weapons. Equally matter of fact was the assumption that new political structures, such as world governance, were required responses to the atomic threat. Young adults would need to rise to the challenge of implementing them. *School and Society*, an educational journal, advised teachers to institute a psychologist-approved curriculum developed in consultation with the Federation of American Scientists, which offered candid assessments of the possibility of another war and the absence of any sufficient military defense as well as the need for international control of atomic energy, international friendship, and peaceful adaptations of atomic energy.[17]

Most youth workers agreed that the best way to ensure the development of healthy personalities was democratic education, equipping young people with knowledge about democracy and its ideals as well as the skills and frame of mind to enact democratic citizenship, and politicians endorsed this method too. Indeed, many adults argued, the way to secure a safe future at home and abroad was for the United States and its institutions, including the Girl Scouts and its peer agencies, to live up to their stated democratic ideals.

President Truman routinely charged educators with the responsibility of developing the "human brotherhood that alone will enable us to achieve international cooperation and peaceful progress in the atomic age." In 1949, he explicitly connected democratic education and internationalism, declaring that the National Education Week theme "Making Democracy Work" meant "broadening our vision to give thought to children of other lands with whom our children must live in increasingly closer relationship."[18] Six years later, Oveta Culp Hobby, the secretary of health, education, and welfare in the Eisenhower administration, called "democratic education" the best hope to protect the nation as it faced not only "obliteration . . . by atomic weapons" but also challenges to the core political values of freedom of speech, opinion, and inquiry.[19]

Girls' institutions followed the research of child experts who advocated democratic education. National Camp Fire executive Ruth Teichmann explained the contribution that these organizations stood to make through teaching about democracy, cultivating spiritual ideals, and promoting the recognition of the dignity of every human being. "Our basic problem is not wholly physical survival," she explained. "What is being consistently threatened and attacked is intangible." Youth organizations could help young people learn to think more clearly about "our democratic way of life, with all its spiritual values" and promote "a real conviction about human dignity and worth."[20]

Martha Allen, the director of the Camp Fire Girls and member of Truman's famine relief committee, agreed that youth organizations had an immense responsibility in "the struggle between the ideals of democracy and totalitarianism . . . especially communism." She elaborated that "an organization which seeks to train girls for citizenship cannot ignore this struggle or operate on the assumption that if we teach children to tie knots, build a campfire and give service, all will be well. Any program which does not help a young person to understand the realities of his world is irrelevant and useless." Not only did girls' organizations need to teach about "the real differences between a free society and a totalitarian one," but they also needed to teach girls, by example, "to value human dignity, democratic practices, free inquiry, and truth even when truth goes counter to some of our cherished prejudices and uninformed opinions." To this end she pledged to make certain that the Camp Fire Girls lived up to its democratic ideals by giving members real experience in democratic practice and the privileges and responsibilities of freedom.[21]

A Relational Approach to Democratic Citizenship

Although programs for boys and girls shared much, gender-based expectations shaped youth leaders' approaches to citizenship training in the atomic age. With girls lay the responsibility for building relationships for peace.

The YWCA's Gladys Ryland, a social worker and professor, believed that gender confusion was super-added to the anxieties about nuclear war and this made the gender-based citizen training fitting. American girls lived in a social context filled with uncertainties unique to them as they struggled to establish their identities. The program directors whom Ryland spoke to believed the first of these was "fear of war and the H-bomb," which led to "frustration, insecurity, apathy, and lack of concern for tomorrow." Girls, however, were also rendered uncertain about proper family and gender roles in a world in which more mothers were going to work, families were moving away from kin, and fathers were commuters and not as often at home.[22] The answer developed in postwar programs for girls was to foster feminine gender identity formation as part of the larger process of producing well-adjusted young people, even as the age called for expanded civic roles for girls and women.

In addressing the problem of juvenile delinquency, Allen did not cast girls as actual delinquents. Rather, she wanted to understand the "role that girls play in setting values for boys as sisters, future wives and mothers."[23] Allen's relational model for combating delinquency reflected the larger social understanding of girls' civic contributions as a product of their relationships.

Most child experts, including consultants for girls' organizations like Evelyn Goodenough Pitcher, director of the Eliot-Pearson School at Tufts University in Boston, favored relational approaches for girls. Pitcher's research on children's storytelling showed that boys created adventure stories set in forests and outer space, whereas girls created home-centered stories that focused on relationships. Pitcher concluded that boys' fantasies prepared them to tackle larger questions of good and evil and to serve as future diplomats and leaders. Girls' stories, however, marked a pathway to motherhood and the important relational role of being the "first educators" of their children. "Men are more likely to be the ones who set the policies in law and labor and diplomacy," she wrote, "while questions of social and personal morality and ethics are more often handled by women."[24] In this context, it was without irony that *Seventeen* promoted heroic leadership to its girl readers in a selection of articles by girls that featured only male leaders but highlighted how girls were trained to help in international community development through traditionally feminine work for others in home economics, sewing, and nutrition.[25]

Girls' duties to the world, then, were based on feminine roles originating in familial and domestic relationships. The Camp Fire Girls' director of field operations, Lou B. Paine, linked homemaking to a girl's patriotic duty, calling a girl "an indispensable member of the most important institution of American life—the home. Girls must continue, therefore, to learn responsibility to give love and understanding and strength to the family structure, which after all, is the fundamental unit of government." Yet Camp Fire leaders saw themselves as modern and open to girls' expanding opportunities. The guidebook directed girls to learn about women in world affairs as they read and discussed global events. Paine added, "It is no longer a man's world or a woman's world. Men and women have one world of responsibility and partnership." Women's and girls' duty, Paine argued, began in the home and extended outward to include the world.[26] Girl Scout officials concurred. Program advisor Louise P. Cochran implored leaders to guide girls to "become better acquainted with their country and the world they live in and to take some responsibility for making them a little better, beginning with the troop and moving on to the community, the nation, and to other countries."[27]

A Y-Teen play written by a committee of West Virginia girls and adult directors framed girls as shaping peace via their relationships and the knowledge of world affairs they acquired through participation in the organization's activities. The homemaker to the world could discuss disarmament, foreign aid, and more. The play opens with a high school boy preparing a speech called "Action for Peace in Our Town." As he gathers advice from his family members, the gendered and age-related expectations of the era emerge. The mother is an idealist and puts her hopes for peace in Christ and prayer. The father is alternately fatalistic and militaristic, explaining why peace efforts are futile and what is at stake in the arms race. At first the boy parrots his father's fatalism, discounting disarmament proposals as "dumb." The teenage sister, however, influences her brother to adopt a middle ground. Together, they represent hope for the future.

The sister works toward peace by being informed about the United Nations and atomic energy while holding on to spiritual faith. She explains the UN Political Committee's proposals for ending the production and testing of nuclear weapons by referring to the minutes of a Y-Teen meeting about international politics. In an allusion to Eisenhower's Atoms for Peace, she declares that nuclear energy does not have to be used for war. She reads aloud how the YWCA USA has gone on record "as supporting an atoms-for-peace plan, including efforts to establish, preferably within the jurisdiction of the United Nations, or under the proper international control, an international pool of fissionable material designed for the promotion of human welfare." Emphasizing her relational approach to world affairs, she states, "We *must* have faith and love, even to loving our enemies, who are people too."[28]

Finally, the boy who is to give the speech says that he has enough "ammunition," using an armaments metaphor to explain how he will argue for peace. He adopts a more militarized position than his sister, but unlike his father, he is optimistic about brotherhood and mutual understanding, although "you have to be more realistic and practical," he maintains. The play ends with lines that sound likely to be in his speech: "We have to do away with our own hostilities and prejudices; we will have to work for disarmament while safeguarding our own security; we'll have to help the less fortunate peoples to realize a better standard of living; we'll have to know and understand others better as they are just as proud of their cultures as we are in the United States. . . . It would help a lot if we studied more languages so we can communicate better with others—even write letters to boys and girls in other countries and exchange ideas with them in their own language. We can be proud of what we tell them about the freedoms and democracy of America if we try to put our own house in order."[29] Although in this play the boy has been identified as the one to give the speech, the girl's influence on her brother, who comes to include disarmament and friendship among his proposals, is clear. The teenagers' voices are knowledgeable, and they propose ways to lead the United States into the atomic future.

Gender and age did shape attitudes, and girls adopted an approach that stressed relationships with others in the international arena. In her essay for a Girls Club Citizenship Award, one young woman described American citizenship for boys as their one day becoming soldiers and fighting for the country, whereas girls showed their patriotism by becoming nurses, "by showing kindness and care to others . . . [by their willingness] to give up [their] time to give someone a few needed moments of happiness."[30] A seventeen-year-old from Ohio explained how one's horizons expand: "The world begins in a little circle around us. But it spreads out to the larger circles in which wars are fought between nations." Urging her fellow teens to think broadly, she continued, "The distance between the circumference of our thinking and circumference of international thinking may not be so great after all."[31]

Cultivating Leadership in Youth Councils and Conferences

As part of the trend in democratic education in the 1940s and 1950s, girls' organizations and *Seventeen* magazine regarded girls as capable and integrated them into adult-style and actual adult roles. The emphasis in American education on youth leadership grew in part from young people's contributions during World War II. Though their work was often downplayed as mere volunteerism, children and teenagers had contributed labor through engaging in scrap metal drives, rolling bandages for the Red Cross, providing child care for women defense workers, entertaining soldiers at United Service Organizations (USO) stations, and cultivating victory gardens.[32] Such activities reversed a trend in American laws and institutions since the late nineteenth century that prolonged childhood by creating a semi-insulated cocoon of adolescence in which children were separated from the world of adults by their school attendance. The inclusion of young people in governance indicates further attempts to allow them to role-play in safely protected arenas.[33]

Girls found other opportunities to enact adult responsibilities in community leadership. Participation in new youth councils and conferences and as actual delegates to decision-making bodies allowed young people to experience adult activities before stepping into their full responsibilities to democracy and the world.

Adolescents participated in national conferences related to their needs and roles. The Midcentury White House Conference on Children and Youth

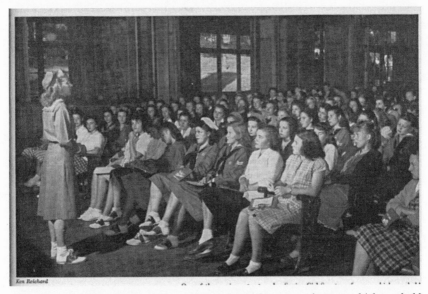

IMAGE 1. One of the sessions at a two-day Senior Girl Scout conference, which was held in the sand dunes studded with Monterey cypress near Carmel, in California.

The American Girl magazine, January 1948, 43. Photo by Ken Reichard. Magazine Collection of National Historic Preservation Center, Girl Scouts of the USA.

was the first that invited young people to participate.[34] The recommendations of Wisconsin's state committee for the conference illuminated the new trend, declaring that "adults should plan *with* youth, not *for* them" and suggesting that youth councils were effective ways to investigate and address problems in local communities.[35]

Camp Fire officials believed that leadership training was more important for postwar children and teenagers than for those of previous generations. "There is good reason to believe that the present generation of young people is going to carry graver responsibility than any generation has yet faced. If our girls are to become responsible, secure citizens in a democratic society they must share with adults the real responsibility for their own organizations, their communities—and their world." Young girls could choose their own activities, and older girls could determine which community service projects the Camp Fire Girls should endorse. Older girls could also serve on camp planning and design committees and set up and plan annual projects at the local level. They could be involved with the recruitment of both girls and group advisors, the choice of speakers for meetings, and the arrangement of special events. The National Council unanimously passed a motion to "secure the active participation of Camp Fire Girls in as many ways as possible, including membership on adult committees where feasible, assistance in planning events in which girls participate, and even in policy-making."[36]

The Girl Scouts cultivated leadership through directed programs, establishing in the 1950s leadership units at youth encampments to prepare the oldest Scouts to become better officers and members of Senior Scout planning boards, troops, and school and community organizations. In the encampment, girls discussed leadership theories and learned through experience.[37]

Such inclusion was not seamless. When the National Midcentury White House Conference on Children and Youth Committee added five youth delegates, they discovered that education jargon was incomprehensible to those not in the field. When the chair asked a seventeen-year-old girl if she had anything to add to a discussion of the committee's objectives, she reportedly responded, "I have nothing to add. I don't know what you people are talking about." Committed to training young people for future leadership and to demonstrating democratic practices at their meetings, the committee resolved to use language that "the lay mind" could understand. Facing similar dilemmas, the Play School Association, Girl Scouts of the USA, and YWCA trained youth delegates so they would understand conference proceedings.[38]

Seventeen also highlighted youth councils as a popular way for high school girls to share their perspectives on community issues.[39] Such councils were established by enterprising teenagers, as well as by a range of adult institutions from city councils and churches to advocacy groups like the National Association for the Advancement of Colored People (NAACP). Special youth councils also addressed international affairs, studied atomic weapon controls, and began to include participants from other nations.[40] Along with offering practical advice on starting youth councils, *Seventeen* connected its support for them to international politics in its glowing coverage of the 1945 London World Youth Conference, the first international youth conference after the war. Unlike many newspapers, the magazine neglected to note that delegates appeared to be between the ages of twenty-five and thirty. *Seventeen*'s article portrayed young people as being in the conference's driver's seat. It depicted young people in Europe, frustrated by the older generation's failure to protect them from war, as deciding to meet during World War II as a means of having a role in shaping their futures.[41]

Out of the London conference emerged a new organization, the World Federation of Democratic Youth (WFDY), and a specific plan of action. Although the WFDY was almost immediately considered by the U.S. government to be a communist front, most news sources initially reported on it positively. *Seventeen* was no exception. In an article, a series of resolutions adopted at the World Youth Conference were considered to reflect the attitudes of the world's young people. These were to support the United Nations "as the most effective method for maintaining peace and raising the living standards of all people"; to support Argentina, Spain, and Portugal in their efforts to defeat fascism; to eliminate fascism, racism, and militarism more generally; to establish the international control of atomic energy through the United Nations; to support colonial people's struggles for independence; to secure the right to vote at eighteen; to work toward full employment at equal pay and without discrimination based on race or sex; to provide free, compulsory primary and secondary education; and to provide relief to young people in developing countries. Pictures of girls and boys from around the world working together suggested that gender equality was part of leading the world toward peace; both boys and girls were leaders. The *Seventeen* article concluded that "today youth at last knows that apathy means death; suspicion and misunderstanding, total destruction. The World Federation for Democratic Youth has put a blueprint for a new era of peace into the hands of young people everywhere."[42] Such articles took girls seriously as community actors and challenged perceptions that they were apathetic and fatalistic.

Informing Girls about the Atomic Age

In addition to promoting civic involvement in youth conferences and councils, girls' institutions offered their members information and addressed girls' willingness to learn about the world as a sign of their maturity. Girls' institutions also produced thought-provoking material that implied girls had a stake and were expected to act.

Girls may have been frightened, or had perhaps grown a protective shell, when they read in *Seventeen* that "all over this land of ours people are in justifiably deadly fear of the atomic bomb," but executive editor Alice Beaton called on her readers to "turn your fear into action. You can help change this ominous thing into the world's servant." She offered specific steps girls could take. The magazine urged them to learn as much as they could about atomic energy, to rouse their friends and acquaintances to join them, and to write to Congress advocating international control of nuclear arms and an end to the arms race.[43]

Seventeen's book review section introduced teenage girls to serious political, scientific, and philosophical works and treated its readers as a unique generation that could affect the balance between policies of war and peace. The magazine pointed girls toward materials that provided chilling but honest information about atomic bombs and fallout. Its 1946 review of *One World or None*, the best-selling compendium published by the Federation of American Scientists, viewed young Americans as having a unique relationship to the bomb.[44] The collection of essays by famous scientists and philosophers detailed how the bomb worked, mapped the scale of a Hiroshima-sized attack against New York City, and presented a case for world government. Noting that many Americans were forgetting the horrors of Hiroshima in their rush to buy new cars, a facet of what historian Paul Boyer calls a "dulled acquiescence" to the atomic age, *Seventeen* remarked, "Most of you young people are still terribly aware" and proclaimed, "This is a book you must read, think about and discuss. You've absolutely got to realize that the problems presented in it are your own, not those of other people." To teenage girl readers fell the responsibility of recognizing that each of them was "a citizen of the world," someone who could "understand this new weapon [and] raise [an] informed voice to demand its best control" if she wanted to live out her life plans.[45]

Seventeen directly countered social beliefs about female ineptitude by claiming that *One World or None* was written by scientists who knew how important young women were. "You may be told to 'leave it to others who understand these things.' You may be told that this is a matter for the military or a highly specialized group of civilians. Don't listen. You can understand; you can act."[46] Such words urged girls to become politically involved with issues of atomic policy as a way not just to ease their own anxiety but to strengthen world security. Throughout the late 1940s, and to a lesser extent into the 1950s, *Seventeen* presented information to girls in a serious, uncondescending way that encouraged them to think of themselves as citizens with responsibilities to the world.[47]

Despite these straightforward informative messages, girls' organizations also encouraged an approach to atomic energy common in American schools that emphasized peaceful applications of atomic science. Government, corporations, and the media also spoke of "the peaceful atom" to "create a more positive—or at least more acquiescent—overall public attitude toward atomic energy" in the late 1940s and early 1950s.[48] In a piece written for the *American Girl*, David Lilienthal, the head of the Atomic Energy Commission, described the science of atomic particles and "how atomic energy, properly harnessed, can bring unimagined benefits to mankind."[49] The Camp Fire Girls published lessons to help leaders teach about atomic energy and recommended books like Robert Palmer's *Young People's Book of Atomic Energy* and John Lewellen and Lois Fisher's *You and Atomic Energy and Its Wonderful Uses* to inform young people about atomic science and careers in atomic energy. In the latter book, with Glenn T. Seaborg as technical advisor, Lewellen's text and Fisher's lively drawings presented atomic science in an accessible way. Fisher's cheery pictures also made atomic energy seem safe and clean. Like most such offerings for children and youth, the book included frank information (but no drawings) about the bomb's destructive capacity while also offering information on scientific advancements. It does not discuss radiation as a consequence of bombing or nuclear tests, for example, but examines it as a positive agent in medicine and agriculture.[50]

Indeed, the arms and space races promoted scientific study and kept science lessons, including those on atomic energy, in front of both girls and boys.[51] Just before the federal government made funding available for science education in public schools through the National Defense Education Act, girls' institutions instituted science education. By 1946, the Camp Fire Girls established a science category for honors called "Frontiers Craft," the name suggesting that science would be the next arena for American triumph. The Girl Scouts instituted a laboratory aide project for older Scouts who wanted to focus on science, and it created a science proficiency badge in the early 1960s. *Seventeen* began running a science column. Atomic energy was just one of the subjects it covered. It included everything from the science of hair brushing to medical developments in blood transfusion.[52]

Girls' materials reflected much that was in children's classrooms. In the second half of the 1940s, textbooks, *Scholastic* magazine, and documentary films reminded students of the threat of atomic war even as they tried to moderate fears by presenting straightforward, authoritative information and discussions of the international control of atomic weapons, world federation, and peaceful atoms.

Only a few social studies textbooks for junior high and high school students ignored the topic. Most included some discussion of international control of atomic energy.[53] Frank Magruder's *National Governments and International Relations*, after cautioning readers that another war would be "ten times as terrible as the Second World War, because of the atomic bomb and jet-propelled missiles," presented the case for international control of atomic energy and the "need of world federation." Magruder warned readers that nations could not expect to prepare for wars and simultaneously enjoy a rising standard of living.[54] Textbooks and other classroom readers matter-of-factly reminded children that their generation had to contend with the bomb. *Senior Scholastic* simultaneously raised fear and hope. One article quoted Secretary of State John Foster Dulles's acknowledgment that "physical scientists have now found the means which, if they are developed, can wipe life off the surface of this planet," but another promoted brotherhood, international cooperation, and a strengthened United Nations as an antidote to world annihilation.[55]

Senior Scholastic as well as other education periodicals and general newspapers published student essays and poems demonstrating that students reared in an atmosphere that promoted support for democratic principles of brotherhood, understanding, peace, and freedom "reflected a strong belief in the country and democracy." They also placed hope in "international harmony," with a few sounding an alarm about nationalistic tendencies in the United States and the world.[56] Their writings, though not of one voice, discussed the threat of atomic annihilation with varying degrees of fatalism and hope.

Although boys wrote about brotherhood, they also expressed more fatalism than did girls. "Laugh and live while you can—," one boy cautioned in 1947, for "your life is the testimony of a gravestone; Your world a burned book; And your name wasted space in the telephone directory." Girls' writings, however, were more likely to counter fatalism with expressions of hope. Peace might emerge through prayer or through cooperation and brotherhood. One 1951 poem placed confidence in children and their future, calling the girl poet's generation "builders of *today; For tomorrow!*" Another girl called on her peers to act. "Look around you," she wrote, "these boys and girls you see now, today, are the men and women of tomorrow. Look at yourself." In 1955, another girl essayist still looked to the United Nations as "the only world organization where countries of all different political beliefs can solve problems peacefully."[57] Such observations were very much in line with the thought being expressed and marketed by institutions that worked with and addressed girls.

On the whole, girls appeared to appreciate readings on the issues of the day. Although *Seventeen* readers asked for more about beauty, founder Helen Valentine believed that marketing surveys demonstrated girls' desire for content about citizenship as well as for wholesome dating and beauty advice. The letters to the editor and girls' creative-writing contributions that *Seventeen* printed indicate that at least some girls wanted both.[58] When one letter from a Brooklyn girl called for more "articles on dates and shyness" in place of the "boring" stories on atomic energy, some of her peers disagreed. *Seventeen* editors responded snidely, "If enough world citizens are similarly bored by atomic energy, we fear that teen-agers may find themselves with no dates left to worry about, no boys to be shy with." Other girls wrote in support of the articles on science and international affairs. One said that stories about atomic energy showed that a magazine for teenagers might have "some point to it." Demanding more from her fellow girl citizens, another wrote to say that the girl who complained that the article was boring had "no sense of responsibility."[59]

Girls also demanded to be taken seriously. *Seventeen*'s editors obliged, printing letters that called attention to girls as capable and serious leaders. H. G. of Brooklyn wrote that even though "adults seem to believe that all teenagers run around behaving like irresponsible clowns and idiots," her peers shared a "serious outlook toward world problems." She was confident they would grow into capable world leaders. The editors agreed and published two more letters by teens attesting to youths' "concern with the future of the world." These girls were interested in fostering world understanding and preventing a third world war.[60]

Many Girl Scouts who participated in a national survey by the National Recreation Association and *Life* magazine were similarly interested in national security concerns and they approached them in a relational way. Girl Scouts' open-ended responses pointed to their interest in "international aspects" such as "concern for world peace" and concern for the betterment and general welfare of all people. Over 70 percent of the Girl Scout respondents believed that the United States should spread the ideals of democracy, but many also thought that the nation should not "force our government, way of life on other people" but influence through example and sharing. Girl Scouts also indicated "the need for understanding of all people, our responsibility for world leadership, the achievement of freedom for all people, and raising the standard of living in underdeveloped countries." A few Girl Scouts mentioned disarmament and "one world, world unity," but these more radical notions of achieving security were not the norm.[61] Another study of Girl Scouts showed that although most did not list "international friendship" among their most sought-after activities in Scouting, the same girls eagerly participated in activities such as pen pal correspondences, entertaining exchange students, and hosting international teas. They demonstrated a strong sense of global responsibility, regularly asking what could be done when they learned about national and international problems.[62]

Some girls criticized adults' passivity. On the anniversary of the Hiroshima bombing, seventeen-year-old Sharman Vaughn, the daughter of United Press Far East correspondent Miles Vaughn, bore witness by writing an essay for *Seventeen* on her visit to Hiroshima. She wondered how other Americans could dismiss the bombings by saying, "Aw, that was six years ago." Vaughn toured the area, witnessing the destruction in the form of mangled buildings (though much had been rebuilt), charred trees, and victims of radiation poisoning, and hearing stories from survivors. It gave her "an uncomfortable sense of responsibility for this wreckage, as if I were partially to blame." She described the injuries sustained by Japanese victims who continued to suffer from radiation poisoning. Still, she was not quite sure how to "atone" and ended up buying a number of atomic "souvenirs," including "genuine atom rocks" and postcards to ease "the discomfort" of the "shriveled" Japanese shopkeeper and his wife.[63] Vaughn's essay explored the need to act but she, like many adults, knew little about how to go about it.

Civil Defense as a Constructive Channel

Some lessons fell under the category of civil defense. When girls' institutions and agencies instituted civil-defense lessons, they mirrored those of the schools and stressed survivability, self-reliance, and psychological composure. But they also continued to support international friendship as the best way to avoid war. Girls' organizations used the need for civil defense to argue for the significance of their programs and attempted to include democratic education and global citizenship as components of civil-defense training.[64]

Youth organizations worked alongside schools to disseminate Federal Civil Defense Administration (FCDA) information. The Department of Health, Education, and Welfare wanted training in civil defense to be "built-in" to everyday thinking primarily through schools and colleges, with which nearly one-fourth of the U.S. population had some affiliation. State departments of education coordinated civil defense education, and the Office of Education supplied technical information that the FCDA distributed.[65] Youth organizations offered their programs.

At a FCDA Emergency Mass Feeding Conference in 1953, Camp Fire representative Arline Broy asserted that youth organizations had knowledge and skills to share with civil defense administrators and with the public through demonstrations. The conference subjects, she explained, "read almost like headings in our own *Outdoor Book*—fire safety, food preparation, outdoor cooking and nutrition, improvisation of equipment and utensils, outdoor sanitation, water purification, and emergency lighting." Moreover, citing the need for courage and self-reliance as necessary for survival itself, Broy argued that "experiences which teach girls skills like those mentioned above make a very real contribution to our national security. We adults in Camp Fire are actually doing an important, timely job almost without realizing it!" Camp Fire Girls' skills would help them feel "resourceful, creative, self-confident, and comfortable under any circumstances," thus bolstering American resilience in the event of atomic attack.[66] Civil defense, then, offered a way for adults to try to protect children and offered a rationale for policymakers to support girls' institutions in line with military deterrence strategy.

In civil defense preparation, girls' institutions followed the national policy of encouraging families to be as self-sufficient as possible.[67] Leaders discussed civil defense with parents, and group activities supplemented family plans.[68] Many civil-defense activities folded seamlessly into the weekly programming for Girl Scouts and Camp Fire Girls. The *American Girl* column Be Prepared offered lessons in ham-radio operations, physical fitness, first aid, and outdoor cooking.[69] The pamphlet *Camp Fire's Part in Defense* suggested "learning emergency cooking, making neighborhood maps, [and] use of play-situations to help younger children develop confidence under unusual circumstances."[70] Younger girls could help with local civil defense programs by stocking service rooms, folding bandages, and providing messenger services, and group leaders could help girls overcome fear of the dark with a night hike. Slightly older girls became versed in survival techniques, taking a Junior Red Cross First Aid Course, learning to read maps and becoming better acquainted with their neighborhoods, and studying "emergency pet care as pets too will need help in an emergency."[71] *The Camp Fire Girl* suggested tying civil defense to nature study by examining the underground lives of snakes, ground squirrels, moles, birds, and insects. Girls might then turn "underground shelters . . . into fun and exploration."[72] Older girls were expected to take more active roles in local civil defense programs, conducting surveys to assess neighbors' civil-defense experience, taking preparatory classes for nursing and for sighting aircraft, aiding at Red Cross blood banks or hospitals, and doing civil-defense clerical and courier work.[73]

Seventeen compared such training to learning to swim before canoeing. The magazine extolled teenagers who had "proven themselves dependable, quick to learn, calm even in the face of emergencies" to enroll in local civil defense associations which needed boys to spot and extinguish fires and girls to serve as civil defense secretaries, watch the skies for enemy planes, look after children, and care for the ill and injured after an attack. Recognizing the various layers of the community involved in planning, *Seventeen* echoed girls' organizations when it said, "You'll be helping to preserve the security and welfare of your family, your friends, your community, and your country."[74]

Girls' organizations elevated their civil defense programs beyond mere preparation for war. The *American Girl* column Be Prepared emphasized "worldmindedness," or "learning how to understand and get along with other people," as the first step in "our defense." It insisted that "we have to defend our country not only from the atomic bomb, but from the evil ignorance that sets person against person, family against family, creed against creed, and race against race."[75] The Camp Fire Girls' list of civil defense activities included making a United Nations flag "for the PTA or other community group as it is a good time to make the community more aware of the UN" and helping to "publicize the People's Section for the United Nations."[76]

In 1950, Allen pledged that the Camp Fire Girls would address "the needs of girls in time of stress" not with fallout shelters and duck-and-cover drills alone, but with a psychological approach that would maintain the American way of childhood and develop healthy personalities, the theme of the Midcentury White House Conference on Children and Youth.[77] She assured members that the Camp Fire program was well suited to times of stress. "Our program is designed to give children and young people the feeling of security which comes from belonging," she said, underscoring the belief that healthy personalities needed to be cultivated especially in anxious times. The Camp Fire Girls, she said, taught resourcefulness and skills that might aid in civil defense, and it taught girls to value the freedom and independence deemed essential to democracy. Echoing child experts who tried to counter fatalism through action, she added, "It gives them opportunity for constructive service and the real practice of democracy; it releases their tensions through play, fun and friendship." Allen believed that these were essential American qualities and that tending to them was just as important to the future of the democracy as was physical survival. Allen looked to civil defense to deepen democratic education for girls, and she highlighted the need to maintain girls' psychological health as legitimizing the Camp Fire Girls' program. By reminding Americans about children's unique needs and stressing that "the children of a nation are its greatest resource," Allen built the case for sustained support of youth organizations.[78]

Girls' Organizations Support the United Nations

In addition to civil defense, girls' organizations and girls' media promoted democratic training through internationalism, global friendships, and confidence in the United Nations—all as what Schwebel had called "therapeutic" channels for action. Training to promote international cooperation, much more than civil defense, responded to the spirit of the call for democratic education.

Support for the United Nations was one way that girls' organizations and *Seventeen* put internationalism into practice. The groups' specific programs in this regard reflected broader educational trends, as they had in civil defense. Schools and youth organizations held annual celebrations commemorating the founding of the United Nations, students took field trips to the United Nations, and juvenile literature such as Lois Fisher's *You and the United Nations*, which was widely recommended by girls' organizations, presented accessible descriptions of the United Nations and its history to middle and high school students. There was also help available to the adults involved in teaching girls. The World Federation of United Nations Associations and UNESCO offered summer seminars for educators on teaching international understanding and cooperation.[79]

Like *Seventeen*, Fisher's book depicted young people as shaping the future, and its feminine imagery might have inspired some girls to embrace its arguments. It promoted the one-world concept and asked students to reflect on global anxiety and commit themselves to supporting the United Nations. A full-page spread of caricatures, each one depicting a stance that Americans, young

Which one are you? Is your mind big or little?

IMAGE 2. Lois Fisher, author of juvenile literature, called on young readers as individuals to broaden their minds and commit to supporting the United Nations.

Lois Fisher, *You and the United Nations*, rev. ed. (Chicago: Children's Press, 1951).

and old, male and female, might take in response to the international organization, asked girls to personalize their choice of how to help. Most of the older
people express skepticism. Several cartoons show girls repeating their parents'
negative attitudes about the potential of the United Nations. Most of the pictures of girls, however, paint them as levelheaded and optimistic. One girl asks,
"Does *my* attitude really affect other people?" Another is already committed, "My
part is small, but I know every person is important." Fisher asks, "Which one are
you? Is your mind big or little?" Children also read that it was not enough simply
to make a commitment; they needed to cultivate a broad mindset, starting with
themselves—a theme prominent in the citizen-building literature. In a warning
quoted in youth organization publications, Fisher wrote, "You must first be at
peace with yourself and your little brother before your thinking is big enough
and clear enough to be a part of a world-wide movement toward peace."[80]

Although the United Nations was run mainly by men, Fisher depicted its
duties in maternal terms that would have been familiar to girls immersed in
the image of the nurturing activist citizen that girls' organizations promoted.
Fisher used the old woman who lived in a shoe as a metaphor to describe how
the Economic and Social Council took care of many children and social services
and included a drawing of the nursery rhyme character. "The Council has many
committees which work on such problems as unemployment, care of children,
freedom of the press, etc." Fisher explained that these "special organizations"
were necessary since "war-torn countries need loans, people driven from their
homes need to be sent back or placed in new homes, and many countries need
to know how to raise more and better food."[81] That UN roles were described
in terms that could be considered motherly might have inspired some girls to
identify with it.

Girls' organizations urged identification with the United Nations. The
United Nations was sometimes treated as an analogue for their organizations.
Robert Staines, the UN director of education, compared the organization to a
Y-Teen conference, and Eleanor Roosevelt compared it to a school club.[82] Girls'
organizations championed their own international networks by claiming that
girls were already part of a multinational organization through their club, troop,
or association.

They also made the similarity explicit. During an international prayer week,
the YWCA promoted the United Nations by comparing it and the YWCA. Just
as the "YWCA around the world works for the welfare of its members" and for a
"better world of peace and justice," its special materials for the week said, "the
United Nations, too, works for people—to prevent war and also to safeguard
human rights and improve living conditions."[83]

The Girl Scouts, too, claimed that the United Nations' multinational
model mirrored their own international organization, asserting that the World

Association of Girl Guides and Girl Scouts (WAGGGS) had comprised "a successful United Nations of their own" since its establishment. In language that was more aspirational than the reality of its complex operations in colonial areas, the Girl Scouts announced that for years, it had worked through WAGGGS toward "better understanding and friendship, based on a common code and a democratic program for all races, creeds, and nationality backgrounds. Even though their nations have sometimes been at war with each other, Girl Scouts have continued their friendships."[84] It explained that UN ideals, which it described again in the most aspirational terms, were consistent with Scouting.[85]

Girl Scout texts compared UN structure and decision making to troop governance. The General Assembly, girls read, consisted of delegates from each member nation, "not unlike your troop's Court of Honor," a decision-making body representing all members through troop and patrol leaders. In addition, "the Secretariat carries out the wishes of the Assembly and Security Council, as plans made by the Court of Honor are carried out by committees and officers of your troop. The Security Council makes decisions that cannot be handled in the General Assembly, just as your leaders, troop committee members, and council must make some plans and decisions for you."[86]

Girl Scout literature acknowledged how difficult it was for the United Nations to build consensus. It reminded girls how hard it could be to get troops to function smoothly: "You must also know how much time, patience, and understanding it is going to take before the time comes when all the nations of the world are working peacefully and happily together."[87] Similarly, Dorothy Groeling, the international education secretary of the YWCA, compared UN debates to disputes in club meetings or between parents and teens. Understanding evolved slowly in each case, she said, as she compared international affairs to personal connections.[88] In these ways, girls' organizations personalized UN proceedings and encouraged girls to see themselves as part of larger multinational governing bodies.

Girls' organizations supported the United Nations' 1947 call to its members to encourage schools to teach about its charter and operations.[89] A year later, when the United Nations called on its member states to disseminate, display, read, and expound upon the United Nations Declaration of Human Rights, girls' organizations printed and publicized it.[90] Girls' organizations found the UN materials appropriate curriculum for expanding girls' horizons and increasing their awareness of domestic and international efforts to improve human relations. The Charter's statement on the dignity of the human person was often cited by girls' organizations and provided a bridge between policy and the everyday practices of youth agencies.

Youth organization literature, such as the *Girl Scout Handbook* and the YWCA program packets that provided quarterly activity and discussion materials to YWCA branches, including the Y-Teens, explained more about the United Nations–related agencies and their purposes, paying special attention to UNESCO, the World Health Organization, and the International Monetary Fund.[91] *Seventeen* did the same. Teaching about the United Nations was one major way girls' organizations integrated internationalism and tolerance into their programs. Through youth organizations, girls gained exposure to UN materials, learned about its functions and structure, and identified with it as citizens. A YWCA survey of teenagers found that over half of the several thousand surveyed had participated in a UN study project.[92]

Formalized relationships between youth organizations and the United Nations also promoted UN awareness and involvement. The Girl Scouts of the USA, the Camp Fire Girls, the World Association of the YWCA, the Girls' Friendly Society, and the Boy Scouts of America had accredited observer status to the United Nations. Observers served as liaisons, gathered information, arranged group visits to, and disseminated information about the United Nations. They attended UN briefing sessions offered by the Department of Public Information and meetings for U.S. affiliates such as U.S. Mission to the United Nations and the Conference Group of National Organizations on the United Nations. The observers received State Department briefings to inform them about U.S. foreign policy. In addition, WAGGGS had observer status with the United Nations and consultant status with UNESCO as well as eight representatives to the United Nations and UNESCO, and Girl Scouts of the USA and the YWCA had consultative status with the Economic and Social Council. Its experts were called to ad hoc meetings when issues arose in its specialized field of education.[93]

In addition, girls visited the United Nations regularly, and *Seventeen* and girls' organization publications covered their experiences.[94] They provided specific steps for those who wanted to get involved. When the Security Council met in the spring of 1946, *Seventeen* explained that the first forty-five people in line gained admittance to the chamber. The 1946 visitors had been overwhelmingly students from New York City high schools who were preparing history and debate assignments or writing articles for high school newspapers. One teen explained: "I don't want my kids to make the world safe—I want it safe when they get here."[95]

The Girls' Friendly Society, a girls' organization within the Episcopal Church, also taught about the United Nations as a means of promoting good "Christian citizenship." In 1952, the organization's districts selected nine teenage delegates to attend a seminar in New York City, tour the United Nations, and visit the opening session of the General Assembly as part of their Christian citizenship training. They heard from Eleanor Roosevelt and Indian diplomat Vijaya Lakshmi Pandit, who the next year would become the first female president of the UN General Assembly, speak about peace, the interdependence of nations, and the role of the international body. They came away committed to serving as individual links in a chain to work for peace and world friendship. Beverly Dempsey of South Carolina compared her own organization's name and its implication of "friendliness" with world friendship efforts within the United Nations. The girls connected their citizenship with their religion, their youth organization, and active support for the United Nations. After the trip, the girls were expected to "spread the message of Christian Citizenship to literally thousands of people via public appearances in churches, clubs, community gatherings, radio, television and the printed word." Their trip had shown them "that the place of the Christian is not only in the Church, but also in the world," and they certainly included themselves in that effort.[96]

Much of the informational content about the United Nations was written in an accessible tone that might have suggested to teenage girls that international affairs was not too complicated for them to understand. An article by *Seventeen* executive editor Alice Thompson describing the Dumbarton Oaks plan is illustrative. She compared international disputes to family arguments, demystified Dumbarton Oaks as "not a mysterious council chamber" but a "country estate," and described the plan for world peace with a diagram that charted the steps to UN action.[97] Such simplification was necessary, according to *Seventeen*'s editors in another article, to prevent "the sands of international politics from closing over the average reader's head (as they do ours when we try to read editorialized accounts of a U.N. debate)."[98] Still, the magazine's coverage of the United Nations included detailed overviews of UN origins within the alliance that opposed the Axis powers, its structure, and its early controversies.[99]

Like Fisher's book, materials prepared for girls adopted a familial theme in describing the United Nations. A 1949 *Seventeen* article's title declared that "the United Nations is a family affair." It described the United Nations as "strengthening the world's families through its specialized agencies" and emphasized the "particular significance for families" in the provisions of the Declaration of Human Rights that articulated special care and protections for children and mothers, promoted the rights of families and homes to be free of arbitrary interference, and defined the family as a fundamental unit of society in need of protections.[100]

In the *Bookshelf*, the YWCA magazine for Y-Teen leaders, before the war's end, YWCA international education secretary Groeling countered a perception that postwar planning was "too remote" for teenagers' experience and "too big" for adolescents to worry about. She offered her readers much detail. She defined political terminology, including *sovereignty*, *nationalism*, and *isolationism*, and outlined the treaty ratification process. Although some Americans called for isolationism, Groeling asked her readers if "the real lesson of this war" was not that representatives of all nations should "preserve peace through joint efforts." She recommended further readings on the Fulbright Resolution, the House

Resolution supporting a postwar international organization for "just and last-ing peace," and the Senate's Connally Resolution, which proposed an alliance of powerful nations. She forecast long debates about power sharing in interna-tional organizations but expected that girls could and would follow the news.[101]

Girls' organizations identified the United Nations as the world's best hope for peace and one that very much included girls. As the 1947 *Girl Scout Handbook* stated, "It is, after all, the *only* world organization there is that has been set up to iron out different viewpoints of nations, and has the authority to do so." Girls' institutions sought to empower their members as political agents by emphasiz-ing their stake in the United Nations. Girl Scout officials pointed out that they were all UN members, since the United States was a member. The responsibil-ity for UN success then fell to each girl, boy, woman, and man to "do his or her best to help the United Nations to succeed."[102] Alva Bernheimer Gimbel, official Camp Fire observer to the United Nations, explained that although some in the Camp Fire Girls thought the United Nations was "something which is only the concern of those who are actively engaged in its meetings . . . actually the United Nations is yours and mine. It belongs to every Camp Fire Girl in every community throughout the nation." Making membership familiar, she added, "It's a family—a family of nations."[103]

During the Korean War, *Seventeen*'s articulations of the necessity of the international body became more emphatic. Against the backdrop of the mili-tary action that the United Nations had undertaken in the Far East, it wrote: "At no time since its inception has the need for a strong United Nations been as imperative (and as apparent) as it is today." Suggestions for teaching peers, neighbors, and other members about the United Nations followed, as did encouragement to participate in UN pledge drives to collect signatures of fellow Americans who placed faith in the United Nations.[104] Girls were also urged to hold UN Day parties to commemorate the anniversary of the establishment of the United Nations.[105] *Seventeen* continued to carry United Nations International Children's Emergency Fund (UNICEF) advertisements with heart-wrenching sto-ries and pictures of children who were grateful even for powdered milk. The ads also urged girls to get involved. "If you want to help realize the ideals of *your* United Nations, then help its future citizens to grow up free from hunger and disease. Start campaigning for UNICEF in your home, your school, your club."[106]

Combating Prejudice in Girls' Organizations

When U.S.-based girls' institutions such as the Y-Teens of the YWCA, the Girl Scouts, the Camp Fire Girls, and *Seventeen* magazine promoted the United Nations, they turned their attention to creating international peace through intercultural tolerance, a strategy that led them to offer lessons about fighting prejudice. These lessons were cast as important steps for girls' healthy personality development. They, nonetheless, often had domestic social implications.

Girls' institutions often used the language of human rights in teaching about and promoting multilateral organizations. The United Nations and the Universal Declaration of Human Rights, especially, became for girls' organizations a manifestation of their internationalist hopes. As important, it provided language and justification for antiracist commitments. Although girls' organizations shied away from identification with radicalism and allowed segregated groups, for example, they still treated combating prejudice at home as a project that was compatible with internationalism and so increased the horizons of mainstream girls and encouraged them to be broad-minded about the diverse peoples of the world and the nation.

Affiliation with the United Nations provided a targeted opportunity to undo prejudice and cultivate understanding of people around the world. Elizabeth Rowe, the editor of the *Camp Fire Girl*, for example, supported the ideal of one world through partnership with the United Nations and UNESCO and stated that the primary contribution the Camp Fire Girls could make was through service, especially talking about and displaying "constructive attitudes" about racial and cultural barriers.[107]

These postwar girls' agencies were responding to the shifts in American attitudes toward racial and economic justice that had emerged from World War II. Indeed, the United States' principled effort against Nazi racism during the war turned attention to racial problems at home and within the military overseas. The Double Victory campaign, to secure victory abroad and justice at home for racial minorities, resulted in heightened awareness of a nascent broad-based civil rights movement. Franklin D. Roosevelt's executive order outlawing racial discrimination in the federal government and among defense contractors was one way of decreasing the damage done by the image of segregated troops abroad. World War II and the Cold War sparked national introspection on questions of race. Conditioned by antifascism to promote tolerance and combat prejudice during World War II, youth leaders in the Cold War drew attention to their efforts to paint a positive portrait of American life for export abroad.

During the war, even as internment forced the evacuation of Japanese American children from their homes and schools and despite the vilification of the Japanese in popular culture, young Americans were taught that hate and prejudice were antidemocratic liabilities for the nation. Moreover, Americans saw children as the nation's future. Concerns about fascist and authoritarian personalities, as well as juvenile delinquency, led some psychologists, sociologists, and educators to argue that fighting prejudice was critical to a democratic American future. Some psychiatrists had been arguing since the 1930s that fascism developed as a result of authoritarian personalities, which they argued were the result of "children with stern, often physically abusive fathers and distant, frightened, and unaffectionate mothers."[108] Child psychiatrist David Levy added internationalism as a potential antidote. His research showed that German Nazi resisters had been reared in homes with more friends and wider international contacts than the more insular fascists had. He deduced that adolescents in a democracy needed exposure to what Katherine Glover of the Children's Bureau called a "liberal viewpoint."[109] In the Cold War world, such lessons on democratic life encouraged a generational commitment to democratic cooperation. Although ethnicity, race, and class shape political ideas and attitudes, such national symbols and values, as child psychologist Robert Coles explains, became part of children's moral and political understanding.[110]

At the same time, evidence of the failures of American democracy to protect all its citizens was revealed in many girls' experiences and was increasingly a focus of scholarship, the press, and youth organization publications. "Because of the intermingling of national and personal identity and the discrepancies between national ideals and sociopolitical realities," Rebecca de Schweinitz writes, "young people who grew up in the period were also potentially more sensitive to violations of American democracy than were their elders."[111]

Midcentury Americans thought about race relations as part of personality development projects, an association that made youth organizations appropriate training grounds. The need of boys and girls to learn to live with others was one of the main threads in the central theme of personality development at the Midcentury White House Conference on Children and Youth. The conference's final recommendations included courses and activities to develop intergroup understanding in schools and youth organizations. One document noted the accomplishments of youth organizations in promoting tolerance across lines of race and nationality and in directly involving the "young people themselves" in intercultural and international friendship activities.[112]

Moreover, racism in the postwar years was an international embarrassment.[113] Secretary of State Dean Acheson bemoaned school segregation's being "singled out for hostile foreign comment in the United Nations and elsewhere."[114] *Pionerskaia pravda*, a Soviet publication for youth, regularly accused the United States of insincere efforts to improve race relations, calling ongoing racial injustice a result of capitalism.[115]

Youth organizations hoped to offer a counternarrative through antiprejudice initiatives. In the words of Martha Allen, "Whenever we fail to practice democracy we hand the communists powerful propaganda weapons to use against us and we dim the faith of people in the goodness of our way of life." She thus urged leaders to value all individuals and "to bring the enjoyment and benefits of the Camp Fire program to all girls in your community who want it—Negro girls, foreign girls, Jewish, Protestant, Catholic, the poor and the rich alike."[116] Girls' media and organizations called on girls to overcome prejudice and to champion inclusion and cooperation.

The YWCA, the Girl Scouts, and the Camp Fire Girls were early adopters of inclusion policies. In the 1910s, they granted access to their programs to girls and women of all backgrounds, but it was not until after World War II that national leaders pushed for integration. They had accepted de jure segregation in the South and de facto segregation even when and where their groups were open. In the 1950s, too, change was slow as challenging prejudice too often took a backseat to local racial politics. Clubs continued to form according to school, church, synagogue, settlement house, or neighborhood; rarely were inclusive local clubs created.

Policies and activities increasingly not only sought inclusion at the organizational level, but also the breakdown of the racial barriers that stood between girls. The Girl Scouts began to desegregate troops nationally in 1951. In the 1920s and 1930s, the Girl Scouts' national office had supported access to all girls but did so through segregated camps and clubs. Although national headquarters restricted registration of "racial groups" to those locations where there already existed a white council, African American and Native American troops were formed throughout those decades in such councils, and in the South, many black leaders had started separate troops that in the 1940s received official recognition as Girl Scouts. Integrated rallies and events occurred outside the South as early as the 1920s. Then in 1951, Girl Scouts began to desegregate its southern troops and camps. The organization moved its first black national staffer, Josephine Groves Holloway, who had run a separate council for black girls in Tennessee, to the main Nashville office. Such efforts earned praise from Dr. Martin Luther King Jr. Even so, the first fully integrated triennial conference did not occur until 1969, almost twenty years later.[117] (The Boy Scouts of America also publicly claimed to be open but allowed local councils to decide if and how they would admit African American boys and men. Discriminatory policies were a problem as late as 1974, when the NAACP sued the Boy Scouts for its racial barriers.)[118]

In 1952, the Camp Fire Girls established a committee to promote interaction and cooperation across racial, ethnic, and class lines. Segregated clubs were increasingly deemed problematic. The Camp Fire Girls' national council resolved to "consciously increase its effort to carry out our already stated membership policy," specifically to provide the "educational-recreational program available to all girls" promised in the articles of incorporation. Officials pledged to "help girls cultivate democratic relationships," to secure "skilled persons of different racial and cultural backgrounds," to build greater intercultural awareness and cooperation, and to select camp counselors gifted at creating cooperative environments.[119] A decade later, the Camp Fire Girls embarked on a major outreach program, the Metropolitan Critical Areas Project, to extend its membership to nontraditional members, particularly minorities and children with mental disabilities.[120]

Like the secular girls' organizations, the YWCA diversified in the 1920s largely in racially segregated branches and then more directly challenged segregation after the war. A 1946 interracial charter committed the YWCA and its Y-Teens to "inclusion of Negro women and girls in the mainstream of association life," a process that proceeded unevenly in the YWCA's many branches. Its own commitment was born of the YWCA's liberal Christian roots, but international understanding played a role here as well.[121] In the prayer and Bible study component of the program, which most distinguished it from the secular Girl

IMAGE 3. The Camp Fire Girls' youngest members present Bibs for Babies to a Netherlands Aid Society representative. Monthly publications of the Camp Fire Girls, the Girl Scouts, and the YWCA highlighted diversity after World War II.

"Picture of the Month," *Camp Fire Girl* 25, no. 9 (1946): 2.
Courtesy of Camp Fire National Headquarters.

Scouts and Camp Fire Girls, the YWCA rejected racism and advocated internationalism. A 1947 prayer in anticipation of an international YWCA conference in China gave thanks to God "for the fellowship we share as members of a World Movement with women and girls of many races and nations."[122] The first postwar Y-Teen guidebook warned girls, "If you don't want to know all kinds of girls, you'd better not join this club!"[123] YWCA authors urged girls to consider what freedom from fear meant for minority girls, who, the authors explained, "are afraid of their future in America," afraid "of not being needed in American life." African American, Japanese, and Jewish girls, the authors argued, saw growing antagonism directed toward them.[124]

Photographic images began to appear regularly in organization publications spotlighting girls from a variety of ethnic and racial backgrounds. A May 1946 "Picture of the Month" in the *Camp Fire Girl* magazine featured three Blue Birds, one black, one Asian, and one white, delivering their contribution of "Bibs for Babies" to a Netherlands Aid Society representative.[125] Monthly publications of the Camp Fire Girls, Girl Scouts, and YWCA highlighted diversity as they reported local and regional club news.[126] (The Boy Scout's postwar manual also featured a drawing of an African American boy, but African American boys did not appear regularly in *Boys' Life* until the 1960s.)[127]

There were, however, distinct limits to the degree to which mainstream girls' organizations supported civil rights. In *Seventeen*, a few African Americans can be found in stories covering high school newspapers and clubs and the music scene, and people with dark skin appear as foreigners in stories about the United Nations and aid. *Seventeen*, however, also featured racist advertisements featuring black servants and did not include multiracial images in its fashion spreads until the 1960s.

The Girl Scouts and Camp Fire Girls directed antiprejudice campaigns at their predominantly white, middle-class membership, girls whose class and racial status freed them to choose to participate in these activities and to support civil rights or not. Camp Fire's programs were designed to help "girls of the majority . . . to understand and respect the accomplishments, native capacities, personal dignity and socio-economic problems of [those in the] minority." The Camp Fire Girl magazine implied that the organization's groups were insular; the magazine encouraged members to take note of their friendship circles and, if they included no minorities, to increase their diversity. Moreover, efforts to include girls of minority groups in citizenship training were designed to socialize them to the middle-class values that youth organizations promoted.[128]

The Camp Fire Girls' 1955 report found that some local leaders were "trying to have girls work together across racial lines . . . to help young people live in a democracy," the organization admitted that "in no Council that we know of, do we have a membership that fully reflects the diverse cultural groups in the community." The Camp Fire Girls, moreover, avoided keeping detailed records of its demographics and relied until the 1960s on anecdotal evidence that the membership was becoming more diverse.[129]

Even the YWCA, which regularly acknowledged the direct experiences of its minority members and the need to fight for their social and economic security, faced at the local level a disconcerting lack of representation from all girls in the community. By 1958, a majority of Y-Teen clubs included girls of more than one race; 70 percent provided interracial experiences. Still, as the 1958 college branch survey showed, although 70 percent of College Y's were integrated, non-white membership often included only one or two members, reflecting the small proportion of minority students on predominantly white college campuses.[130]

Although the effect of changes in policy and imagery had definite limits, girls' institutions encouraged a citizenship model giving each girl the responsibility to foster tolerance in herself, her community, and her world. Efforts to build bridges were often grounded in international understanding. This framework of concentric circles that girls' organizations used to describe girls' citizenship responsibilities allowed links between the rings of domestic and international tolerance. Each girl's responsibility to herself and her family grew outward to incorporate the entire world. According to the constitution of the Girl Scouts of the USA, the organization was "dedicated to helping girls develop as happy, resourceful individuals willing to share their abilities as citizens in their homes, their communities, their country and the world."[131] A girl started with herself and her local community and built peace from there. A Girl Scout booklet about international friendship explained that combating prejudices locally was a precursor to international activism and that girls who failed to confront their own unacknowledged prejudices were "not ready for an international program."[132]

The circles of extending responsibility allowed girls' leaders to use personality development as a tool to connect girls to international activities by linking tolerance to maturity, popularity, and charm. The question in a title of a *Seventeen* magazine article from the spring of 1945 connected internationalism, antiracism, and girls' personality development: "What Kind of World Do You Want?" The article reminded a hypothetical teenage girl whose older brother serves with the military overseas that his experience has put him into close contact with "boys" from the "other side of the tracks" and that "what counted" in a fox hole "doesn't have anything to do with what church [the other fellow] goes to, or where his folks were born. . . . Your brother's muddled prejudices have worn off in battle." This neglected the fact that U.S. troops were still not integrated in World War II. Next *Seventeen* asked, "What about you? Have you stood still meanwhile, hanging on to all the little dislikes you had as a child?"

In the remainder of the article, *Seventeen* offered personal and international cautions. The girl would not only fail to grow into a loving, successful adult if she ignored her prejudices, but she would also undermine world peace, since fascist propagandists, like the Nazis, exploited racism to destabilize the nation. As the war drew to a close, girls, like their overseas brothers, learned that adults connected their personality development to the fight for democracy and that they could choose what kind of world they wanted.[133]

In her pamphlet *At Home with People: Ways of Banishing Prejudice*, Y-Reserve secretary Elise Moller used materials from sociology, psychology, and other fields to train groups and leaders to set up activities to battle prejudice. Moller began with a girl's developing personality and the relationships she had with others in her Y-Teen club. Clubs, Moller argued, should help girls find "recognition and security" so that they can "readily expand their world to include persons 'different' from themselves without fear for their own well-being." She encouraged activities that crossed racial boundaries to introduce young people to those outside their social circle. She also told leaders to target "the adolescent girl's absorbing interest in her own popularity and 'charm.'" Because racism tarnished an attractive personality, girls were encouraged to figure out what kind of prejudices they harbored and how those "interfere with . . . developing a pleasing personality" so they could change them.

Yet even as girls' leaders emphasized the personal, they paid attention to structural factors and world affairs. A few pages after admonishing girls to "examine how you behave," the booklet asserted that avoiding another world war depended on combating prejudice. Moller added that personality alone was not sufficient to undo racism and that economic insecurity exacerbated the problem. "Intellectual understanding, religious conviction and personal experience will have to be supplemented with action on the economic bases of prejudice—the fear for oneself and one's family caused by too few jobs for too many people." She invoked the four freedoms, the principles of freedom of speech and religion and the freedoms from fear and want outlined by Franklin D. Roosevelt and Winston Churchill in the Atlantic Charter, and explained, "We have been fighting for a world in which all peoples will be free and secure from fear and want, and in which all human beings may reach their full stature."[134]

Girls' organizations not only printed their own materials for combating prejudice but also published the messages and printed reading suggestions of well-known social scientists whose writings bolstered the idea that eliminating racial prejudice began with the individual and extended through the club and around the globe. The Girl Scouts recommended Hortense Powdermaker; Ruth Benedict and Gene Weltfish's *Races of Mankind*; and Moller's pamphlet

At Home with People, which had been put together for the YWCA; and invited Ethel J. Alpenfels as a national speaker. The Camp Fire Girls printed articles by Alpenfels and Margaret Mead. And the YWCA's suggestions included Gunnar Myrdal, Mead, Alpenfels, Powdermaker, Benedict and Weltfish, Walter Lippmann, and an Anti-Defamation League comic book titled *About People and Fair Play*. In the 1950s, conservatives extended their condemnation of some of these authors and their writings to the girls' organizations for promoting them, but the readings remained a regular component of the groups' recommended literature for girls.

Alpenfels, an anthropologist and associate professor of education at New York University and the author of the juvenile pamphlet *Sense and Nonsense about Race*, regularly spoke about race and war before educators, students, home economics associations, and youth organizations such as the Girl Scouts. Her writings for young people stressed the need to debunk myths about the purity and superiority of races, to move toward intercultural cooperation and international cooperation in order to prevent a third world war.[135] With no sentimentality about the innocence of children, Alpenfels tasked girls' leaders with helping children break down their racial prejudices at the club level and to begin to build intercultural networks of association. Leaders, she believed, played an active role in shaping girls' racial attitudes.

She advised introspection about the prejudices that existed in each group's community and cautioned leaders that such beliefs likely resulted in cliques forming along racial or ethnic lines even within integrated clubs. First, prejudices needed to be "unpacked" through acknowledgment and discussion. Second, leaders should break down the cliques clustered around "one national, economic, or racial background" by "choosing partners for trips, for committee work, or for games." Next, cross-cultural activities should be promoted by leaders so that girls met people from different backgrounds. The step of meeting new people was important because, she wrote, the young might dislike one another for a multitude of reasons other than prejudice, but they needed experience to "know enough people of English, or Negro, or Methodist backgrounds" so they could realize that "we can dislike some without being prejudiced against all of them."[136]

In homogeneous areas, clubs were encouraged to "visit other communities" and "bring in speakers and discussion leaders from all races, religions, and nationalities." Invitees were asked to talk about general topics, not just their ethnic or national background. "If . . . you bring a Chinese girl to speak," Alpenfels warned, "it is wise not to have her talk about what it means or feels like to be Chinese. Rather let her talk about a common problem or demonstrate a skill in which she is talented." She also suggested reading books that present people whom the girls would not otherwise meet. Through specific strategies, Alpenfels believed, girls' leaders actively designed girls' racial attitudes.[137]

Anthropologist Hortense Powdermaker, writing near the end of the war, also directed writings to teenage readers and advocated that they work on the personal and community levels first. She saw such work as necessary to creating national and global change. All three girls' organizations recommended *Probing Our Prejudices*, Powdermaker's popular book for high school students about challenging stereotypes.[138] The Bureau of Intercultural Education and III educators and interfaith leaders in twenty-five states also endorsed the book, which schools across the nation and interfaith leaders adopted for their work with young people during and after the war.[139] Powdermaker argued that prejudice harmed not only its targets but also the prejudiced person, whose personality became "small and mean." She believed high school students could do much to work on their own prejudice and to improve the climate in their own schools.[140]

Still, most of her solutions were institutional and structural. "The battle is not only on the personal front," she cautioned. "It is not enough to just look at ourselves." So although *Probing Our Prejudices* taught students how to evaluate their own biases and challenged them to think about the role played in stereotype formation by family, friends, movies and radio, and books and magazines, Powdermaker offered systematic analysis of recent race riots, interrogated false generalizations, examined economic uncertainty as a cause for prejudice, and detailed the harm done by what a later generation of psychologists and sociologists would call microaggressions. Powdermaker pointed to civic organizations as useful tools for coordinating protest and urged readers to act through labor unions, churches, social or civic clubs, and the chamber of commerce.[141]

Powdermaker urged readers to embrace a cosmopolitan outlook. She wrote that human history included an ever-expanding sense of community with others. Village identifications gave way to national identifications and had culminated in "the feeling of closeness that we have with millions of people we have never seen . . . our allies in this war." She predicted in the postwar world "the development of a feeling of internationalism, as expressed in the concept of the Four Freedoms for the whole world."[142]

The intertwined messages of internationalism and antiracism also appeared in YWCA program packets. The fall 1948 packet theme was "Building a World of Free Peoples," and it emphasized advice on international observances, UN programming, and world fellowship festivals. Nestled between these ideas and news about Indian workers' struggles was a section on U.S. civil rights written by YWCA and National Council of Negro Women leader Dorothy Height. Her message was twofold. First, American racial and religious discrimination were international news that caused outrage and despair, especially in the "colored world." Second, true understanding of people and races was the only basis upon which to build peace. Height outlined actions for girls to take to further her vision. Reminiscent of Angelina Grimké, who had urged southern white women excluded from electoral politics a century earlier to read, pray, speak, and act to end slavery, Height urged all girls who were similarly excluded from direct channels of power to read, pray, and use moral suasion. Height recommended that girls clip newspaper articles about race relations, read pamphlets such as Benedict and Weltfish's *The Races of Mankind* and Benjamin E. Mays's *Seeking to be Christian in Race Relations*, and persuade others through personal conversations and by joining groups that promoted cross-cultural understanding.[143]

Height also urged girls to "make friends with persons of different racial and religious groups." She continued, "Remember, creating a genuine friendship is always hard work; it is even harder when you reach beyond the confines of your own 'race.'" Height advised majority members to invite more than one minority person along to avoid making someone an "exhibition" and told minority members that the sincerity of the majority member might be difficult to ascertain but extending the hand of friendship was everyone's responsibility. Girls could also challenge voluntary segregation and speak up in restaurants, workplaces, and schools when they saw injustice.[144]

Finally, she offered a reminder of how antiracism and pacifism coalesced as a focus for women. Height wrote to Y-Teen directors that it was their responsibility to "train your children and others." Developing your child's openness to "other races, religions and nations, is good insurance that he will not want to participate in another war." Height illustrated this idea by describing a school tableau in which the girl child stands, head uplifted, and holds in her palms a lighted globe, holding "the world in her hands." Girls undertaking specific tasks on the personal and local level were imagined to be political actors with the potential to teach behavior, build character, and create peace.[145]

Refugees in the Teenage Social Circle

Building on the idea of concentric circles of responsibility, girls' organizations cultivated support for immigrants within the United States as an extension of the one-world ideal proclaimed by UN supporters. The *Girl Scout Handbook* of 1947 praised global migrants within the United States as an asset to treasure rather than a foreign element to be feared. Girl Scout officials explained that because the United States was a nation of immigrants from whom girls could learn about other countries, they had "a greater opportunity than any people of the world to promote international friendship."[146]

The YWCA also saw immigration policy as a realm for girls. Their personal connections in their schools and communities, YWCA leaders believed, could have international implications. In the fall of 1945, two million displaced persons were living in Western Europe and more were coming from the East, but most Americans did not want more immigration and were untouched by the refugees' living conditions. President Truman sent Earl G. Harrison to investigate the displaced person camps, and Harrison's report in the State Department *Bulletin* described Jews who were still living behind barbed wire. Although many of them wanted to immigrate to Palestine, some sought refuge in the United States. Only 5 percent of Americans thought there should be more European immigration than had been permitted before the war and 37 percent wanted fewer immigrants. When only about five thousand displaced persons were admitted in 1946, Truman sought legislation to admit refugees, many of them Jews, outside immigrant quotas. Seventy-two percent of Americans opposed such a policy, and Truman's announcement led to six years of public debate.[147]

For the YWCA, immigration was an issue that involved combating racism within the United States and playing an active political role to change policy. The National Board of the YWCA worked alongside the Citizens Committee on Displaced Persons to liberalize the displaced persons laws and to increase the number admitted to the United States. Both groups called for the removal of the discriminatory preferences for farmers and specialized occupations that prevented women and children from coming to the country, and they called for the admittance of Jews, Catholics, and Protestants in proportions that reflected the population of the displaced person camps.[148]

Y-Teens were expected to learn about the displaced, ask school principals and religious leaders if any had moved to their communities, and reach out to the newcomers. If new immigrants were teens, YWCA authors suggested that Y-Teens help the newcomers get acquainted with the school, invite them to the Y-Teen club, and include them in the teenage social circle.[149]

When its opponents filibustered the displaced persons bill, the YWCA urged girls to examine how racism and the filibuster worked together in Congress to hobble inclusiveness.[150] As part of the awareness campaign, YWCA officials recommended materials that would humanize the displaced. It especially promoted *Answers for Anne*, a film made by the Lutheran Resettlement Service in a displaced person camp near Nuremberg. The film featured camp residents who shared their stories.[151] By supporting the war's displaced, the YWCA provided girls with specific plans for engaging in political action. The bill that finally passed in 1948 represented a limited success for immigration reformers, allowing only 202,000 non-quota visas over two years, and those were mortgaged against future quotas. In 1950, Congress extended the Displaced Persons Act for two more years, admitting another 200,000 during that period.[152]

The concrete ideas for girls to combat racism at home intertwined with broader ideals about world peace. Girls began with their own personalities, talked with friends and family, and then moved outward, embracing "fundamental human rights, in the dignity and worth of the human person," as the Universal Declaration of Human Rights puts it, in the community and around the world.

Girls Define Peace

Youth organizations and *Seventeen* encouraged girls to formulate concepts of peace and security that included tolerance and to understand their commitments as beginning with themselves and extending outward. Articulations about peace by many girls reflected these ideals.

One New York girl wrote to the editor of *Seventeen* to lay claim to the idea that her generation was distinctly suited to bringing tolerance and blaming her parents' generation for obsessing over nationality rather than the character of individuals.[153] A seventeen-year-old from Central City, Nebraska, similarly despaired that her generation was the first that could not "make the mistakes which our forefathers made without the earth opening up and swallowing us." She said her generation was ready to take on the responsibility. Evincing hope and exclaiming over youths' importance for the future, she ended with "We are the world."[154]

At the 1947 National YMCA-YWCA conference for high school students, teens demanded "a major emphasis be placed on the development of educational programs on World Peace and World Understanding." They held schools and other community institutions responsible for providing courses pertaining to world understanding and for encouraging interest in the United Nations.[155]

In 1952, when girls served as delegates in their own right at the Y-Teen conference, they demanded that peace be a key topic and they adopted an expansive definition of peace and security. Young people, the women directors wrote, identified peace not only with the absence of war but with "no prejudice and discrimination, and happiness—food, shelter, and security."[156] Y-Teens wrote and presented a pageant for the opening session called Peace in One World, which "portrayed the need for mutual respect among individuals, groups and nations" as a "first step in the building of a peaceful world." In a general session led by the New York University School of Social Work professor Nathan Cohen, girls identified as common obstacles to peace "the desire of nations and individuals for power and money; lack of understanding of other people; and failure to practice the principles of democracy in daily life." In a follow-up session, teens expressed the need to start locally by working toward peace within families, friends, and community groups. These Y-Teens agreed that they had responsibility to work for world peace, which began with the self and the family and extended outward.[157] Although these proclamations were made in the setting of a conference with girls' leaders in attendance, they nonetheless demonstrate girls' familiarity with the peace discourse their leaders sought to teach them.

Girls clearly did define peace in terms consistent with what adults expected. In an essay contest for which teens wrote about what the YWCA meant to them, the winners demonstrated the ability to articulate the YWCA's integration of civil rights and internationalism. The winner recognized her involvement in "a

world-wide Christian fellowship of women and girls" through which her "prejudices are being removed through association with people of other races, religions,
and nationalities." She noted that she was learning about the world and its people
and said, "Because I am a Y-Teen, I am related to a larger world in which I hope
to be a good citizen of tomorrow."[158] The runner-up in the category for twelve- to
seventeen-year-olds emphasized the YWCA's recreation and social activities but
also wrote that she "mingle[s] with all kinds of people," and "I picture myself and
my local YWCA linked with girls and women all over the world who are working together within the YWCA to create a better, kindly, more Christian world."[159]
Girls understood that their organizations connected them to an international
movement, and they believed it had the potential to make change.

Y-Teens were not alone. *Seventeen* reader J. W. from Salt Lake City signaled
her commitment to work "with people of all races" and to "get to know the
family around the corner" in order to find "we like them and . . . have much
in common." This she connected to turning an armistice into true peace and
"fighting for a better world—and not with weapons."[160] Laurendale, Pennsylvania, Camp Fire Girl Helen Schoener's club visited UN headquarters in 1949.
Three years later, Schoener participated in the National Triennial Conference
of the Camp Fire Girls, where peace was among the topics. She explained, "The
United Nations suddenly became very vivid to me. In order to develop international understanding we must begin at home. By eliminating prejudice from
our schools and communities, we form attitudes which eventually bring about
world friendship. Camp Fire Girls can play an important role in foreign relations
by including activities in their program which promote understanding of other
peoples."[161]

A YWCA survey on teenagers' commitment to citizenship gave further evidence that girls merged internationalism and antiracism in their thinking. Y-Teens
distributed approximately three thousand surveys to their schoolmates, members
of church groups, and other peers ranging in age from twelve to seventeen. The
surveyed teens voiced broad support for intercultural learning and understanding,
and many believed that "only through true understanding and appreciation of all
people for each other can world peace ever be attained."[162]

Conclusion

U.S. girls were taught about the United Nations during the early Cold War as
their own institutions incorporated the language of human rights and invited
young people to read about and discuss the international body and to bring
its themes to bear on ordinary program activities. When asked if the world
would descend into destruction or if peace would prevail, the internationalist girl citizen was trained to respond that international friendship and world

understanding provided answers. She would ward off fatalism and protect her brothers and boyfriends from delinquency through her vision of democracy and world peace. She would commit herself and her club to knowledge about atomic energy, the United Nations, and world citizenship, and she would ready herself for the future's demands through democratic activities in her group and participation in youth councils and national conferences. Still, her world was a gendered one. Her duties would be primarily relational. She would influence her brother and her boyfriend and be an advocate for peace, but she rarely was encouraged to imagine herself as a future Security Council delegate.

As the atomic bomb awakened her political activism and led her to raise her voice for "one world," the internationalist girl citizen would, *Seventeen*'s editors believed, become aware of other ways that her voice was needed to bring about "one world." Editor Alice Beaton explained, "You'll get very impatient with that thing called 'national pride'"; "You'll want decent housing for all human beings"; "You'll want to understand your neighbors across the barriers-that-are-no-longer-barriers."[163] As American girls learned about internationalism, they also learned the language of international cooperation and human rights. Girls' organizations and girls' magazines taught an international outlook that supported the United Nations. The human rights claims led to a concept of fellowship amenable to opposing prejudice, a principle that transformed girls' organizations over the next several decades.

2

"Hello, World, Let's Get Together"

Building Global Conversations through
Pen Pals and Aid Packages

After World War II, girls' organizations linked letter writing and providing relief to world friendship. In March 1948, one year after President Truman announced his plan to "help free peoples" around the world through economic aid with the Truman Doctrine and just months before U.S. military aircraft delivered supplies to civilians in Soviet-blockaded West Berlin, the Camp Fire Girls celebrated the organization's birthday with an international project called Hello, World, Let's Get Together. Girls in the Eastern Massachusetts Council responded by initiating relationships with girls in Czechoslovakia, France, Germany, Belgium, Italy, Ireland, and Jerusalem by writing letters and sending relief packages to orphan homes, private families, and schools. Local executive director Doris Foster fastened a letter of thanks from fourteen-year-old Marie Kulova, of Frystatn, Czechoslovakia, into her scrapbook. Marie wrote, "I was feel very happy that people in such a far country are thinking about us and helping us as much as they can. I shall never forget it. I enjoyed learning about the U.S.A. at our school about their great presidents and their democratic principles. I am sorry not to know the [E]nglish language so that I could read the book you sent me. I shall learn it now. I am an orphan, am 14 years old. One more many thanks, harrah for the United States."[1]

Marie's letter provides a glimpse into the postwar contacts that girls forged after World War II, illuminating the burgeoning interests of Americans, including youngsters, in forging personal links with other countries. Girls wrote to, and provided assistance to, peers overseas, and girls like Marie began to contend with U.S. world leadership by learning English and studying "great presidents and their democratic principles." Marie's salute to the United States at the end of her letter provides insight into how U.S. girls saw their nation reflected back to themselves. It promised international friendship and the reassuring gratitude of the world.

Girls' culture and international politics met in pen pal letters and in shipments of school supplies and children's clothing. Educators and youth organizers asked girls to correspond with and send aid packages to war-stricken children and families to rescue children from the suffering caused by war, to cultivate peace through human contact, and to spread Western democracy by telling girls in other lands about their lives in the United States. Humanitarian aid—public and private—advanced an image of the United States as moral and generous, an image needed for Americans as well as foreigners to legitimate the nation's new-found global leadership. The picture of American military strength could be moderated by expressions of human rights and respect for "the dignity and worth of the human person," aspirations found in the Atlantic Charter, the United Nations Charter, and the Universal Declaration of Human Rights. Even if girls did not recognize the larger national interests at stake in their letter and gift exchanges, their organizations saw such beneficence as fulfilling the responsibility to help others and as a fundamental part of the era's expressions of humanitarianism.[2]

Adult educators, youth workers, and political leaders promoted girls' international correspondence and gift shipments as a gender-appropriate activity. In the late 1940s pen pals were seen as a way to foster mutual understanding and world peace. Camp Fire program specialist Lucille Hein endorsed the emerging correspondence between Japanese and U.S. girls as "helping to foster world friendship in a little way."[3] By the mid-1950s, politicians also identified girls' contacts as an element of supporting international alliances and creating respect for the United States. By writing neat, friendly letters, girls would share their part of the American story. The world would see through their own words how, in contrast to the imagined robotlike children who served the Soviet state, healthy, happy, generous, educated girls were produced by American capitalist democracy.

But the letters did more than present only the story that adults intended. On the one hand, letters and packages promoted lopsided relationships that placed American girls in superior positions to their overseas peers. On the other, personal contacts were not easily controlled, and girls' relationships produced honest, candid accounts of American family life, education, race relations, and consumerism that challenged official Cold War messages. Pen pal friendships and presents to girls abroad represented the new relationship of American girls to the world and a space where they could present their own opinions.

A History of Youth Pen Pals

For Americans, writing to a pen pal, a correspondent with whom the primary relationship is through letters, emerged as a popular pastime in the interwar period and was immediately regarded as an activity appropriate for children and youth. Children of the Junior Red Cross, the Camp Fire Girls, and the Girl Scouts had sent supplies to Allied civilians during World War I, and many began to exchange postcards as well. A Red Cross official described these activities as "welding links in a chain of international friendship that disputes between the two Governments cannot break."[4] Likewise, the Girl Scouts established an office they called the International Post to match Girl Guides and Girl Scouts with pen pals. In 1926, on its first Thinking Day, an annual event intended for contemplating international friendship and world peace, girls sent fellow Scouts and Guides around the world postcards. As the pen pal hobby spread in the interwar years, teachers began to introduce pen pal projects. Iowa schoolgirls Juanita and Betty Wagner were introduced to Anne and Margot Frank in this way in 1940 and exchanged a few letters before Anne's family was forced into hiding. Pen pals also began to appear in girls' popular culture with the publication of the Dutch fiction series by Cissy Van Marxveldt, whose teen character Joop ter Heul writes letters to her friend "Kitty," the name Anne Frank used to address her adolescent diary. In 1936, when her professor at Wellesley commented on the isolation of America's young people, Edna MacDonough founded the International Friendship League, eventually the largest of the pen pal matching services and one supported by the federal government.[5]

After World War II, diverse youth groups sponsored pen friendships, often with a political intent. Before and after Israeli independence in 1948, Reform Jewish schools in the United States asked students to write to students in Israel as part of a political project to "cultivate empathic bonds between Reform youth and Israel." At the same time, the Boy Scouts and Girl Scouts wrote hoping to link the children and teenagers of the United States to Cold War allies, and educators sought ways to supplement their traditional geography and history curricula. Overall, pen pal letters surged. In 1953, the Girl Scouts established a pen pal proficiency badge that nearly 160,000 Girl Scouts earned over the next decade, and the YWCA had a correspondence division that included many teenagers.[6] In 1956 the Eisenhower administration capitalized on the trend's popularity and urged Americans of all ages to share America's story abroad through letters as part of the People-to-People program. American adults and children sent 330 million personal letters abroad each year in the mid-1950s.[7]

Relief projects and writing to pen pals were closely related activities. San Francisco schools used the children's Red Cross support as a "springboard" from which to build an international education program that included hundreds of children writing letters overseas. One teacher exclaimed, "I am sure many enduring friendships are going to result from this correspondence."[8]

Conditions after the war prompted action by caring individuals and organizations with the resources to help. Throughout Europe and Asia, World War II

had brought devastation. In 1945, vast populations were homeless. UNESCO estimated that there were 8 million children in Germany (both the displaced from
other countries and Germans), 6.5 million in the Soviet Union, and 1.3 million in
France, all with no place to call home. Urban infrastructure had been destroyed.
Vienna, for example, lacked transportation and electrical services, and its hospitals were in disarray. An estimated thirteen million European children had
lost one or both parents. Families throughout Europe were separated and so-
called wolf-children wandered streets in packs looking for sustenance.[9] Over
the next decade, U.S. and British relief efforts through the United Nations Relief
and Rehabilitation Administration, the Marshall Plan, and private international
agencies helped while European economies struggled.

In Asia, conditions were similarly bleak. In Japan, standards of living were
estimated to be 65 percent lower than before the war in rural areas and 35 percent lower in urban areas. Following the devastating bombing of Japanese cities, nearly 30 percent of the population was homeless in Tokyo and Hiroshima.
"The streets of every major city quickly became peopled with demoralized ex-
soldiers, war widows, orphans, the homeless and unemployed—most of them
preoccupied with simply staving off hunger." Both the Occupation government
and after 1952 the reconstituted Japanese government responded slowly and
with "scant grasp of the dimensions" of the problem as the poor conditions
continued years after the war. In some areas only 10 percent of students reached
middle school and food crises shortened students' schooldays.[10]

In 1950, the Commission on the Occupied Areas reported on 176 U.S.-based
civilian organizations involved in international relief, international correspondence, and education, ten of these specifically recruiting young people below
college age. In 1949, the commission reported that U.S. agencies had sent over
eleven million dollars to occupied countries alone, probably a vast undercount
since only 44 percent of listed agencies could provide data.[11]

In their relief and correspondence programs, girls' organizations worked
both alone and in collaboration with such other organizations as UNICEF and
the Cooperative for American Remittances to Europe (CARE), which one year
after its establishment in 1945 sent one million packages to hungry European
families. CARE later expanded its activities beyond Europe and became the
Cooperative for Assistance and Relief Everywhere.[12]

The Camp Fire Girls undertook a wide range of international projects. In
1948, girls in Washington County, Oregon, "adopted" a French orphan, and girls
in Sacramento, California, adopted a twelve-year-old Dutch girl to whom they
sent the considerable sum of fifteen dollars each month, which, along with a
box of clothing, candy, vitamin pills, and school and toilet articles, would provide the girl's necessities.[13] Girls in Tyler, Texas, collected "gifts of clothing"
for Danish children, and girls in Quincy, Massachusetts, shipped thirty food

parcels to Camp Fire Girls in England. A club in Holland, Michigan, established a "chain of regular correspondence" with Dutch girls, part of what Camp Fire officials boasted were pen friends in thirty-seven different countries.[14] Alva Bernheimer Gimbel, the Camp Fire Girls' observer to the United Nations, encouraged cultivating ties to specialized UN agencies, such as UNESCO, to promote "the immediate rebuilding of libraries, museums, schools, etc., and the 'human reconstruction' of young people." She envisioned direct contacts with girls exchanging letters as well as American girls sending recreation kits, and school supplies, activities she hoped would lead to international travel and visits.[15]

Girl Scout officials similarly praised their members' dedication to projects of international scope. According to one report, "These have included sending tons of Friendship Bags containing scarce items to Girl Guides and Girl Scouts in other countries; 130 Play Kits, filled with books and toys from 35 states, to Greece; 10,861 cases of canned food to Europe from 228 different communities; 3,000 Thinking Day Boxes of school, recreation, and food supplies to Girl Scout headquarters abroad; 2,328 pounds of seeds in family-sized packages to help replant the fields of Europe; [and] 10,000 blankets. In 1947, 1948, and 1949, the

IMAGE 4. The Central Los Angeles Council of Girl Scouts prepares Kits for Korea, 1954. Collection of National Historic Preservation Center, Girl Scouts of the USA.

Girl Scouts aided 150,000 children in Europe and Asia through their Clothes for Friendship project."[16] These numbers represent a fraction of what the Scouts provided.

In the late 1940s, *Seventeen* magazine pointed girls to additional agencies to which they could contribute to relief efforts and make contact with girls overseas. Although the editors did not match pen pals or collect packages to send abroad, regular columns advertised service programs that did; these included the Foster Parents' Plan, UNICEF, Save the Children Foundation, Youth of all Nations, Youth Out for UNICEF, and CARE.[17] Endorsements of the United Nations and advertisements to support children through international agencies such as the Foster Parents' Plan and Save the Children Fund became part of the political culture with which young people identified. Certainly some of the 361,000 CARE packages Americans sent to Europe in November 1948 alone were inspired by advertisements in the *American Girl* or *Seventeen*.[18]

Although many of the early efforts focused on Europe, as Cold War policymakers turned attention to the developing world, so did U.S. agencies. Letters and relief offerings traveled to an increasing range of countries beyond Europe. Both reflected the pattern of cultural exchange that the State Department and United States Information Agency (USIA) used to wage cold war by promoting positive images of the United States abroad and warm relations with potential allies in new Cold War regions of interest. Organizations like the Children's Plea for Peace, which matched 21,152 American children with foreign correspondents in 1957, also distributed school supplies to children in countries like Cuba.[19] The Camp Fire Girls' 1957–1958 Meet the People project, collections of photographs and stories about American life put together in local communities, traveled to places like Egypt, Lebanon, Pakistan, Nigeria, Ghana, India, and Israel. That same year, two thousand Girl Scouts came to Philadelphia City Hall to support a book drive for Morocco and Tunisia.[20] Just as the State Department sponsored music and dance tours featuring jazz superstars, among them Louis Armstrong, Dave Brubeck, and Duke Ellington, and the Martha Graham dance ensemble in the mid- to late 1950s, girls served as young cultural ambassadors who could reach a new generation of allies.[21] Although the State Department did not directly commission girls' letters and relief packages, the American Council on Education and youth organizations sought the advice of and collaborated with the Department of State, Office of Wartime Information, military officials, USIA, and President Eisenhower's People-to-People program to facilitate international exchange.[22]

Gender, Girls, and "Humanitarian Impulses"

Pen pals and humanitarian relief were understood to be appropriate activities for girls. Aid was consistent with women and girls' caregiving duties. The YWCA presented humanitarian aid as a responsibility of girls in a play outlining the duties of the youthful postwar citizen. In it, a high school boy claims that nations receiving aid are ungrateful: "They distrust us and think we've just helped them to increase our own power." His father concurs, remarking, "Sure, our foreign aid program is based on our own security," cementing alliances and preventing the spread of communism. His mother, however, disagrees, insisting that some is also given from "humanitarian impulses" that derive from the Golden Rule. The girl reminds the male family members that "individuals help, too, by sending CARE packages abroad; and in our own YWCA we share in other ways through world fellowship projects. None of these is connected with government."[23] Y-Teen literature, then, showed the choice to give aid to be a private one made by agencies and individuals that cared about the world.

Not only was service to families and children through international aid akin to traditional arenas of girls' civic activity, but youth organization literature also conceived of girls as especially able to cultivate personal relationships around the world. Because it built personal connections, pen pal letter writing appeared as a major activity of girls' organizations and as a pathway to larger projects and citizen roles. The Camp Fire Girls' 1946 manual opens with a narrative intended to introduce the central activities and themes of the program. Pen pals are mentioned twice in the opening section. A hypothetical club decides to put on a Christmas pageant that they learned about in letters from their Camp Fire pen pal friends in England. A few pages later, these imaginary girls receive another letter, from girls in China, which the leader promises to read aloud.[24] The letters not only established one-to-one relationships between girls, but they also had the potential for connecting groups, thus broadening their effect.

In contrast, pen pal correspondence was less noticeable in the postwar Boy Scouts of America and boys used it to transmit militarized values as well as brotherhood. In 1945, *Boys' Life* touted that boys could get pen pals from a geographic swath ranging from West Africa to the Netherlands and again in 1954 the magazine described pen pals as something fun and adventurous and as a way to make "less trouble in the world." Overall, however, *Boys' Life* mentioned the activity far less than did girls' literature.[25] Despite the formation of the World Brotherhood of Boys, a pen pal network established in the 1910s to awaken boys from their provincialism and prejudices, the 1948 Boy Scouts of America handbook carried no mention of pen pals.[26]

When the Boy Scouts did get involved, some of the gifts they sent had a different tenor. Some gift packages, for example, used military imagery. When the

Boy Scouts of America sent World Friendship Funds to Scouts overseas, they sent them in a package they called an "Inter-continental Brotherhood Missile, a projectile of friendship and good will." They did not let the packaging describe itself but explained that "the nose of this ICBM is loaded with training scholarship, equipment, and literature from the Boy Scouts of America." At each meeting, boys held a "five minute 'blast off'" where members made coin contributions to the "ICBM envelope." Similarly, the YMCA Youth Department developed an "ingenious missile shaped coin card called 'YMCAnik'" to distribute among Y groups to inspire fund raising. (Coin cards were envelopes in which fund-raisers kept coin donations.)[27]

Evidence of how gender shaped the internationalist ethos, sometimes in subtle ways, also comes from the Girl Scout and Boys Scout proficiency and merit badges for interpretation. Both groups offered such a badge and counted letter writing in a foreign tongue as an activity toward the achievement. Girls' activities included interpretation in the context of writing to others, whereas boys' activities focused more on skill building. The Girl Scout manual for 1947, for example, suggested a back-and-forth correspondence, one that might advance world friendship, whereas the Boy Scout manual focused on acquiring the ability to write in a foreign language. Boys were required to write a letter in a foreign language on a topic of the counselor's choosing, but earning their badge did not require that they send it or even have a foreign recipient in mind.[28] The focus for girls, then, was development of relationships whereas boys built skills for future leadership roles.

Pairing Pen Pals

The institutional structures that girls' organizations set up to pair pen pals provide evidence of how seriously these youth leaders regarded the activity and the ways pen pal networks intertwined with military, missionary, and U.S. foreign policy aims. Girls found pen pals through a variety of mechanisms. Some of these friendships were sustained for several years. Others were short-lived because of circumstances beyond the control of the girls' leaders or teachers. Using connections with churches, schools, correspondence societies, and other youth organizations, the Camp Fire Girls and Girl Scouts matched their groups to Camp Fire Girls and Girl Guides in other countries.[29]

The Girl Scouts had an International Post correspondence matching system that boasted of its ability to pair American girls with those from forty countries and refugee camps in the Ukraine. Girls twelve and over could write to Girl Guides in other countries using the International Post, and leaders of girls under twelve could use the system for group letters. The International Post Box maintained a file of the names, ages, and addresses of girls from abroad who

sought pen friends in the United States. To requests for correspondents in countries for which the Girl Scouts had no listings, staff sent the names of those
inquiring to the Post Box secretaries in those countries. The process of matching
girls as correspondents often took two or three months.[30]

Despite the ambition of educators and youth organization leaders, a variety of barriers made it difficult, and at times impossible, for girls to sustain
correspondence. Lack of resources in Europe and Asia dictated against corre-
sponding with American girls because of the costs of mailing letters abroad and
the expense related to reciprocating with photographs and occasional presents.
Thus, when the Girl Scouts pioneered international friendship troops, or "sister
troops," in 1944 through correspondence and exchange, the program expanded
slowly because of the paucity of girls abroad who were ready to take part.[31]

Language was another barrier. Although some correspondence societies
and charities, such as Foster Parents' Plan for War Children, offered translation
services, girls' organizations and schools rarely did. Pen pals commonly relied
on the foreign language abilities of one correspondent, and in the United States,
instruction in foreign languages for young people was limited. Hence, many girls
asked for English, Scottish, Australian, South African, and Canadian pen pals.[32]

Youth organizations tried to prevent language barriers from undermining
pen pal relationships. Girl Scout guidebooks instructed those seeking a pen pal
to avoid listing only the countries that interested them, but also to consider
carefully the "languages that they know or for which they can find translators."
Some girls, lured by the fantasy of writing to pen pals in faraway places, failed
to anticipate the problems of writing to girls who knew only languages they did
not. The Girl Scouts encouraged the study of foreign languages and writing in
those languages but also warned, "Don't ask for a pen pal who speaks a language
you cannot speak unless you have a genuine curiosity to learn something of her
language, and unless you can arrange for a capable and willing translator in your
community."[33]

One popular pen pal country was Japan, but in the late 1940s, few U.S. girls
knew Japanese, and few Japanese girls could write in English even as educated
girls were beginning to learn English. Correspondence societies and teachers
promoted correspondence with Americans as a way to learn about the United
States.[34] In the late 1950s and early 1960s, Mary Alice Sanguinetti, a Camp Fire
Girl in Bakersfield, California, wrote to several international pen pals and
remembers the language difficulties. It was easiest for her to correspond with a
pen friend in Australia. She also had a pen pal in Germany, but that correspondence faded. "I tried to write in German and that was really, really hard, so that
kind of died," she remembers. She also wrote to a Japanese girl for a short time
and suspects that the efforts got to be too much for the Japanese girl, who tried
to write in English.[35]

Camp Fire officials made some effort to get around language barriers through translation partnerships. The president of the San Gabriel Valley Area Council of Camp Fire Girls in California sought help from the Japanese-speaking population in the region.[36] She hoped that "the Japanese Camp Fire Girls could write their letters in Japanese, and then we would get friends in the San Gabriel Valley who are of Japanese descent to translate them for our girls." She urged her contact in Japan to find translators in Japan, as well, so that the American girls could write their letters in English. "We followed this plan in connection with our Community Service Project for French children last year," she explained, "and found it worked very successfully."[37] Such programs helped girls exchange letters, but sustaining a long friendship in this manner was a burden for all involved.

As the decade proceeded, plans for international friendship became more robust. Some organizations, such as the International Friendship League, tried to solidify friendships through follow-up visits and sponsored travel. In the summer of 1958, a group of teenage American girls visited their pen friends in Western Europe. They lived in the homes of their European pen friends to "learn firsthand about their families and way of life."[38]

Corresponding with Communist Countries

Even as the number of ties to Western European girls grew and contacts with children in developing countries began, pen friendships with girls in communist countries became more difficult to set up and maintain. American girls had written to girls in Czechoslovakia and Poland right after the war, but by the 1950s, Cold War tensions hindered correspondence with girls in communist-dominated countries. In 1947, a Rialto, California, Camp Fire Girl club had adopted Polish families and one group tried to maintain correspondence with a Polish girl who had lost her father in a Nazi concentration camp.[39] Poland, however, was experiencing "terror and chaos." Jews returned from the death camps to face renewed anti-Semitic violence, and in 1948, "Stalinism proper triumphed in Poland" as the one-party Soviet satellite had fully emerged. In 1949, the Polish communist party shut down Western youth organizations and charities and tried to take control of the Catholic Church.[40] Most communist countries eliminated open Scouting and Guiding by the end of the 1950s. Even as Guiding's internationalism blossomed in the West and in developing countries after the war, the Guides were being forced underground in communist Hungary, Poland, and Czechoslovakia in the early part of the decade and in China, Cuba, and the Baltic States by its end.[41] Without familiar church and youth organization networks operating openly in communist countries and with increased surveillance and closed borders, U.S. girls had little opportunity to correspond with pen pals in those countries.

Cold War anticommunism within the United States further limited the range of pen pal correspondents to those deemed politically appropriate. When the Camp Fire organization received an invitation from the Japan LPF Club to set up pen pal connections, Camp Fire officials asked their correspondence society contact, Heihachiro Suzuki, to find out if the club's "aims and purposes are good and democratic." After Suzuki warned that the organization was likely the Japan International Pen-Friends Club, which he believed was run by "ex-communists" who were antagonistic toward U.S. policy in Japan, Camp Fire officials did not accept the invitation. Even had they been comfortable with the arrangement, such relationships would have been too dangerous in the anticommunist political climate in the United States of the late 1940s and early 1950s.[42]

As the Khrushchev thaw that followed Stalin's death in 1953 made cultural exchange a new strategy to win the allegiance of neutral populations, the U.S. government provided new opportunities for pen pals in communist countries. USIA officials aided Letters Abroad, a pen pal–matching organization for adults and children, in its efforts to write content favorable to the United States and to connect Americans, including students in school classes who wished to write to pen pals behind the Iron Curtain.[43] People-to-People committees claimed to have arranged 227,203 correspondences with people behind the Iron Curtain in 1958.[44] Still, pen friendships with those living in communist countries were pursued only with great caution. By 1959, the People-to-People Letter Writing Committee was receiving an increasing number of requests from the Soviet satellites. Such requests were "handled on a highly selective basis," as communists, it was believed, used pen pals to disseminate propaganda. (Americans' own attempts to promote a favorable image abroad, by contrast, were viewed as informational.) Similar caution was used with regard to suspect organizations in the free world that sought pen pal affiliates.[45]

Ambassadors of Friendship

The contents of girls' letters varied widely. Some, like Marie's, were solitary thank you letters that appear in club records. Others were introductions that began a correspondence. Sometimes girls sustained intimate and detailed correspondence over months or even years.

Pen pal letters, like much of children's writings, have often been lost in the intervening years. Many adult women interviewed for this project remember writing to girls in other countries but did not save the letters they received, let alone copies of those they composed. Still, some survive, as do the instructions provided to the girls taking part in such programs. Schools provided model letters to teachers so that they might promote internationalism. The Camp Fire Girls' headquarters saved several introductory letters from girls in Japan, and individual groups included pen pal letters, especially thank you notes recognizing their service, within scrapbooks.

The intimate and lengthy correspondence of Elizabeth "Liz" Frank, the Jewish American daughter of a Hollywood producer who grew up to be a Pulitzer Prize–winning author and English professor, and Lore Petzka, a Catholic Viennese girl whose father suffered psychological wounds as a Nazi soldier on the Eastern front, reveals how candid and mutually supportive girls' letters could be. The girls, both born during the war, met briefly in Vienna in 1957 and developed a close friendship through their nearly six-year correspondence. Lore saved all of Liz's letters. Although Lore's letters were not saved, it is possible to piece together many dynamics of the relationship.

Although many girls certainly decided what to write in their letters, those produced within schools and clubs, where teachers and leaders supervised the writing, did not necessarily reflect children's unfiltered expressions. Many pen pal letters cannot be considered a "spontaneous phenomenon."[46] A 1945 district curriculum resource for the intercultural program in the San Francisco Unified School District included several model pen pal letters written by children in the United States and Scotland. One such letter attested to the author's civic pride and awareness of the United Nations, especially since the child's city hosted the 1945 UN conference. His letter described the activities of a class that was busy making charts about the "Dumbarton Oaks Plan for World Security" and "Our School Plan for Democratic Living." He also discussed world peace. "We must have an understanding of other people and countries," he explained. The model letter ended with an invitation to respond: "I would like to know your ideas on this subject. Don't you think we, the children, have a part in this world friendship idea?"[47] Such letters, perhaps written by children and perhaps not, were then circulated in the district so other teachers could instruct their own students to follow the idealistic style in international correspondence. Such letters may have been dictated or copied from a chalkboard or merely used as inspiration.

The Camp Fire Girls' project announcements explained that leaders helped girls, especially the younger ones, write their letters during group meetings.[48] Parents also helped, and adults regularly read the letters that girls received. A Girl Scout publication pointed out that the letter to a pen pal "will be seen not only by her but possibly by her friends, her family, and her teachers."[49] Letters were not intended merely as private correspondence but as an activity of good citizens. The American girls might well have paid heed to their adult audience as they wrote. Indeed, one American pen pal asked her correspondent to avoid commenting on the former's references to sex and romance because she did not want her mother, who read the letters she received, to know she was sexually active.

Content mattered because a girl could serve as "a kind of ambassador," girls' leaders announced, by making friends for America and telling the nation's story abroad.[50] In the late 1940s, manners were stressed as a way to make friends, but in the 1950s, as U.S. government officials grew increasingly concerned about the United States' image abroad, girls were encouraged to share everyday stories that reflected positively on American democracy and capitalism. Whereas relief showcased American generosity and sympathy, letter writing made the girls cultural ambassadors who would build world friendship and complement the United States through correspondence.

Girls received advice from youth organizations on how to make friends and increasingly on how to portray themselves, and by extension the United States, in a positive light. Good manners would extend friendly world relations. Girls were cautioned, "Not you alone but your troop, all Girl Scouts, and your country will be judged by the things you write, the way you write, and the neatness of your letter." The Girl Scout handbook encouraged girls to write about things that would interest girls abroad and things that portrayed daily American life such as "what you do in your troop, about your family, your pets, your hobbies, your everyday life, and special celebrations." Girl Scouts read that their pen pals "will be pleased to receive pictures of you, your family, your town" and reminders to include stories about camping.[51] Sometimes instructions on what kinds of things to write were implicit but obvious, as when the Camp Fire handbook told the fictive tale of the arrival of a letter from China: "[The letter] just came and [our pen friend] answered all our questions about her school and her home."[52]

Another Girl Scout publication further instructed girls to demonstrate interest in the lives of their pen friends and not to write only about themselves. Girls should incorporate knowledge from their study of the other country into a letter if they could. In addition, the handbook reminded girls that, "with the exception of girls in Central and South America, Australia, South Africa, Switzerland, and Canada, you are writing to persons whose countries for years will probably feel the effects of the terrible devastation of war." Girls could "promote international good will by being thoughtful and tactful." They could send gifts, especially magazines like the *American Girl* and *Seventeen*, but the handbook advised against "luxury items if food, clothing, sewing materials, and writing supplies are most needed."[53]

Because American girls' culture was becoming more focused on consumerism, new concerns about girls as ambassadors emerged. Girl Scout and Camp

Fire officials warned against exhibiting consumer culture too proudly. "Don't refer to your country and your possessions as the 'richest,' 'biggest,' and 'best.'" Instead, girls were told, "write about the things that will interest your friend" not about "*you, you, you.*"[54]

Although girls' organizations wrote many of the guidelines for the content of correspondence in the 1940s, the government also made suggestions in the mid-1950s. Beginning in 1950, the Common Council for American Unity (CCAU) sponsored "Letters from America Week" and published articles and stories about American life as topics for letter writing and released them to the foreign press. The letter-writing week soon won the endorsement of the Eisenhower administration, and the Ad Council announced the initiative, mobilizing Americans to send thirty-five million letters for "better understanding." The council suggested writing to at least one overseas friend or relative and including "some example of the American way of life from your own experience or events in your community," to "answer criticisms and hostile propaganda" about U.S. bellicosity, materialism, and exploitative big businesses. "Don't brag about our material advantages," it warned. It also suggested showing interest in the correspondent's country and life overseas.[55]

As ambassadors, girls could combat the stereotype of the ugly American, made infamous in William Lederer and Eugene Burdick's novel of brash, condescending, and incompetent statesmen, by avoiding self-absorption and materialism in their letters.[56] In this light, a 1953 *Seventeen* magazine article demonstrated that American letter writers had their work cut out for them. It published an account by seventeen-year-old Victoria Langford of New York City, who described her experience with Youth of All Nations (YOAN) and encouraged other readers to get involved. American girls were needed to "*prove*, in letters, that we are full of friendly feeling toward youth elsewhere." Langford reported that *Mirror for Youth*, the YOAN magazine of international letters, demonstrated the hope for international unity among young readers but also dangerous misunderstandings of American life. A teenager from the British Gold Coast (Ghana) in Africa wrote that Americans "can do wonderful things" but are "rascals and very wicked." An Indian wondered if Americans all carried revolvers as they did in the movies. And a Filipino wondered why Americans "discriminate [against] those of the brown race." In response, Langford urged teens to become their own "Voice of America" and write letters to improve America's image abroad.[57]

The People-to-People's Youth Activities Committee organizers knew that personal relationships were not easily controlled. They recommended "adult guidance" of children and teenagers involved in international contact, since "there is very little, if any, possibility of control once it has started." The committee's resource guide noted that "thoughtlessly worded letters can actually do more harm than good" and therefore suggested that youth leaders coordinate "group letters" as a "training process for the individual" correspondence and consult for suggestions and appropriate topics a CCAU pamphlet on how to be a "spokesman for the United States."[58]

"I Can Tell Her Everything"

Many girls created reciprocal friendships that lasted years or even lifetimes. Some heeded adult advice to produce chatty, friendly letters about school and home that showcased healthy, happy American girlhoods. Some were candid about American culture in ways that challenged official Cold War descriptions of American life. Much correspondence, especially that connected to relief projects, promoted asymmetrical relationships that mirrored the United States' power in the world.

Although numbers are difficult to recover, about one-third of girls in organizations likely wrote to pen pals. One-third of the Camp Fire alumnae interviewed for this project who were asked about pen pal correspondence remember writing to someone. A YWCA survey of Y-Teens and non-Y-Teens also found that a little less than half had participated in international friendship projects like international correspondence.[59]

Not all were enthusiastic. Ann Chenall, an elementary school student in the early and mid-1950s in Corvallis, Oregon, remembers writing to a pen pal with her class, but a later student exchange experience was much more meaningful for her understanding of the world. She wrote to a girl in Turkey because her teacher required it. "I know in elementary school I had a teacher who was really into pen pals. And we did it a little bit, and I can't even remember. I think the girl was from Turkey, but it wasn't a significant part of my life particularly. My mother ended up taking in a young girl from Thailand who came as a student to Oregon State, and that was a lot more a part of my understanding of the world than being a pen pal."[60]

It could be difficult to get girls engaged, but leaders persisted, and many girls did get involved. When a Massachusetts Camp Fire leader wrote to an organization official about her group's international correspondence, she explained that "somehow, it has been hard to get my group warmed up to the project." Perhaps the lengthy process of acquiring pen pals discouraged her girls. They had initially approached a group in England but had not heard back, so they contacted Chinese and Dutch families and sent party kits to England and the Netherlands. The leader noted, "Practically every girl, or her family, is now sending clothes parcels over seas. . . . Now they are well keyed up, and seem 'raring to go' on the subject."[61]

Girl Scout leaders also sometimes had trouble getting girls to sustain their correspondence. One leader in Nottingham, England, wrote to a Xhosa-speaking South African leader. They hoped to engage their clubs in an exchange of letters, and although the two adult women maintained a correspondence and friendship that lasted about a decade, the girls' letter writing was short-lived, in large part because of language difficulties.[62]

When girls did become involved, as was the case for many, they generally wrote about everyday activities such as school, their families and pets, and their activities with the Girl Scouts and the Camp Fire Girls—topics the organizations hoped would show American life and institutions as attractive. Barb Kubik, a Marysville, Washington, Camp Fire Girl in the 1950s and 1960s, had pen pals in Scotland, South Africa, and Germany. Her topics included the familiar terrain of family and recreation, and since she was studying German, she "was curious about their school system" and wrote about that. Barb's letters talked about Camp Fire activities because these were important in her life, but none of her pen pals were in youth organizations. She explained that she wrote because she enjoyed it, but even as a girl, she recognized also that it taught her about cultural differences, which she had been interested in exploring. "I loved to write letters, and it was a wonderful way to write another girl somewhere else. It was fun." She continued, "So I was conscious of the fact that people in other countries didn't do things the same way we did things. So some of the questions we shared back and forth were, 'This is how we do X; how do you do it?' Things like school: 'This is how our school system works; how does yours work?' So I knew there were differences, and I was curious about those kinds of differences and where my pen friends fit into those differences." She credits the letters as one root of her broader interest in international exchange, which she later pursued with the student exchange program Youth for Understanding.[63] Kubik's reminiscences describe letters that largely fulfilled the Cold War project of telling the world about the strengths of American domestic institutions. Families, schools, and girls' clubs nurtured happy, healthy, protected girls, who could represent American promise.

Letters did foster international friendship for some. And the girls' relationships sometimes fostered adult connections. The daughter of the *Boston Globe* reporter John Harriman had a pen pal in France to whom she wrote about her family life and daily experiences. When her father traveled to France for work, he looked up the girl's family. He reported, "Suddenly I was talking about home, my children, and finding that this French family knew all about us in Cambridge—how Jane was doing at her school and where she hoped to go to college . . . even about our two cats and our little dachshund." Although he may have been unsettled by what or how much they knew, he also explained that "I was no longer a traveler in a strange land eating in cafes and hotels, but a man sitting down with friends in their home."[64]

Some friendships were long lasting ones among confidants. Liz called Lore her "perfect friend."[65] Their letters explored hopes and expectations for the

future—college, marriage, and motherhood along with romance and the violence and tensions of the times. In one letter, Liz confided that she was about to
write in her *tagbuch* when she realized that instead "my friend Lore can be my
diary. I can tell her everything."[66] In part the idea came from Liz's fascination
with Anne Frank, whose name was the same as Liz's mother's.

Liz felt a kinship with Anne, who in the diary was, like her, just beginning
to menstruate and starting to develop a political understanding of her world. Liz
came to understand the war through Anne's writings. As an American Jew, Liz
was keenly aware of the suffering and discrimination that Jews in Europe had
experienced during the war. For these reasons, Anne Frank was an important
literary influence on the budding writer, and references to the late girl regularly
appeared in Liz's letters. Although deemed too young for the part, this daughter
of a Hollywood producer was allowed to try out for the role of Anne Frank in
a play and met Otto Frank. When Liz did not get the part of Anne Frank, she
fancied that Lore could be Anne. "I thought that you would be perfect—you are
sensitive and have a high personal opinion of yourself and others—and that is
Life—you are in love with life. Your whole character—from what I know of it—
is like a beautiful poem. You are blessed with beauty, and a charm, and love."[67]
At other times, too, Liz called Lore her "little Anne Frank."[68] Though Lore was
Catholic, Liz saw her as a European girl in dire circumstances who had under-
gone tremendous suffering. Thus, Lore became Liz's "Kitty," the diary in which
Anne Frank recorded her daily thoughts.

Still, one might imagine that a young American Jew might harbor anger
toward the daughter of a former Nazi. Liz did indirectly ask for reassurance
from Lore, writing, "I am a Jew—I suppose you are a Catholic." She continued,
"I respect others and their freedom—and they may worship as they please."[69]
Although Lore's response is absent, a few months later Liz wrote to say she was
"very glad to know that you are not against Jews—indeed."[70]

Through their friendship and correspondence, Liz explored her anger about
the war and clarified in her own mind the difference between civilians and leaders. "I don't know what side your parents took—and I don't care—because we are
all friends now and that war is a nightmare (bad dream) in the past." Instead of
harboring anger toward individual soldiers and their families, Liz included them
among Hitler's victims, writing:

> I guess I do not really know how the people of Austria suffered during the
> war. I can only guess, and hate one single person, HITLER. I don't really hate
> very many things, but I do hope that this monster (horrid thing) [could]
> die a thousand deaths. I know that I should not have such bitterness in
> my heart, but how can I help it, when I see men in Vienna without limbs
> or eyes, begging—a poor country, torn to pieces by this cruel person.

Think of your own poor father—in shocks because of the war—Ah Lore, let us hope that war shall never be again.[71]

Although the legacies of World War II, of which the girls were too young to have firsthand recollections, figured largely in their writing, theirs was a Cold War story, as well. Liz's letters from the United States to Austria dealt regularly with the heightened tensions of the era. When American troops entered Lebanon in late July 1958, Liz asked, "Are you worried about what is going on in Lebanon? I am. I hope we don't have another war."[72]

Through their new relation to the world, girls challenged official Cold War narratives. Liz did not accept the rigid position that Americans were "better dead than red." Her early letters referred to fascism and communism together as systems that hurt people, but when tensions increased in Berlin in 1961, she worried that the events would draw the world into war. She asserted, "I would much rather live under communism than be dead" and chastised Soviet and American leaders for not having learned better lessons from World War II.[73] Instead, Liz championed world peace. When her family moved to Europe in 1960, she explained that she was studying Russian. "Either Russia and America will live peacefully together or else they will kill each other, and I am an optimist—always, so I am learning Russian in hopes for world peace."[74]

Girls expressed sentiments that show their letters were not easily controlled in more common ways as well, for the authors gave their candid impressions of family, school, consumerism, and race relations, often ignoring the careful guidelines that girls' organizations and the government laid out for them.[75] Quite ordinary teenage annoyance at a mother's perceived nosiness and at parents who bickered challenged depictions of cozy family togetherness.[76] Liz's characterization of American schools as lacking "intellectual stimulation," her peers as "stupid and [caring only] about clothes and boys," and her teachers as prejudiced gave credence to a common foreign criticism that American schools were disorganized and lacked discipline.[77] Her descriptions of her own daily life, which included a sprawling Los Angeles home with a swimming pool, a boyfriend's sports car, and a servant, hardly honored the girls' organizations and USIA pamphlets' injunction to avoid excessive materialism.[78]

Girls' letters did address the political issues of their day, at times airing dirty laundry their governments might have preferred remain within borders. Kubik remembers that although most of her correspondents "talked about the kinds of things girls talk about," especially school and siblings, her South African pen pal "danced around issues of apartheid."[79] Liz spoke candidly in her letters. She did not ignore anti-Semitism in the United States. On Herbert Lehman's departure from the Senate, she claimed, "If he wasn't a Jew, he could have

been a president, but people are very prejudiced in the USA."[80] Liz a
her frustration about the slow pace of desegregation: "I am very an⌐
the people in the South who don't want Negro children to go to school with the
white children."[81]

The USIA frowned on the airing of the United States' racial problems. Still,
the agency's inability to squelch press reports about events like the confrontation that attended the desegregation of Little Rock Central High School in 1957
led to its adoption of a narrative of progress that characterized racial strife
as a regional problem that the United States was making tangible strides in
overcoming.[82] Liz's portrayal of America's racial problems fit this pattern. She
regionalized the race problem as she condemned the South, and a sophisticated
observer might have seen her own youthfulness as suggesting a generational
change in racial outlook. She almost certainly did not hear the nuances when
she tried to prove her own commitment to tolerance by exclaiming her love for
her family's "Negro servant, Gussie, who has been with my mother even before
I was born, and I love her almost like my mother."[83]

Other letter writers projected a different image of American racism. Southern girls sometimes mimicked segregationist adults who argued that integration
harmed white children by lowering educational standards and pointing to popular stereotypes of black people as morally lax, hypersexualized, and criminal.
In the wake of the 1954 Supreme Court's *Brown v. Board of Education* school desegregation ruling, one high school girl exclaimed, "I'd rather go to no school at all
than to an integrated one."[84] Such sentiments found their way into girls' letters.
The race narrative, and many other narratives, could be quite uncontrollable
when in the hands of ordinary Americans writing to friends.

The Lopsided Relations of Rescue

Although girls' international contacts at times produced mutual friendships
and challenged official Cold War narratives, they were also often lopsided relationships that reflected the United States' economic and military power in the
postwar world. Relief packages and letters were deemed appropriate for girls
because they reflected a historic space in Americans' relationships with foreigners for women who sought to rescue others. Although rescue often assumed
a colonial population as its target, the deprived populations of Europe fit the
overall understanding that it was appropriate for women to aid and assist suffering women and children abroad. Such ideas were ideologically connected
to missionary activities, where Americans accepted women and children's
presence in foreign lands as a civilizing and uplifting force in the world. U.S.
women and girls were thought to model modern gender roles for their contacts
abroad, furthering the rationale for the women and girls' presence in foreign

and sometimes tense regions. The theme of rescue, however, depended upon unequal power, with American women and girls appearing as culturally and materially superior and with something to teach their peers.[85]

Moreover, most types of cultural exchange operated asymmetrically. Travelers and students came to the United States from countries that, except for those in Europe, most Americans rarely visited. In addition, Americans sent cultural emissaries abroad with the hope that this effort would have a transformative effect on ideas and attitudes toward the United States. Although educators hoped for increased tolerance, Americans rarely anticipated a radical transformation of their own values from pen pal correspondence.[86]

Liz's letters and those of others reflected the class positions of their authors as well as the privileged position of the United States in the world. Although schoolchildren from all backgrounds wrote letters, it is reasonable to assume that more children of the middle class wrote and sustained correspondence because of the encouragement they received from youth organizations and in foreign language classes. Even as high school enrollments expanded toward near universality in the postwar era, less than a quarter of all students studied foreign languages, and those who did tended to be in college preparatory tracks.[87] These students, like the majority of youth organization members, were disproportionately white and middle or upper class.

Letters to Europe and Asia after World War II could take a patronizing tone, for American girls were encouraged to think of themselves as rescuers of suffering children. Liz's letters to Lore have some of this character to them. Although the girls gave each other foreign language instruction, as they got older, Liz gave advice to her Austrian pen pal that seems odd given that Lore was the older girl. Fifteen-year-old Liz advised her eighteen-year-old European counterpart on careers, boyfriends, and having fun. "Do you have any boy-friends, Lore?" she asked. "It's about time you started having them, n'est-ce pas? . . . It's time for you to start having some fun! Now Lore: you are out of school; what will you do?" Then living in London with her family, Liz counseled, "I think you ought to do some work where you can use your English." She suggested the embassy or Amerika Haus, the United States Information Service (USIA abroad) library in Austria and Germany. "You really must travel and see the world and meet people."[88]

Since the letters from Lore were not preserved, it is impossible to know the degree to which the advice was solicited or if Lore gave the same kind of advice in return. Either way, this American predilection to offer counsel appears in *Seventeen* magazine as well. Articles contrasted U.S. girls' wealth and independence with the poverty and more limited social lives of teenagers around the world. Some American girls presumed they had something to teach the recovering and developing regions. It is likely that Liz saw herself as having sound advice to offer a girl whose social life had been kept from developing by the harms of the war.

American girls came to see themselves as rescuers and benefactors of people who had little opportunity to reciprocate. American girls often dwelt upon "the dreary circumstances in which [their pen pals] lived."[89] Camp Fire Girls in New York and Texas, for example, wrote to girls quarantined with Hansen's disease in the Philippines. Clubs had been started in the so-called leper colonies in the 1920s to promote camaraderie and belonging among the inhabitants, and they were reestablished after the war.[90] U.S. Camp Fire Girls overcame their trepidation about contamination from the disease and became pen pals. New York girls sent shipments of books and bedspreads that were purchased with their gift exchange money, a project that exhausted the group's treasury, and Vernon, Texas, girls sent Christmas gifts and first aid kits.[91]

Through the sacrifice of their Christmas money, the U.S. Camp Fire Girls learned the responsibility of rescue. The stories told by Camp Fire officials and the Filipina Camp Fire leader Euphrosinia Pizons stressed the importance of privileged girls' providing charity through aid. The *Camp Fire Girl* narrated a glum plot of the poor girls' expectation that they would not receive any Christmas presents. It told how the Filipina Camp Fire Girls "decorated the stage for some visitors to come and give gifts to the Woman's Club organization" but added that the girls "stood aloof from the others because they knew they were not a member of the organization. There was not even a piece of candy for them."

The narrative shifted as Pizons explained what happened next: "On the following morning we were notified that we have packages and, my, they did not finish their breakfast. They ran to get the packages. When we opened each box everybody was silent. They have all big eyes and long breaths as they saw the nice bedspreads and beautiful jewels." After having their sympathies aroused, U.S. girls could rest assured that their treasury had been bankrupted for a good cause. Finally, Pizons expressed her gratitude with sentiments that showed how lopsided foreign exchange could be: "I could not sleep the whole night. I was in tears. What a great gift you have given us all. You have satisfied our wants, our needs. You have let us feel the real feeling of 'belong.' How can we ever repay you?"[92] Pizons would clearly not be able to repay the U.S. Camp Fire Girls. Projects could foster alliances and raise spirits, but they also signaled U.S. strength, prosperity, and power.

Into the 1950s, *Seventeen* published European girls' letters, which described continued despair and appealed for American girls' aid. One letter from Paris described French orphans who received dolls from the United States: "If you had seen the cold, cheerless, highly regimented Home in which these children live, you would understand what the sight of those brightly clothed dolls meant to them." From Finland, *Seventeen* readers learned that "the life of our children has been a prolonged, often quite agonizing, struggle for their daily bread and, most of all, they need just that joy and happiness that their young American friends have now sent to them."[93]

Sometimes the costs of shipping goods to struggling countries were higher than the worth of the goods themselves. Camp Fire Girls discovered this when they tried to help peers in the Philippines. Yet they persisted, though youth organizations and schools sought reputable charities through which they could send items abroad with greater certainty that the items would arrive and at less cost. In fact, the Girl Scouts and Boy Scouts were among organizations recognized as "operating agencies" able to "receive and transfer funds, materials, or services, and to supervise their allocation and distribution through their own representatives abroad or through affiliated agencies."[94] American girls and their leaders found enough value in collecting and sending items to war-torn countries to outweigh the costs of postage and the difficulties of coordinating shipment, and they sometimes chose to do this rather than simply sending funds.

Girls' belief in their duty to serve derived from their understanding of themselves as citizens of a global power. In her Camp Fire record book, Linda Lou Harris counted among her citizenship and service projects sending seven dresses and fifty cents from her allowance to the Methodist Committee for Overseas Relief and writing to an English pen pal from whom she received three letters.[95] Similarly, a local newspaper quoted nine-year-old San Diego Camp Fire Girl Stephanie Duntop regarding the organization's annual project theme Make Mine Democracy. She said, "We have all the warmth and clothing we want, and all the food. We can go to all the churches we want and we can join our own organizations. We Blue Birds sell doughnuts and Christmas cards so we can give to the poor. We send packages of clothing to the Dutch."[96] Her sentiment underscored how deeply young Americans had internalized the idea that democracy meant freedom from want or access not only to food and clothing but also to luxury items like Christmas cards and doughnuts.

At a time when U.S. parents urged children to eat everything on their plates because those in Asia and Europe were starving, girls' institutions presented American abundance as a global good to share with others. Girls' gifts aided the rebuilding of educational infrastructure, provided toys to restore playful childhoods, and supplemented the wardrobes of their adolescent peers. An advertisement for CARE in *Seventeen* implored girls to think of those beyond their borders: "Here, with larders overflowing and closets gay with spring finery, it's so easy to forget the millions in a score of countries whose cupboards are empty and who carry their pitiful wardrobes on their backs."[97]

Girls' organizations encouraged American girls to make donations, sew, or supply food or goods to remedy the suffering of children worldwide. They helped meet the greater needs of educational infrastructure and recreation that would put Europe back on a footing toward thriving consumer capitalism. As the Girl Scouts presented it, play kits, books, and toys were as important as blankets and food if the goal was to establish freedom from want and a model of childhood where children went to school, played, and were unencumbered by labor and adult responsibility. Girl Scout publications reminded readers that people everywhere "want and work for the things that we in this country want and work for—homes for their families, education for their children, interesting jobs, leisure to enjoy the good things of life."[98]

Many gifts were for play and parties, underscoring the identification of childhood with fun. American Girl Scouts shipped duffel bags filled with stuffed animals through the American Friends Service.[99] Despite the obvious need for school supplies, food, and warm clothing, Camp Fire Girls from Melrose, Massachusetts, assembled a "party kit" for a group of girls in Stourbridge, England, and "shipped everything necessary to throw a party: crepe paper, a lollipop decorated maypole, fudge mix, Crisco, and Kool-Aid."[100] The Melrose project reflected the American girls' own priorities rather than basic postwar needs in Europe. On the one hand, the Melrose girls' shipment may have done more to disseminate evidence of Americans' ability to spend their income on consumer goods than to alleviate postwar struggles for necessities. But on the other, it was very much tuned in to American girls' organizations' philosophy that play must be maintained as an essential part of childhood. Having no parties, just like having no toys, was to be deprived of a basic element of modern childhood. No doubt the Melrose girls identified parties with freedom from want before they packaged up decorations and sweets for their peers overseas.

Exchanging gifts with pen pals also could signal inequities, although U.S. girls usually sent modest presents, often ones they made themselves. Gail Oblinger, a San Francisco Camp Fire Girl of solid but modest means, wrote to Girl Guides in England in 1945 and recalled the time and effort that went into preparing relief packages. Many of the American girls learned to knit, and it was Gail's first attempt. The result, she said, was "this god-awful, horrible scarf. Knit and purl, your first attempt at it, you can imagine what it looked like. . . . I knitted it forever and it went in the bag with all the stuff. It was a box that went." As a result of sending the relief package, Gail became pen pals with a London girl slightly older than she was. The Londoner reciprocated with personal photographs and "a little tourist package" about her city on miniature postcards. At Christmastime, the girls exchanged presents, and the London Girl Guide requested nylons, a symbol of American prosperity, since they were not available in Europe after the war. Gail enlisted the help of her mother to deliver the sought-after gift. The two lied at the post office, saying that the gift was handkerchiefs, since sending nylon, used for military purposes, was still

prohibited from the United States.[101] Gail and her pen pal shared gifts and letters on relatively equal terms, but Gail's pen pal assumed that an American girl
would have access to what were still scarce items in the United States as well as
in Europe.

Long-term pen pal relationships had a greater capacity for mutual exchange.
Liz and Lore also exchanged gifts. Liz sent an anthology of English literature
and an English-German dictionary that became the basis of the Austrian girl's
English training. Aware of the poverty her correspondent faced as a result of
losing her father during the war, Liz pleaded with her not to send anything in
return: "The only return gift that I want is that you take pleasure in reading it."[102]
Lore, however, did reciprocate, sending photographs, combs, and compacts
for the American girl's birthday. Their sharing of experiences, thoughts, and
dreams created a mutual friendship, but it appeared to be important to Lore
that she participate as an equal. Similarly, when a Scottish girl wrote admiringly
of U.S. soldiers stationed near her home, flattering her reader that their presence made her want to visit the United States, she also included a face-saving
side note that invoked mutuality and evened out the exchange: "But I guess you
would love to be over here."[103]

Invoking women's historic role (and justification for civic and political
involvement) in providing service to women and children, magazines played on
their connections to other women and children, and emotional appeals emphasized "tearful" orphans in need of donations and a "personal contact." *Seventeen*
asked U.S. girls to imagine themselves in the place of girls in war-torn Europe
and the colonies. A *Seventeen* article on the 1948 appeal for the American Overseas Aid–United Nations Appeal for Children featured an eight-year-old French
girl forced to care for her younger siblings while her parents worked. The message called on American girls as babysitters (and therefore consumer-cash earn-
ers) to relinquish their "babysitting money" or the dues from their "Gay Girls'
meeting" so that the "not-so-gay girls [of Europe] won't have to fight over a
garbage can for their one-meal-a-day."[104] Girls regularly sent their own money or
money they had earned through fund-raisers.

When U.S. girls' clubs and schoolchildren "adopted" families or children in
other countries, their relationships reflected the unevenness of U.S. alliances
that made other nations "client states." Such "adoptions" meant a sustained
commitment to provide supplies and donations to a child or family in war-torn
Europe. The familial concept underscored adoption as an appropriate form of
international service for girls and women. The Foster Parents' Plan, a nonprofit
established after the war with which girls' organizations collaborated, created
the model for establishing a relationship between donors and recipients of aid.
They did this by providing each donor with things like pictures and biogra-
phies of a particular recipient to involve the emotions more deeply and, the

charity hoped, open further the pocketbook of a given donor. The term *adoption* implied a parental obligation on the part of the donor and a form of dependence on the part of the recipient, an especially striking status when the families that were adopted included adults as well as children and when the adopters themselves were children.[105] A *Seventeen* article underscored the unevenness of the relationship, at first recognizing the oddity of teens adopting children: "Would you like to adopt a child? We're serious." It then magnified the distinction between correspondents. Americans might write to "Georgette, a foster child in France"; "eight-year-old Yvonne"; or another poor French war orphan. The children, *Seventeen* promised, will write, "Chère Marraine (dear foster mother)" in their return letters and send "charming" watercolor pictures.[106] Such adoptions promoted service and international awareness but scarcely represented relationships of equals. Even when efforts to provide care often came from the heart, international correspondence affirmed U.S. girls' privileged position in the post–World War II world as benefactors, or rescuers, of people who had little opportunity to reciprocate fully. Girls' organizations along with *Seventeen*, then, promoted actions that reinforced Americans' inclinations to see themselves as part of a benevolent and generous world power.

Conclusion

When the Czech girl, Marie, and the Boston area Camp Fire Girls exchanged gifts and letters as part of the Hello, World, Let's Get Together project, they played the roles adults promoted for girls in the postwar years. American girls became caregivers and friends, if not the rescuers, of children living in countries that were European and Asian Cold War allies of the United States. Pen pal and relief package projects became central to youth organization programming and school curricula in the immediate postwar years as young people acted in the hope of hastening world peace in the same spirit that guided the Marshall Plan and aid to Asia. In the same way that foreign aid promoted asymmetrical relationships even as it produced allies, girls' involvement in international exchanges reflected the power dynamics of the postwar world, especially given that most letter writers were white and middle class. Girls' letters were seen as playing a role in shaping the image of America abroad, one that might aid U.S. moral credibility both within the United States and abroad, credibility that legitimized global leadership. As the next chapter shows, a related goal advanced by girls' correspondence was the reimagining of former enemies as Cold War allies.

3

"Famous for Its Cherry Blossoms"

Reimagining Japan and Germany in the Postwar Period

In 1948, against the backdrop of the search by nations for reconciliation and efforts by American adults to create a psychological opening for such a rapprochement, Japanese teenager Masako Ina wrote a pen pal letter to an American Camp Fire Girl. She introduced herself and related information about her school and family, her summer vacation, and her nation. "Perhaps you have heard of Japan where Tokyo is," she wrote. "Japan is famous for its cherry blossoms."[1] The letter casts one angle of light on how girls reimagined former enemies with the reemergence of peace.

During World War II both girls had been adolescents, and images of the enemy in wartime propaganda would likely have darkened their feelings toward each other. Those who had been children in the United States during wartime later remembered having been very frightened of the "loathsome buck-toothed little yellow savages" depicted in popular culture. They recalled their parents smashing toys made in Japan and of other adults speaking easily of killing "Japs."[2] Japanese women were caricatured as having been "taught to shoot" to contribute to the war effort and at the same time as "still 'slaves,' in the world of the male Jap." In Japan, people were told the West was corrupt and decadent; Japanese were presented with caricatures of Americans who were all "tall, ugly, and noisy."[3] Masako's friendly gesture in opening this correspondence, mentioning cherry blossoms and not mentioning the war, cleaned the slate for a different kind of relationship by shifting the image of Japan from that of a militarized enemy toward a picture of a peaceful nation filled with flowers and potential friends.

Reconciliation—the process of replacing hostility with friendly relations—involves ordinary people, not just political agreements. Individuals rethink their nation's and their own relations with a former enemy. Recent scholarship shows that in the postwar period, reconciliation discourse employed gender and age to recast the Japanese and Germans in a new light.[4]

Subordinate groups—symbolic or real—of women and children were less threatening. Shifting the lens to girls' culture enables us to see that peace was reconstituted through girls' connections as well as between adults. As in wartime, adults determined what stories to tell children—whom they saw as the future of the nation. Images and stories were disseminated through schools, youth organizations, and media. As global ambassadors of friendship, girls not only symbolized the hope for peace but also made personal connections as they questioned, configured, and adopted new understandings of former enemies.[5] This chapter examines the inclusion and participation of girls in this process.

As wartime propaganda gave way to peacetime messages, repairing the relationships of the United States with Japan and Germany relied heavily on how Americans perceived women and children in those nations. Although perceptions of Japan and Germany differed following the war, media and policymakers promoted images of children and women that fostered U.S. sympathy for both countries. It is hard to know if children's communications contained intentional propaganda or simply reflected their notions of how to make friends, but their letters clearly reflected the larger society's efforts to cultivate peace.

In these postwar messages, nineteenth-century models of a feminized, infantilized, and subservient Japan remerged alongside newer liberal arguments that emphasized how the "backward" Japanese were maturing into democrats. Images of tea sets and women in kimonos with babies on their backs replaced the vicious soldier to create a fanciful, diminutive, feminized Japan susceptible to and dependent on U.S. influence and guidance. Japanese children asking American occupation soldiers for gum and candy, and orphans tugging at the heartstrings of reformers, were regular fare in stateside media after World War II. Japanese women were depicted as both submissive and bighearted, thus offering a lesson to American women on how to please American men, even as Japanese women were seen as in need of American help in reforming backward gender roles.[6]

Meanwhile, the feminine and child-related side of Germany became more accessible as well, making it easier for Americans to see Germans as dependents worthy of assistance and in need of protection. American GIs who had remained in occupation zones after the war encountered a population devoid of its young men. They saw suffering women, children, and elderly citizens struggling to survive in ravaged towns and cities. This Germany was "weak, submissive, and disproportionately female." As American soldiers saw victims, they began to question the wartime assumption of common German guilt. Moreover, racial and cultural affinities led to interactions between male soldiers and German women and children and placed GIs is the position of father figures—at times literally—and protectors.[7] American GIs came to see themselves, and ultimately the United States, as providers, a view that was shared by stateside Americans, including children, and that culminated in support for the Marshall Plan and the Berlin Airlift, as Germany was understood to have been defanged and broken.

Keeping the peace meant teaching young people to reimagine enemies, a strategy that made sense in terms of both the idealistic aims of youth internationalism and the shifting geopolitical context of the emerging Cold War. From 1945 through the first two years of the 1950s, economic and security concerns meant that Japan and Germany emerged as key commercial and military allies. To minimize Soviet influence in Asia, the United States carefully shut out the Soviet Union and other nations from playing a role in Japan's postwar reconstruction. Japan, under General Douglas MacArthur's occupation government, adopted a new constitution that renounced war and established women's political rights. To prevent the spread of communism within Japan and to ensure an Asian market and military outpost in Asia, especially as China's nationalist government faltered, the United States increasingly built up Japan's industrial economy. In 1951, Japanese sovereignty was reestablished, but the ongoing U.S. military presence was guaranteed in the Treaty of Peace.

Meanwhile, Germany was at the center of diplomatic disputes between the Soviet Union and the West. By 1949, the United States and western Germany had achieved a cultural rapprochement at the level of official policy. Critics remained, but rebuilding the German economy and creating military security alliances were the primary concerns of U.S. policymakers. They came to accept and promote not only the industrial buildup of Germany as the cornerstone of a strong European economy and a guarantor against the spread of communism in Western Europe but also the rearmament of Germany and ultimately, in 1955, West Germany's integration into the North Atlantic Treaty Organization (NATO).[8] Foreign policymakers needed the support of Americans of all generations to reshape the world.

U.S. women and girls actively shared American Cold War gender values, especially those connected to girls' education and roles in a democracy. At the same time, a larger gendered discourse of rescue justified international action and made contact with former enemies an appropriate girls' activity. Many Japanese women and girls welcomed the partnership.[9] Women's status in both Japan, where they were thought to be both deferential dolls and beasts of burden, and Germany, where the Nazis had relegated women to *Kinder, Küche, Kirche* (children, kitchen, church) to produce children for the regime, were considered justifications for intervention by American women, who would uplift foreign women to "American-style housework."[10] Moving beyond the home, American girls were invited to consider the questions of how much Nazi youth were capable of learning about democratic citizenship and what they might teach Japanese girls who were embracing women's rights. Girls' media and youth organizations made the feminized Germany and Japan, especially the child and female victims of war, appropriate targets of girls' international friendship.

American girls' culture was part of the discursive development of new ideas about former enemies, of reimagining Cold War allies in gender- and age-specific ways. Pen pal letters, such as Masako Ina's, along with textbooks, girls' literature, and the efforts of youth organizations to establish clubs in Japan and Germany, cast former enemies in a new light. *Seventeen* magazine's July 1945 issue, before the war in the Pacific was over, began to build sympathy for enemy youth even as it pointed out the rights for which Americans were fighting. *Seventeen* reminded U.S. girls that they had much to be grateful for as children in a democracy. "[German and Japanese youth] never had to think about what to wear, where to go, what to study. . . . Hans didn't need to study his newspapers and magazines to determine what kind of a world he wanted and what he would personally do to get it. Miss Tojo had no decisions to make about what she would do to earn a living and how she could make her one small life mean something. The individual was nothing."[11] American girls, by contrast, *Seventeen* noted, were called to play an active role in shaping the postwar world. Rethinking the American relationship to Japan and Germany and American girls' relationships to girls in those countries became part of postwar girls' culture.

The Image of Japan and Germany in Textbooks and Girls' Literature

Just as American diplomats and journalists used gendered and infantilizing imagery to neutralize Japan as a no-longer-fierce enemy, girls' institutions reimagined Japan in ways that made an alliance nonthreatening. They created images of the girls of Asia, especially those of a harmless Japan, that suggested fantasies of exotic tourism and the possibility of friendship. Moreover, as Americans during the course of World War II came to denounce overt racism and associate it with fascism, persecuted groups such as Japanese Americans began to receive more favorable treatment in the media, including girls' media. The YWCA magazine for Y-Teens, for example, included news updates on girls in the Japanese internment camps that reflected the editors' positive view toward Japanese Americans. That might be an analogue for the response to women in Japan when the war ended.

Textbooks read by girls and boys in middle and high school redrew the images of enemies. They moved beyond portrayals of Japan as the "hungry" aggressor that had devoured Pacific Islands and parts of China while breaking treaties. During the war, the enemy nation had been described as "pygmy Japan," which had nevertheless "maimed the United States' fleet at Pearl Harbor."

Seldom did textbooks distinguish Japanese imperialists or militarists from the Japanese people in general, even as these books began to distinguish Hitler from the German people. Students read little of specific Japanese leaders, creating the impression that all Japanese might be categorized and blamed together.[12]

After the war, textbooks maintained old images as they introduced new ones. On the one hand, they reminded readers of Japanese treachery (and U.S. heroism) during the war. On the other, they assured readers that the conquered Japan, under U.S. influence, was occupied and submissive. Texts did remind American students of the intensity of wartime feelings. The popular *History of a Free People*, which the USIA adopted for foreign distribution, quoted President Roosevelt and the Joint Resolution of Congress to describe Japanese actions at Pearl Harbor in the worst light, as an "unprovoked and dastardly attack" that was "thrust upon the United States."[13] In 1961, another important U.S. history textbook used the voices of key figures of the war to capture the mood of that era and to cast enemies in a negative light. The text quoted Harold Ickes, who was known for his over-the-top language, calling Hitler a "maniac," and Roosevelt referring to Japanese, Italian, and German aggression as "armed banditry."[14] In describing the events leading up to Pearl Harbor, a third textbook characterized Japanese actions as "treacherous."[15]

Textbooks also offered frank, vivid descriptions of the stakes of the conflict, focusing on the threat that imperial Japan and fascist Germany had posed worldwide to free institutions and self-governance and the right to live in peace. Textbooks made clear that hostile invasions in Asia and Europe put all the world at risk. "There was little time to lose," one exclaimed. "[In 1942], Germany and Japan were so close to dominating the great 'heartland' of Europe and Asia that it almost seemed as though nothing could dislodge them." Students read hostile slang that argued that "if the Jap war lords could have held out, they would have ruled the most populous empire the world had ever seen."[16] Still, authors separated such depictions of a masculinized aggressive wartime Japan from what followed after peace had been declared.

Stark comparisons between imperial Japan and occupation-era Japan treated the occupation in ways that reenvisioned the former enemy for a new generation of American school children. Although U.S. history texts portrayed wartime Japan as strong, militaristic, and dangerous, they portrayed postwar Japan as an emerging democracy and emphasized the United States' paternalistic role as a humble, generous, yet reluctant world leader.[17] Under Allied occupation and under General MacArthur's leadership, one 1954 text explained, Japan had turned a new leaf:

> Under his able direction Japan underwent a remarkable period of
> reform. . . . Political democracy was advanced by the abolition of secret

police, by the promotion of civil rights, by a new constitution, and by woman suffrage. The Mikado remained as a symbol of Japanese unity, but was no longer to be regarded as a god. . . . The educational system was altered to provide more equal opportunities and to teach democratic ways instead of blind obedience to authority.[18]

Referring to what historians now call the reverse course by which the United States abandoned plans to have Japan pay reparations to its Asian conquests in favor of a quick economic buildup that would make Japan the key bulwark against communism in the Far East, the text continued, "At first the idea had been to force Japan to pay reparations, but the economic difficulties of the island kingdom proved so great that eventually the United States sent Japan nearly two billion dollars in economic aid." No longer an aggressor, Japan became a fanciful, benign "island kingdom," a phrase that invoked a common understanding of Japan as stuck in a feudal past and that erased the technological threat that Japan had posed in the war. The text suggested as well that aid was more a product of American benevolence geared toward helping Japan grow than it was motivated by direct national self-interest in securing capitalist allies abroad.[19]

Moreover, texts described Japan as compliant: "The Japanese displayed courtesy, even friendliness, toward their conquerors, and seemed to take kindly to [Supreme Commander of the Allied Powers's] reform program." The United States' role as benefactor and guide received attention as well. About the 1951 Treaty of Peace with Japan, in which Japan stated its intention to join the United Nations, renounced its claims to Korea and other territories, and accepted a continued U.S. troop presence, *History of a Free People* explained, "It was as yet too soon to know whether the reforms of the occupation period would prove permanent, but few would deny that the United States had been generous in victory."[20] Such descriptions celebrated the ongoing military presence as benevolent and encouraged American children to think the United States had much to teach Japan. Other U.S. history textbooks had similar regard for McArthur in the 1950s. One 1954 volume also noted the growing threat of communism in Japan and so offered a new reason for the necessity of MacArthur's reforms.[21] In 1961, however, another textbook did not mention the occupation at all, implying that the issue of occupation, and therefore the degree of the Japanese threat, was settled.[22]

Further suggesting Japan's subordinate status, textbooks like *History of a Free People* described preimperial Japan as naturally submissive and compliant. Characterizing Commodore Matthew Perry's 1853 fleet as "penetrating" the island kingdom that had been closed to international interaction, the text explained how the "elaborate presents for the ruler of Japan," which included a telegraph and a miniature railroad, provided the "mixture of courtesy with the threat of force" that had persuaded the Japanese "to carry on relations with the rest of the world." The United States, the text made clear, used "no actual violence" in forcing the emperor's hand.[23]

Indeed new images of a Japan were not limited to textbooks. Whereas such depictions suggested that a feminized, receptive Japan was a natural state, a Girl Scout publication late in the war declared that "lots of people wish, now, that Japan had stayed shut!" The article shifted attention away from Japan to the conquered Ryukyuans, the ethnically mixed island people of Okinawa who would soon be free from Japanese occupation.[24] The Okinawan focus may have also eased reconciliation, since the Okinawans were technically Japanese nationals but had faced Japanese colonization and second-class citizenship.

Seeking to entertain as well as to educate, articles in the *American Girl* by the late 1950s noted that the Japanese were now peaceful and eager to learn from Americans. In one piece, the daughter of an Air Corps man described her visit to a high school in Okinawa. The English teacher asked her to read aloud and before she "knew it, the windows of the room and the doors were jammed with children, all anxious to hear an American read."[25] Okinawans were used to demonstrate that the Japanese were eager to learn from Americans, including girls.

Other articles in Girl Scout publications covered the historical progress women and girls in Japan were making. Whereas the history books of the 1950s—not known for covering women's pasts—did treat women's rights as a marker of democratization, they tended to describe it as the product of U.S. paternalism and the wise fatherly MacArthur without noting Japanese feminism. The *American Girl*, however, recognized the agency of Japanese women. Although the magazine still painted Japanese women as "[struggling] against the teachings of centuries of slavery" and noted MacArthur's significant prodding of Japanese men to support voting rights for women, girls read about suffrage leader Fusaye Ishikawa of the League of Woman Suffrage and her decades-long efforts on behalf of women's rights. They also learned that like their peers in the United States, Japanese women had made significant contributions to the wartime work force and as a result were demanding the education that would allow them to become scientists, teachers, and doctors.[26]

Postwar articles and plays for YWCA girls also tried to dispel stereotypes that the Japanese girls' world was backward and crimped and to dramatize the opportunities for girls in Japanese families. In one short play, Michiko Sato, a member of the Japanese YWCA who was studying at Springfield College in Massachusetts, compared a historic scene to her present time. The first act showed a 1930s meeting of Japanese YWCA girls pondering their futures. They are pressured into arranged marriages, and their fathers rule the house. In the second act, set in the early 1950s, the next generation of Japanese girls appeared as modern. They attend a coed high school, and one girl's mother has taken a job as a teacher. Each girl talks about plans to work or take classes after graduation and to be a "useful woman for the community as well as a faithful daughter."[27] Just like the American girls who would read the play, these Japanese girls find the walls surrounding them have expanded to include the world.

Still other articles in Girl Scout publications presented Japan as an exotic and feminized culture, inviting to tourists. An article on Girl Scouts around the world noted that Girl Scouting in Japan, though modern, was layered upon a traditional, feminine culture. U.S. girls became tourists of the exotic as they read about "Machiko," a "Gaaru Sukauto," or Japanese Girl Scout, whom the magazine described as "graceful" and "dark-eyed." A "study in contrasts," the girl could sing American song lyrics as well as she could make flower decorations following a thousand-year-old tradition. The *American Girl* emphasized the mix of modern and exotic, calling her surroundings "a fascinating mixture of the very ancient and the up-to-date." Next to "fairyland gardens and richly ornamented Buddhist temples can be seen near modern new shops and signs advertising American movies!" Girl Scout reporters explained.[28] U.S. girls could be touristic voyeurs of a magical and nonthreatening island kingdom, one that seemed perhaps more peaceful since American teen culture had, like Perry, entered the island kingdom.

Seventeen magazine provided similar descriptions. Representations of girls and images for girls neutralized militarized wartime depictions and instead pointed to tourism, beauty, and fantasy. Betty Eikel, an American teenager living in Gifu, Japan, with her army father, wrote an article about her experiences. Images of war vanish as the article described the "beautiful valley" near the army camp and Eikel's travels beyond its gates to Kyoto. Eikel wrote of the women she met at lavish parties and restaurants. Waitresses and "geisha girls" in colorful kimonos and obis with "centuries-old" hairstyles, carrying "exquisite fans" populated her narrative. These Japanese women were made accessible to American readers, inviting the Western gaze but also remaining mysterious. The "stringed instruments . . . sound off-key to Western ears," wrote Eikel, who admitted, "We couldn't understand the symbolism" of the dance.[29]

Although boys read the same textbooks as girls and encountered many of the same postwar images, Boy Scout literature, as it emphasized masculine Allied wartime heroism, also exposed them to continued depictions of Japanese treachery and deception. *Boys' Life* presented postwar boys with war stories about Japanese soldiers "scurrying" like rats from caves and the heroic Allied soldiers who "picked off" the Japanese enemy.[30] Boy Scout literature highlighted American, Allied, and underground heroism. The *Handbook for Boys* recounted Scouts' own wartime contributions to civil defense, salvage, and emergency service patrols. Typical of the fiction in *Boys' Life* was a 1946 story of the heroism of French, Belgium, Dutch, and Norwegian Boy Scouts who helped the American troops when the Americans stormed Normandy.[31] Such short stories suggested that girls and boys had different roles with regard to reconciliation. Girls especially were positioned to create friendly relationships.

Partnering to Establish Girls' Organizations in Japan

Assistance from American women reformers in occupied Japan was important to the new relations between the nations. This partnership extended to the establishment of girls' organizations in Japan that offered a Western framework for Japanese women engaged in their own critique of Japanese gender roles and seeking partnerships with and assistance from U.S. women. The Japanese reformers developed close relationships with American women who had a vision of liberating their peers in occupied Japan.[32] They worked within the framework of U.S. domestic containment as the American women shared a model of sex-segregated organizations that offered girls an education that included maternalism, homemaking, and the treatment of boys and girls as essentially different. At the same time, American girls were taught to admire Japanese women for their supposed doll-like feminine features even as they saw their own girlhoods of coeducation, outdoor adventure, and school activities as markers of the superiority of American gender equality. Japanese women became worthy, if unequal, partners.

As part of the U.S. policy of promoting worldwide democracy, youth organizations expanded overseas to teach American democracy and gender roles and, in the process, foster long-lasting connections. Leaders of girls' organizations started clubs in occupied Japan with the idea that democracy would be fostered through the shared democratic experience of Scouting. Often working under the aegis of U.S. women reformers, many of whom had prior Camp Fire or Girl Scouting experience, the organizers were among the half million Americans who went to Japan within two years of the war's end. Many were involved in reform through their own or their husbands' work in the Red Cross, YMCA, and occupation agencies. Others were the wives of soldiers stationed in Japan.[33]

As part of the broader development of civic agencies in occupied Japan, the Girl Scouts successfully organized. Adviser to Girl Scout troops in Japan Harriet S. Calkins explained its significance: "We believe that getting Japanese Girl Scouts to know and work easily with different groups will result in miniature democracies where all can practice the essentials of decent living." Membership grew to over 125,000 in 1950. There were about three hundred Brownies and Girl Scouts in about twenty-five troops in Tokyo alone. The U.S. Girl Scout organization had funded field agents for six-month stints to establish troops, and although they may have built upon their prewar reputation in Japan, they had to start fresh given that troops had been disbanded during the war.[34] The Camp Fire Girls' more limited efforts to expand, despite their lack of financial resources to send staff abroad, were important because of their focus on gender-specific education.

The founder of the Camp Fire Girls in postwar Japan looked to U.S. girls' organizations to further international friendship and to develop gender-specific educational experiences for girls in democratic Japan. Heihachiro Suzuki, a Japanese businessman and the director of a correspondence society he intended to foster world peace, established a Camp Fire Girls club along with his niece Yoshiko Suzuki near Tokyo in 1948. In explaining his interest in girls' organizations, Suzuki cited the need to promote democracy in Japan and to find a proper educational model for girls. He first learned of the Camp Fire Girls when he saw a program booklet in a United States Information Service center in occupied Japan and began the process (which required authorization from the Civil Information and Education Section of Allied Command) required to bring Camp Fire clubs to Japan. Along the way, the Suzukis established a pen pal network in which several Japanese girls (including Masako Ina) took part. By 1949, Suzuki and his contacts had started a handful of clubs in occupied Japan.[35]

Suzuki was especially interested in the Camp Fire Girls and not the Girl Scouts, which then had stronger roots in Japan, because he perceived that the Camp Fire organization stressed the female role of nurturer of her family and community more than did the Girl Scouts. Although both organizations socialized girls in the acceptable midcentury femininity, which emphasized domesticity and service to family, it was hard to squelch the popular perception in the United States and abroad that the Girl Scouts and Guides copied the Boys Scouts.[36] Despite the promise of equality for women in the new Japanese Constitution, equal rights and roles proved elusive. Traditionalists held to a family system that honored "good wives and wise mothers" and limited the public ambitions of individual women while holding them up as national mothers serving the family and nation, a framework not unlike what Camp Fire officials called homemaker to the world.[37] In the Camp Fire Girls, Suzuki found a model that adapted the "good wife and wise mother" to demands for the increased civic involvement of girls and women in democratic Japan. He explained, "It is very helpful to introduce to our Japanese what the Camp Fire Girls are and let them know how [girls'] education should be."[38] In particular, the Camp Fire Girls emphasized women's "concern and ability in connection with their homes; their experience in organization and household management; their concern for the health and well-being of their children; their ability to create an atmosphere of charm and graciousness in their homes."[39] In other words, Suzuki hoped to import to Japan the Camp Fire Girls' model of maternalist citizenship and its emphasis on domestic roles.

The establishment of American girls' organizations in Japan may have been an adult project, but the groups allowed Japanese girls to present new images of Japan to American girls. In the United States, the Camp Fire Girls wrote about the Japanese group in its national publications and planned an exhibit at a national conference to show how Japanese Camp Fire Girls did such projects as memory books and crafts similar to those of clubs in the United States. Japanese girls sent paintings they had done to Camp Fire headquarters for display and for circulation among their peers in the United States.[40] The message that girls shared experiences internationally countered wartime stereotypes in ways that lent public support to postwar reconciliation.

Letter Exchanges

In addition to the common experiences of Camp Fire Girls in both nations, letters created a new image of Japan for U.S. girls, one of a Japan interested in Western gender roles and American life. Japanese girls' letters combined assertions of emerging equality with requests for information about American democracy and institutions. In the letter of introduction that she sent through a correspondence society, Mitsue Chinone, who identified herself as a seventeen-year-old "girl of the Taga Dressmaker's Institute," said of her country, "Japan is in ruins, but we endeavor to build up world peace by American help. Women in Japan have been negative and have submitted ourselves to men by a damnable militarism. Therefore we are anxious to learn American thought and manners. Please teach your thought. Do you like anything?"[41] Phrases like "damnable militarism" reflected the postwar Japanese renunciation of the force blamed for drawing Japan into war. Although I found no letters in which Japanese girls expressed remorse for their nation's recent role in the war, they did adopt the stance of the occupation government, the newly installed Japanese officials, and educators who taught the Japanese people to blame military leaders for all they had suffered. The occupation authorities even broke up youth groups that supported militarized activities like judo in order to rid Japan of remnants of militarism.[42] Still, the letters provide evidence that Japanese girls reached out to American girls with a new portrayal of Japan, one that advanced friendly relations and suggested that they were adopting democratic practices much like their own.

Yoshiko Suzuki, the woman who had started a Camp Fire club near Tokyo, echoed the belief that the status of women was improving. In a letter to Camp Fire officials about possible pen pal correspondence between her group and U.S. girls, she explained that "as you know pre-war Japan was not the country of the same right of both sex. . . . But since surrender, their posi[ti]on have been elevated and males became very gentle." Japanese women, she wrote, were advancing in politics, business, and education.[43] This letter and others refashioned images of the Japanese enemy as a nation reforming itself, creating a new vision of a worthy Cold War ally.

Boys' letters from a Christian school in Japan express a similar hope for peace but pay little attention to women's rights. Middle school student Shin-ichiro Ishida of Kyoto wrote to a young Indiana school teacher, "I am very don't like war. I hope we maintain peace." He told of school and his aspirations to be a doctor but did not address gender equality.[44]

Girls' magazines also carried assurances that Japanese girls wanted peace. A letter to *Seventeen* magazine from a sixteen-year-old Japanese girl carried the assertion that Japan sought peace, but also hinted to the American audience about the degree of devastation wrought by American bombers, which had killed three hundred thousand civilians and injured another five hundred thousand.[45] After explaining that she used *Seventeen* to study English, she turned her attention to the war: "It has passed five years since the war ended, but the memory of the terrible air raid will not be effaced forever. Wishing not to let anyone else have such an experience, we Japanese teens are eager to take part in the restoration of world peace."[46]

Although evidence of girls' responses is limited, the letters altered at least some perceptions. The mother of an American Camp Fire Girl reported to the national office on her daughter's letters with a Japanese girl. Although U.S. cultural superiority underlies how she described her child's experience, she illustrated that pen pals could and did successfully counter the villainous stereotypes of the Japanese that had been carefully crafted by American wartime propaganda. In addition to writing about her school and church, her daughter decided to help her pen pal and her family by sending the girl some money, an action consistent with youth organization service activities such as gathering contributions for the poor and for children in war-torn countries. The money was soon returned. Although it is not clear why—it may have been an act of pride for the Japanese girl and her family to reject charity—the American mother and daughter viewed it as a surprising gesture of honesty (one might presume that the Japanese girl would keep the money rather than go to the trouble and expense of retuning it). The American reportedly told her mother, "We call ourselves Christians, yet we listen when we hear people say that the Japanese can't be trusted. I just wonder how many of us would be that honest and considerate."[47] The pen pal relationship had provided a new way—though not necessarily more accurate—for the U.S. girl to think about Japan.

At the same time, these letters were part of the larger enterprise of the exportation of American values. The American mother was also writing to Japanese women, and she proudly reported to Camp Fire headquarters that some of them had converted to Christianity. Although additional factors (among them the Japanese families' proximity to the missionary networks, correspondence societies, and Red Cross Centers that had probably approached them about becoming pen pals in the first place) likely prompted their change in faith, the example illustrates how pen pal friendships operated within the larger context of Americanization efforts abroad.[48] Still, letters could provide a way for writers to recast their national image and for correspondents to begin to see each other as more alike than not.

U.S. girls read in their textbooks, girls' organization monthlies, and popular magazines that Japan was friendly, feminized, and modernizing. The establishment in Japan of girls' organizations such as the Camp Fire Girls and Girl Scouts promoted the idea that girls around the world shared common interests and that democratization advanced girls' and women's rights. The contact that pen pal letters created and the support of girls' organizations for internationalism fostered new images of recent enemies, furthering reconciliation and supporting the new Cold War military and economic alliance.

Reimagining Germany

The process of reconciliation with Germany differed somewhat. Whereas Japan was regarded, on the one hand, through an Orientalist framing that positioned it as fundamentally Other and that allowed for a much greater degree of exoticization or, on the other, as a child growing toward mature democracy, representations of Germany in girls' culture fit three types. Germans were alternately seen as European victims of war and of Hitler, as educable transgressors, and as recalcitrant Nazis. German women and children were depicted in ways similar to other Europeans whose lives had been disrupted by war and who were in need of care.

As American attitudes softened, voluntary aid began to flow from civilian agencies to German women and children in 1946. The first relief sanctioned by the Treasury Department was through the Council of Relief Agencies Licensed to Operate in Germany and orchestrated by a New York German-language newspaper, *Staatszeitung und Herold*.[49] CARE, which enabled private citizens to donate, began sending aid to Germany in June of 1946. By 1947, 60 percent of CARE packages went to Germany, demonstrating the rapidity of the shift in American public opinion. In addition, Americans of German descent, who had more resources than the Japanese Americans rebuilding their lives after internment, often sent packages. The Red Cross also offered to help Germans locate family members in the United States who could aid them.[50] New York Girl Scouts sent four hundred pounds of Christmas toys. The press release noted only that they wished to help Europeans who had no toys of their own, ignoring any unique regard for Germans.[51]

Children and youth were the first recipients of relief. As the military's fraternization ban forbidding friendly relations with Germans was weakened shortly after the war, the army worked with young people to establish youth programs, especially in sports, to teach about the United States and provide a constructive outlet for young people disillusioned by war who might other-wise become delinquent. Youth organizations like the Boy Scouts and Girl Scouts soon were reestablished. Occupation authorities asked Girl Scout staff member Gertrude Burns to stay in Germany to train Girl Scout leaders.[52] The YWCA also declared that "young people in Germany are learning from the YWCA workers what it is like to live in a democracy" as the YWCA and YMCA recommenced pro-gramming in Germany.[53] The occupation government also organized *Kinderfests* and American holiday parties. In 1946, Army Santas "saw themselves no longer as occupiers of a hostile country but as paternal providers for a people ravaged by hunger and deprivations."[54] American GIs saw German children much like other displaced persons, as victims in need of aid.

Children elicited sympathy and former enemies were reconceived on friendly terms. Indeed, images of innocent-looking German children chasing the "Raisin Bombers," U.S. planes whose pilots dropped treats en route to land-ing with their deliveries at the air field in 1948 and 1949, conflated ongoing war recovery with Cold War threats after the Soviet Union closed supply lines to West Berlin. Children's dependency "invited the image of Germans as victims rather than villains."[55] In 1954, the textbook *Our Nation's Story* described the Ber-lin blockade as the turning point in German-American reconciliation. Although the text stressed the larger geopolitical and military context of the looming Soviet threat that cast Germans as worthy of U.S. support, the view of Germans as key allies was clear.[56] As anticommunism replaced antifascism, the crisis, with its prevalent images of children, solidified a new relationship between the United States and Germany, one in which girls' outreach to German children through pen pals and aid projects seemed appropriate and worthwhile.

Closely related to the idea that Germans were simply another population suffering from the effects of war was the widespread demonization of Hitler, which shifted attention away from collective German guilt as Americans forgave or overlooked the wartime actions of Germans and Austrians. This view could be found in materials written for girls and in their own reactions to the postwar world. Textbooks covered the theme of Germany's militaristic past, but by treat-ing Hitler and Nazism as aberrations, they also countered the fear that Germany would rise again. Most textbooks in the 1950s referred to Hitler and the Nazis and only occasionally to the "German Army" or German people as a whole.[57] The government and politics textbook *National Governments and International Rela-tions* placed sole fault in Hitler, stating that although most nations preferred peace, "one man like Hitler can create a world war."[58] *History of a Free People* regarded Germany as having a bellicose past and argued that Pan-Germanism was the main threat to peace during the period before the First World War. The text emphasized Hitler, and not a generalized German mindset, as the cause of aggression in the period preceding World War II. The text highlighted the 1931 economic crisis in Germany, suggesting sympathy with the German people's having had experiences similar to those of Americans during the worldwide Great Depression.[59]

Making Hitler an international symbol of evil enabled Americans to reconcile with German and Austrian civilians, especially those who were too young to have taken part in the war. By the end of the war, Allied officials regarded Austria as the first victim of Nazi aggression, and its division into occupation zones until 1955 magnified the victim status. Still, many Austrian citizens served the Nazi government. Liz, an American Jewish girl, channeled her anger and rage toward Hitler in letters to Lore, her Austrian pen pal and the daughter of a former Nazi soldier who had lived her early childhood in the Soviet occupation zone in Vienna. Liz's letters expressed empathy for the suffering of Austrians during and after the war, pointing specifically to the ways that the war had torn Lore's family apart and left her father with deep psychological troubles. Liz squarely laid blame on "one single person, HITLER."[60] Placing the blame squarely on Hitler's shoulders allowed Liz to avoid questioning her friend's parents' role in the war. Not only had Liz rendered another girl innocent; she also had come to see Austrian Nazi soldiers as among Hitler's victims. Such gestures by girls seem small, but they reflect the notion of reconciliation through human relationships that their youth organizations stressed.

Nonetheless, the anger toward Germany was hard to shake and regularly emerged in depictions of brazenly unrepentant Germans, including women and children who tried to take advantage of American aid and sympathy. Their dependence softened the anger somewhat, and girls' institutions emphasized the reeducation of former Nazi youth as a way to remake a generation, but even in girls' literature this view did not go uncontested. Americans saw Japan advancing toward mature democracy but Germans as pathological.[61] Thus, although both Japan and Germany were reimagined after the war, the process of reconciling with Germans involved girls in more direct debate. By the mid-1950s, however, the acceptance of Germany as a key Cold War ally was well accepted by girls coming of age in that decade.[62]

In addition to thinking about German children and women as worthy recipients of aid, U.S. girls dealt earnestly and sympathetically with the question of whether Nazi youth could be reeducated and turned into democrats. Immediately following the war, a *Seventeen* magazine article about high school students' views of education began to articulate the role of young people in reconciliation. Four students, two British and two American, "agreed that education in the postwar era should be designed to achieve world friendship" and should break down prejudice. All believed that it was necessary to reeducate Nazi youth, whom they did not distinguish from German young people more generally. Although the British students feared it would not be possible to change

Nazis older than twelve, the American teens hoped that by working with democracies and possibly by being taught by American teachers of German descent, Germans "could be taught to value human life."[63] These American teens were cautious, but hopeful that especially the youngest Germans could learn to live as democratic citizens.

Yet amid debates about reeducation, girls' magazines reminded readers of German guilt. War correspondent and *Seventeen* contributor Dickey Meyer (Chapelle) wrote an article in 1947 about displaced persons in Germany in order to teach young people in the United States about what others in their age group had experienced during the war. It focused on those Polish, Jewish, and Czech children who had been victimized by the Nazis and urged American girls to take responsibility by building awareness and empathy: "It is part of your job to understand that bitter attitude and do whatever you can now and later to overcome it." Meyer saw girls as building connections that would make peace possible. "For it is with these teenagers that you must work toward an assurance for them and for you that nothing born of hate can ever happen again," she editorialized.[64]

Meyer built sympathy toward displaced Czechs and Poles inside Germany and reminded readers of German guilt. Readers learned of a Czech boy who was "looted" by Nazis. He had been assigned to live with a family near Salzburg, and although the couple provided for him and pretended they were his parents, they also overworked him and forbade his speaking Czech or talking about his past. Meyer's other heartrending stories included one about a German Jewish girl who had lost her family in a concentration camp and survived more than two years there working as a laundress who cleaned the clothes of friends who had been killed in the gas chambers.

Meyer also told of "Gretel," a German girl who had been "a good Nazi" socialized through the Bund Deutscher Maedel, or League of German Girls, the girls' auxiliary within the Hitler Youth, to accept Nazi ideology and to lionize Nazi officials and Hitler. Now that the war had ended, Gretel was "out of place in the world" and looking "for cigarettes and candy bars." Although the article implied that her Nazism made her guilty, it also pointed sympathetically to her vulnerability to delinquency and the broader social dangers of such behavior. Meyer's *Seventeen* article complained that "Gretel . . . does not think that she is meant to help in the dirty, but so vital, business of removing rubble, although this would be one way to get a bigger food ration." American girls were told that this former Nazi still thought herself better than others and sought an easy way out of her troubles by marrying an American.[65] Two years after the war, girls' media continued to describe German atrocities and unrepentant youth. Although some articles evinced faith in reeducation, others exhibited serious doubt.

American girls responded to *Seventeen*'s piece through letters to the magazine. Although the editors no doubt culled responses to promote active girl citizenship, some girls appeared willing to accept responsibility for promoting world peace and expressed a newfound understanding of what their age cohort had experienced internationally during the war. P. L., from Tankton, South Dakota, wrote, "I really sat up and took notice. . . . I hadn't realized how close those children from other countries are to us." E. E., from Spring Lake, Michigan, concurred: "We need [articles such as 'How Could They Be Like You'] to remind us of the bitterness and cruelty of the war days. To remind us that we must fight and keep on fighting for world peace."[66]

As late as 1949, with the Berlin Airlift in full swing, public opinion was still not completely comfortable with seeing Germany as a hapless victim in the same league as other aid recipients. *Seventeen* magazine featured the struggle of Lee Kane, a Jewish refugee from Germany living in Cleveland. She wrote, "because of our beliefs, my family . . . was ordered to leave Germany" and several extended family members were "burned alive." Kane had received letters from former associates of the family back in Germany asking her for assistance. She had no evidence that the people requesting aid had turned her family over to authorities, but she resented their silence and believed their complicity had contributed to her family's suffering. *Seventeen* asked readers if Kane should help her family's former acquaintances.[67] Three of four girls who responded answered that the girl should help the people in Germany, and their letters treated German civilians much like the victims of war throughout Europe. One girl from Trenton, New Jersey, wrote, "Yes, send food and clothing to Europe, for this is one way to world peace." She personalized her concern by adding, "My brother will have to go to war if there is another one." Another teen asserted that "we should feed the starving, regardless of their nationality, and show them we are their friends." Her addendum intimated connection to the letter's author and claimed moral authority to speak on the matter: "My relatives died at Dachau and Buchenwald." Several respondents were more reluctant, their letters boiling over with bitterness, but asked that the children be fed and clothed and taught a new way.[68]

Other girls, however, used the forum as a space to vent their continued rage at Germany and its people. A New York City teen cautioned, "A trip to Germany this summer gave me the answer. Despite the cruelty and misery they inflicted upon others during the last war, the Germans regret only that they did not win." A girl in Syracuse concurred, writing that "every German is responsible either by direct action or because of his lethargy and acceptance." Another held that while forgiveness was important, aid should go first to the countries that Germany had harmed. A U.S. girl wrote from the occupation zone in Germany that "the people are not starving" and therefore not deserving of the same level of sympathy as others across Europe. She argued that the German people's participation in black markets and unwillingness to follow government quotas was the only thing still preventing Germany from recovering from the European food shortage. Still another remembered the lessons from the interwar years, cautioning that Germany would wait until it was strong and would then attack again.[69] Thus, as policymakers increasingly treated Germany as a crucial Cold War ally, girls' responses varied. Although many endorsed a new sympathetic image of Germany, others continued to view it as unrepentant, hostile, and threatening.

Although concern about reeducation was not unique to girls' agencies, as with other internationalist themes, the Boy Scouts of America dealt much less directly with issues of reconciliation. *Boys' Life* mentioned German Boy Scouts attending jamborees, but short stories in the magazine left the World War II relationship unchallenged. One article, for example, told of the Scouting underground in occupied Belgium and of two courageous Belgian Scouts who risked their lives serving the Resistance.[70] Little mention was made of boy Nazis other than that they were indoctrinated in the Hitler Youth and that Scouting had been forbidden under German occupation. The magazine did not address questions of Nazi rehabilitation. *Boys' Life* instead printed stories about Allied heroes shooting down Nazi planes and the postwar capture of former members of the Nazi SS (Schutzstaffel).[71]

When it came to aid, *Boys' Life* continued late into the 1940s to focus on helping those harmed by Germany and Japan and did so in ways that highlighted the idea of a militarized brotherhood combating fascism rather than on the peace building and rehabilitation seen in girls' media: "When our troops invaded the beaches of Normandy they needed trusted friends. They found them in the French Boy Scouts who in spite of death penalties went all out to help the Americans. So did the Belgium, Dutch and Norwegian Scouts. They showed the real spirit of world brotherhood. Now they and Scouts in every other corner of the world, where the iron heel of Nazi and Jap oppression tried to stamp out Scout ideals, are very much in need of friends."[72] *Boys' Life* called on U.S. boys to help rebuild world Scouting through a World Friendship Fund set up to revive the Scouting movement that had been devastated by German and Japanese aggression in Europe and the Philippines. Although girls' media likewise blamed Germany for others' suffering and Boy Scout troops sent aid to Germany and Japan, *Boys' Life* reinforced divisions between worthy victims and the suffering of former enemies, images that girls' media was reevaluating and reformulating through girls' relationships.

Conclusion

Girls' organizations and literature in the United States helped Americans to reimagine Japan and Germany. Both boys and girls were called on to take up world citizenship roles after World War II. Boys, however, were more likely to be envisioned as future warriors. Their role as "defenders of democracy" would keep the word safe, whereas girls were expected to create peace through international connections. Masako Ina ended her letter with a request to "please tell me about yourself, and school and country." As she offered a new image of Japan to her American pen pal, she invited a letter in return and a relationship outside of war. Although we cannot be certain what Masako meant when she wrote about cherry blossoms rather than the disruptions of war, her letter and others tell us something about how enemies reconciled following World War II. Institutional support in the United States and in Japan made it possible for girls' culture to engage issues of reconciliation and—wittingly or not—support foreign alliances.

Common girlhood experiences were part of girls' organization imagery and helped Asian enemies to be reimagined as nonthreatening. Moreover, U.S. girls saw their nation and themselves represented as providers of knowledge and the model for gender roles in a democracy. Japanese girls and women also initiated partnerships with U.S. women. The relationships they formed reified the Western two-gender system and left the somewhat less narrow confines of gender roles in the United States unexamined, but they also broke down the hostile stereotypes of wartime.

The image of Germany as enemy was harder to displace. Because of racial similarity in the dominant populations of the United States and Germany, Americans did not exoticize Germans, and U.S. girls' institutions had a tougher time casting Germany as a submissive and controllable Other. Still, in the mid-1950s personal connections and representations of German children and women as being capable of rehabilitation had begun to transform the image of Germans for U.S. girls, who came to see them as worthy of friendship. Girls' political culture shifted blame away from the German people to Hitler as their leader and a symbol of evil, a move that helped reconcile former enemies and shift new attention to the battle against communism. The textbooks and magazines that girls consumed had prepared them to accept Germans and Austrians as allies, and their personal expressions indicated that a new relationship was possible. This reflected and supported the nation's acceptance of Germany as a military ally. As the next chapter shows, these new relations of U.S. girls to the world also found expression in and through consumer culture.

4

"Playing Foreign Shopper"

Consuming Internationalism

From the late 1940s into the 1960s, American girls were urged to accept internationalism by being consumers. Girl Scouts, for example, learned to "play foreign shopper," a guessing game in which girls pretended to buy "colorful article[s] from a foreign country."[1] Similarly, the Y-Teens hosted international festivals where they played a form of charades in which girls acted out items they might buy in Paris and other foreign cities. Along with the international shopping games, girls consumed goulash and spaghetti, although these were hardly foreign or exotic foods in the 1950s, and then had a dessert of Armenian cookies, Czechoslovakian cookie rings, Italian knots, or Scottish white girdle scones.[2] Playing foreign shopper was meant to teach girls tolerance and acceptance of global cultures as they exercised their citizenship responsibilities. U.S. girls consumed internationalism in a variety of ways that fostered a cosmopolitan identity as they related to girls beyond their borders through private purchasing, collection, and display.[3]

Businesses and youth organizations also urged girls to share consumer culture with their peers in other countries by sending magazines and consumer items abroad. In addition, images of American girls went overseas, often intentional marketing for the American way of life. Although sending magazines and gifts had the potential to create mutual understanding and ease global want, the activities reinforced normative gender roles. They also fit well with that aspect of U.S. Cold War policy focused on rebuilding foreign markets. Advertisers and girls themselves sent images of American girls as part of a larger message that those abroad might secure the American teenager's standard of living if their countries followed the American plan. Such images might spread envy of, as well as admiration for, American life, but either way, they showcased the success of American political, educational, cultural, and economic institutions.

That girls' internationalism was tied to consumption is unsurprising given the emergence between 1945 and 1970 of "an economy, culture, and politics built around the promises of mass consumption, both in terms of material life and the more idealistic goals of greater freedom, democracy, and equality." By equating consumer goods with higher standards of living, policymakers, business groups, labor leaders, and civic groups (including girls' organizations) depicted "their nation as the model for the world of a society committed to mass consumption and what were assumed to be its far-reaching benefits."[4]

Since prosperity under capitalism offered a deep contrast to the deprivations of communism, buying was a citizen's duty, for a "consumer satisfying personal material wants actually served the national interest, since economic recovery after a decade and a half of depression and war depended on a dynamic mass consumption economy." *Seventeen* magazine posed a question to girls in an article titled "What Kind of World Do You Want?" It echoed a refrain heard regularly in the press and in advertisements that promised to give consumers "what you want." Articles in the *New York Herald Tribune* and *Harper's Magazine* detailed the exploding field of market research and used phrases like "nine out of ten of you want" to suggest consumer capitalism was democratic with the popularity of products depending on the choices of consumers.[5] The phrase connected consumer choice and democracy, suggesting that buyers voted for market outcomes.

After the war, teenagers were included in this democratization of consumer choice, and girls were treated as full participants. Consumerism and assisting national regeneration were understood as appropriate for female roles. During the Cold War, girls' images predominated in media and advertising that showed children. Advertisements often pointed to parental duties to protect innocent daughters or highlighted girls' expected futures as mothers and consumers. The kitchen debate between American vice president Richard Nixon and Soviet premiere Nikita Khrushchev, about whose country had the better economic system, emphasized home appliances and how much housework women did, and so also signaled the importance of women's consumer choices to international Cold War politics. Long before they would have kitchens of their own, girls heard of the importance of consumer choices as part of their role in a capitalist democracy.[6]

The growth in disposable funds after the war increased the role of teens by giving them more to spend, and youth involvement in consumer culture took deep root. Producers, advertisers, and magazine articles began to market directly to teenagers. Like their parents, adolescents were "consumer citizens."[7] Indeed, American teenagers spent $3.03 each week in the 1950s, and $9 billion during

1956, money they accumulated by working as well as from gifts and allowances. Twenty-three percent of teenagers had after-school jobs in 1956. According to the Bureau of Advertising, a majority of girls bought their own lipstick and at least influenced the purchases of their clothing and other cosmetics.[8] As marketers recognized girls' purchasing power, they legitimated a subcultural female teenage identity.[9]

Economic abundance stood with political freedom as an indication and symbol of successful U.S. governance and business, and American girls were themselves a vivid symbol of that success. Their access to education, recreation, and consumer goods was showcased when girls shared this model of consumer girlhood with girls abroad by sending letters, magazines, and aid, thereby spreading positive images of American abundance and culture that aligned with U.S. goals to cultivate consumer democracies abroad.

International consumption and sharing reinforced normative American gender roles. The ordinary girl that magazines depicted (and so marketed both at home and abroad) was a middle-class, heterosexual, civically engaged consumer and citizen. There were variations, though, on racial inclusivity. The YWCA, Girl Scouts, and Camp Fire Girls began to show African American, Latina, and Asian girls in their magazines in the 1940s, but *Seventeen*'s fashion models were white, and the membership of girls' organizations was predominantly white, too.[10] The typical girl these magazines depicted dated boys and planned to marry, but not right away. She cared about fashion and appearance, and she was engaged in her school and community through service, clubs, or student government. She sometimes had misunderstandings with her parents, siblings, and teachers, but she was a wholesome American teenager.

The YWCA and the Camp Fire magazines in the 1940s and 1950s carried no advertisements, but *American Girl* and *Seventeen* did. They situated the readers as future wives and homemakers as well as recognizing them as teenagers with significant leisure time for fantasizing about their futures. *American Girl* featured school fashions and cosmetics, feminine hygiene products, and snacks. The ads also spoke to girls' hobbies, showing friendship photos, bicycle equipment, stamp albums, and a science kit. *Seventeen* carried ads for clothes, department stores, sterling for bridal registries, cosmetics, records, and soda pop.

In addition to showcasing the American good life, girls' international involvement mimicked U.S. foreign policy. American policymakers held that they needed to ensure stable economies in Western Europe and Japan both to create markets for American goods and to offer European consumers an attractive alternative to following the Soviet Union.[11] In this spirit, American girls sent books and pencils to rebuild educational infrastructures. They also sent party items, magazines, toys, and other consumer items that fostered a consumer ethic and leisure activities. In sharing consumer items, girls promoted the ideas of American free enterprise even as they helped it grow through their purchases.

American business and political leaders taught young people that American power and prosperity were rooted in the nation's particular blend of capitalism and democracy. President Truman described the Atlantic Charter's freedoms of speech and worship as bulwarks of capitalism. "Throughout history," he asserted, "freedom of worship and freedom of speech have been most frequently enjoyed in those societies that have accorded a considerable measure of freedom to individual enterprise."[12] It followed for many that freedom from material want and economic abundance derived from free enterprise as well. As businessman J. C. Yeomans argued in a speech to the National Association of Manufacturers, schools needed to "indoctrinate students with the American way of life" and show that "the American system of free enterprise has done more for human comforts than any other system."[13] Media and organization literature for girls, as well as their pen pal letters and scrapbooks, demonstrated a gendered consumption-based internationalism that reflected the Cold War understanding of "freedom from want" as built upon free enterprise. Although earlier conceptions of "want" included the security of food, clothing, and basic needs, the Cold War's promotion of capitalism placed more stress on Americans' high living standards.

Concern about equity and access to middle-class standards of living led girls' leaders to broach consumer advocacy and antiracism alongside internationalism. The global girl citizen, however, was typically quite traditional, conforming to standardized heteronormative gender roles, consumerism, and nationalism. Although the right wing would attack the YWCA and the Girl Scouts in the mid-1950s for alleged radical influence, the internationally aware girls these groups wanted to create helped champion the American way of life and advance (both explicitly and implicitly) the national project of internationalism launched in the postwar period. American girls were told they fostered peace and tolerance as they accepted the responsibility to extend service to the world; they also reinforced the nation's political commitment to free enterprise and its global extension in the postwar period.

Fashion and the International Look

Major consumer media like *Seventeen* magazine supported the internationalist concept, offering it as a moral identity for girls to choose with their purchases and global service. *Seventeen* made internationalism and civic responsibility elements of its so-called *Seventeen* look. The girl who had it wore the clothes and accessories advertised in the magazine to achieve the "bright, shining, beautiful look you all want," but her beauty also reflected a "curious, eager desire to understand and fit into and be a part of and a credit to the world which awaits you." Invoking the saying "pretty is as pretty does," it made civic-mindedness part of beauty. The girls who knit for war-stricken Korean children as well as the girls busy serving the American Cancer Society, the Red Cross, their schools, and church organizations "have the special glow of the look" too, the magazine's authors explained.[14]

Further, youth organizations and magazines framed shopping as coming from an essential female desire that could further global mutual understanding. *Seventeen*'s July 1953 issue made the point that shopping had international uses, in "Yankee Teens in Tokyo," a story that profiled two American girls dressed in kimonos on a Tokyo shopping spree. Girls around the world were connected through their desire to shop, readers learned, since "Saturday shopping is a world-wide institution." A caption related how an older Japanese woman paused to give her approval of the girls' selections and thereby suggests that international female interaction and bonds could be built through consumer activity. The girls not only acquired "a pin-dot taffeta and a Paisley silk for spring" but also shared in a supposedly universal female culture of appreciation for fine products.[15]

Seventeen was not alone. *American Girl* also treated shopping as an activity inherent to being female. Its special features on foreign girls displayed them in "native markets" and in "handsome" new "dime stores" in cities like Colombia's Barranquilla.[16] A YWCA pamphlet on the organization's fellowship week used this supposedly universal world of shopping to encourage women and Y-Teens to learn more about their peers around the world. Although the week was devoted to prayer and friendship, the pamphlet advised women and girls to celebrate the week by taking "a quick shopping trip around the world" by investigating how and what they might buy in places such as Britain, Chile, India, and Africa.[17] Shopping, it suggested, offered a peek at the interdependence of people worldwide.

Models wearing clothes influenced by Italian, Mexican, English, and even American pioneer fashions suggested readers could show international spirit (if not commitment) by selecting the right look. *Seventeen*'s fashion spreads invited the viewer to copy romanticized, ethnic trappings sanitized of their complex histories and the voices of their cultures.[18] *Seventeen* presented different styles for girls' various moods and expressions. For flirtatious adventure-bound girls, Mexican-style "vacation" clothing in "brilliant contrasts" and "torero pinks" looked "glorious with tanned or natural complexions." By contrast, English garden clothing would fit girls with a taste for gentility.[19]

Girls could also find American fashions that were inspired by foreign styles and still experience the exotic, fulfill their desire for adventure, and create cultural understanding. A 1955 fashion spread in *Seventeen* featured Indian-inspired clothing "fit for an Oriental princess." The gold-accented designs and "pure silk sari cloth," the piece claimed, were "sari-inspired" and brought East and West together.

"Fiesta colors" in another fashion feature invoked friendship with Mexico as well as parties and fun. These caricatures through fashion offered girls stereotyped images of global cultures in marketing what they implied was cosmopolitan sophistication. *Seventeen* promised its girl readers that foreign attire offered fun and flirtation, a chance to "dance anywhere in the wide, wide world."[20]

Fashion was also a marker of American abundance and capitalist success, and it was sometimes contrasted with the condition of girls' closets elsewhere. A 1945 article in *Seventeen* noted the lack of consumer items available to South American girls and explained that all "señoritas" share the "big ambition" of coming to the United States. "Drug stores with soda fountains—Latin America

IMAGE 5. "¡Ole! Shirts, with Mexican Touches." *Seventeen* magazine's fashion spreads favored cosmopolitan styles.

Seventeen, April 1962, 109. Courtesy of *Seventeen*.

doesn't have 'em. Clothes—those marvelous clothes ready in the store for you to try on and wear out—they don't exist. Everything must be pinned and fitted and tried on again and again at the dressmaker's, which means that nothing is finished in less than months."[21] In this way, girls' media highlighted access to consumer goods on demand against a backdrop of global struggle and old-fashioned production methods.

In 1950, highlighting U.S. economic advantages, *Seventeen* discussed the paucity of clothes in Europe in comparison with what its fashion-rich layouts suggested was available to American teens. Its readers learned that middle-class French girls bought just a few ready-made items and that many of their clothes were handmade. Inviting American girls to compare themselves with their peers abroad, *Seventeen* inventoried the wardrobe of one French girl: "three skirts, four blouses, three sweaters, three day dresses and two evening gowns," the gowns being a luxury that, it pointed out, were bought for two weddings in her family.[22] This picture of middle-class French girlhood contrasted favorably to the previous month's article soliciting contributors for the Foster Parents' Plan, a piece that described French children as still lacking basic clothing and food, and contrasted favorably to that of many American girls. Still, *Seventeen* implied that the French girls' purchasing power was behind that of American girls. Indeed, on average American *Seventeen* subscribers purchased four sweaters, two skirts, two school dresses, and one party dress in the year 1944 alone.[23]

Seventeen also drew attention to the purchasing power of an American girl as a source of her worth as a citizen, suggesting that adults took her seriously because she was a consumer. The magazine noted a French girl's astonishment as she looked at its pages: "Do they pay, actually, to advertise to girls like me?" In France, she complained, "we are not considered very important people until we are grown up."[24] A British girl's letter expressed similar amazement at U.S. girls' consumer culture. English children were not respected as "responsible citizens" as American girls were "right from childhood," she complained, conflating consumer choice with responsibility. She also longed for a teenage magazine that would display the fashions in England in more than two pages "tucked away at the end of a woman's journal."[25]

The message to girl readers in the United States was that their inclusion in consumer culture was another way that they were taken seriously. They mattered because their spending—and their parents' spending on the girls' needs and desires—mattered. In a context in which free enterprise and consumer choice were understood to be the products of and fuel for democracy and prosperity, *Seventeen* could champion itself as evidence of girls' significance in a capitalist democracy.

Just as girls learned that their own abundance was linked to democratic institutions and capitalism, elsewhere in *Seventeen* girls read narratives of women's progress that linked greater rights and freedoms to engagement with Western markets. In the war's final year, *Seventeen* readers learned that the lives of women in allied China were being transformed through education and wartime service. Compared with their grandmothers, who, *Seventeen* reported, had been forced to bind their feet, Chinese girls had new opportunities. The latter were educated and wore blue jeans.[26] That girls were depicted as wearing denim underscored the connections made domestically by mainstream youth institutions, between the consumer economy and the expansion of democratic practices.

In 1950, with Japan an important Cold War ally, a Japanese reader of *Seventeen* promoted the image of Japan's embrace of democracy by describing girls' adoption of new fashions. T. S., a girl in Tokyo, criticized the wartime styles of school uniforms as pleasing only to the "warlike totalitarians" and complained that regulations kept girls from expressing their own "individualities" and kept them from wearing clothes and accessories they would have preferred, such as hair ribbons. In poetic prose that may have been edited by an adult, she reported that after the war, however, Japanese girls had come to embrace American fashions: "On the very day of American victory, all these unhappy restrictions and arbitrariness were blown away" as women gained "liberty . . . suffrage, individuality, personality and strive for beauty." She ended her letter by noting that Japanese women's fashion sense "makes progress every day."[27] That *Seventeen* presented women's fashion and consumer choices as equal to political rights and freedom made a kind of sense during the Cold War, when women's comforts and consumer choices were seen as evidence of the strength of the nation's political and economic system.

Exhibiting the International Scene

In addition to suggesting that fashion could express an internationalist identity, youth organizations implied that displaying foreign clothes and collectibles was a way to show interest in the international scene. They took a page from women's organizations that used fashion shows to promote charitable causes and offered activities with a particular emphasis on girls' culture by discussing dolls and teenage fashions. A 1949 YWCA program packet, which was used for both women's and teen groups, for example, called fashion shows "an immensely popular way of raising funds for our foreign program" and suggested holding a "Ball and Round-the-World Fashion Show."[28] Organization literature also recommended dressing dolls in international fashions, wearing international costumes, and exhibiting international souvenirs. Individuals, clubs, or entire community festivals might display foreign collectables. A YWCA Program Packet advised making an exhibit on a country or region by gathering "postage stamps, miniatures, doll costumes and all the galaxy of treasures and oddities that delight [collectors'] hearts." The guidelines told readers to investigate gifts sent home from brothers who were abroad in the service and the heirlooms that older people had "brought from the old country."[29]

Such festivals and their exhibits were modeled on the interwar cultural gifts movement in which liberal Americans, responding to nativists' reactionary

IMAGE 6. Camp Fire Girls host a party with an international theme.

Reprinted from *The Book of the Camp Fire Girls*, 1946.
Courtesy of Camp Fire National Headquarters.

attitudes, celebrated immigrants' and minorities' cultural contributions to American life with the hope of shaping "children's attitudes so as to eliminate prejudice in the next generation." Like these earlier efforts, the postwar projects of girls' organizations tended to overlook the complexity of ethnic cultures and emphasize those traits that were easily compatible with American middle-class values.[30] Although girls with immigrant backgrounds had a special opportunity to explain and demonstrate the traditions of foreign cultures and to teach their American peers, interaction with foreign people in consumer settings was minimal.

Organizations combined fund-raising and consumption to raise money for domestic or international charities. YWCA program packets explained that part of any festival should be "Things for Sale!" and suggested offering homemade as well as such imported items as handicrafts, aprons, and heirloom treasures. One festival in Lansing, Michigan, became a "colorful two-day market" with "wandering musicians, vendors, portrait sketchers, [a] fortune teller, [an] international doll show, sweetmeat and gift shops . . . [as well as] exhibits and demonstrations of puppets, folk songs and dancing."[31] Organizations capitalized on immigrant communities to showcase the former's international commitment and to raise money. Cities such as Lansing had become home after World War II to many refugees from Latvia, Poland, Lithuania, Estonia, and Ukraine fleeing communism who joined older communities such as Germans, Dutch, and French Canadians. YWCA women intended such festivals to "highlight the cultural and artistic expressions of people of many racial and national backgrounds" both from within the United States and internationally.[32]

Folk Dance and Tolerance

Such festivals regularly included folk dancing, which had been an activity of girls' organizations since their establishment in the early twentieth century, when leading youth workers held that it better suited girls' need for exercise than competitive sports like basketball. Believing that folk dance represented the primitive spirit untarnished by modern industrial society, its practitioners sought to create a version of modern American life that meshed tradition with progress. Indeed, the founders of the Camp Fire Girls believed that through traditional folk dance, girls developed valuable psychic and regenerative connections to women of the past, preparing them for healthy motherhood. Dances might come from all over the world, although those that "contradicted gracefulness" and Middle Eastern "love dances" were excluded as inappropriate.[33]

The postwar years saw a period of folk dance revival in the United States with ties to interwar pacifist groups. Girls' organizations backed folk dance for promoting "the one world ideal" by creating a "better understanding of the cultures of this world." Practitioners of its many varieties met regularly in YWCA facilities. Although some Americans emphasized English country dances and their Anglo roots, ethnic clubs from Poland, Latvia, and elsewhere danced to build and retain community and cultural identity. International folk dancers might incorporate pieces from thirty countries in one evening.[34]

Folk dancing could, of course, carry political affect. Fiercely nationalistic in Nazi Germany, folk dance has generally been associated with progressive internationalism in the United States and England. Internationalists danced to highlight American tolerance, whereas members of ethnic groups danced as ethnic Americans, their dances symbolizing and asserting the freedom and inclusivity that let them be ethnic in the United States. In the 1950s, these seemingly "liberal and radical political expressions" were sometimes coupled with declarations about the importance of proletarian folk culture, and folk songs and folk dances regularly provoked the suspicion of anticommunists.[35]

Collecting Knowledge about Girls Abroad

Through collection, girls came to possess and believe they knew something about the foreign world and demonstrated international spirit. Youth organizations, for example, also encouraged stamp collecting. Postwar Boy Scouts earned merit badges for the hobby, and the Girl Scouts added a stamp collector proficiency badge in 1963. To earn this recognition, both boys and girls collected either national historical stamps or international stamps, especially topical ones on a subject of global interest like agriculture. They might also gather commemorative stamps issued by Scouting organizations in different countries (and even some by Scouts in displaced person camps). In addition, girls collected postcards that had been designed by the Scouting and Guiding organizations for distribution to peers around the world on Thinking Day, Robert Baden-Powell's birthday. Although foreign stamps might come on letters from pen pals, *Boys' Life* advised searching stamp collector catalogs and visiting dealers to buy stamps and getting ideas from other collectors, especially members of the American Philatelic Association. The *American Girl* carried stamp dealers' advertisements. Youth organizations regularly described collecting as a way of creating cultural awareness and feeling "at home in the world."[36]

Far more common than stamps, however, were invitations for girls to collect and display dolls and to outfit them in foreign costumes.[37] To emphasize the personal connections between Girl Scouts and Girl Guides around the world, the Girl Scouts suggested displaying dolls in the uniforms used around the world and sending dolls dressed in American uniforms to friends who lived abroad.[38] In addition, girls often made doll clothes and sent the dressed dolls to children in war-torn Europe and Asia. Camp Fire Girls in Rialto, California, combined display and charity by hosting a doll contest and exhibit before sending off the dolls that they had sewn.[39] Just as folk dance played upon multiple traditions, doll collecting and exhibition taught girls about other traditions. It tapped into a progressive cosmopolitanism, even as it may now be understood as having appropriated other cultures' traditions for consumption rather than copying them to learn about and honor others.

Girls' fiction also promoted doll collecting and encouraged girls to dress their dolls and furnish their dollhouses according to the national origin of the doll. Rumer Godden's stories often shifted to the dolls' perspective. Miss Flower, for example, wonders if her owner will know that "a Japanese house should have walls that slide open like windows."[40] The dolls serve as props for Godden to teach her readers about Japanese customs, including the Japanese doll festival, an elaborate event whose display included dolls representing the imperial court.

Many girls' organizations used the festival as a model for their own exhibitions. In 1953, Japanese American Girl Scouts in San Francisco who had never lived in Japan held a Japanese doll festival and invited non-Japanese troops from the area to honor international friendship. They dedicated hours of research to the project, consulting books and local Japanese residents to "make their festival authentic."[41] Girls' fiction and articles on exhibitions suggested a universal love of dolls among girls even as cultural differences, such as kimonos, the preference for bowls rather than plates, and the use of floor cushions instead of chairs, were depicted as romantic and unique.

In 1954, *Seventeen* bridged the world of charitable giving and consumer culture, turning girl citizens into potential entrepreneurs by joining with the Ideal Toy Corporation for its annual Save the Children doll-making campaign and contest.[42] The winner was chosen by former first lady Eleanor Roosevelt, singer Marion Anderson, and actress Deborah Kerr, along with representatives from the company. Marketability was critical in the choice because Ideal planned to put the doll into production. The girl who designed it got royalties, and the Save the Children Foundation would also share in the profits. There were several categories, including baby doll, character doll (which went to a Snow White figure), and fashion doll, for which they selected a "Negro doll, Taffy." (The girl who selected the name may have been invoking a light shade of brown or simply suggesting the doll was sweet.) The teenage designers won trips to New York City, where they appeared on television shows and received honors from the U.S. Committee for UNICEF.[43]

Not only did the girls travel, but the dolls also served as ambassadors. As symbols of world friendship, the collected dolls went to "free China" and to the Marienfelde Refugee Camp in Berlin, which housed East German families fleeing the Russian sector. The fourteen-year-old grand prize winner, Joan Shelton from Missouri, traveled to Europe with the baby doll she had designed. After Joan visited and toured Marienfelde, a letter in *Seventeen* from a Berlin woman explained that "international friendship can be started with our children." The visit had etched the image of "a pretty girl holding a beautiful doll in its christening robes" in the minds of refugees as their image of the United States.[44]

This cooperation between a company, a children's organization, government, and a specialized agency of the United Nations was not unique. The United States Department of Commerce cited the Camp Fire Girls for their "outstanding public service to the United States Government" after the Camp Fire Girls contributed a donation of American dolls to the 1957 U.S. International Trade Fair program.[45]

Such gestures simultaneously displayed American generosity and exported a narrow image of American femininity. Although some dolls, like "Taffy," were African American, the winning blue-eyed doll in her christening robes upheld a narrow definition of white feminine beauty and exported it as part of the Cold War's expansion of American capitalism and democracy.[46]

The International Menu

Cooking foreign foods was another form of international consumption consistent with the gendered programming of girls' and women's organizations. The Columbus, Ohio, YWCA hosted an "Old World Market" that served cafeteria-style fare of Hungarian, Swedish, German, Italian, Indian, Japanese, Spanish, Chinese, Turkish, Greek, and American origins. YWCA advice underscored the notion that international consumption created world friendship. "Festivals," the YWCA promised, "are traditionally 'feast days,' and good food is always an easy and pleasant way to people's hearts."[47] Food festivals tapped into the role of the girl as hostess and her service to her family and social circle and extended it to the world. Indeed, foreign culinary preparations offered an activity consistent with gender-specific expectations that females purchase and prepare foods for their families and friends.

They also enabled girls to cultivate internationalist identities that could extend to their families and clubs as they cooked for them. Advertisers connected foreign food purchases with a "debonair, modern, and paradoxically American" identity that left rigid customs behind. Indeed food choices have symbolic power to demonstrate social affinities and identities, including cosmopolitanism and tolerance.[48]

YWCA materials advertised that fun and adventure came with a cosmopolitan gastronomical identity. "Your international event offers boundless opportunities for interesting adventures in eating," a 1948 program booklet enthused. Girls were prodded to "consider the appeal to imaginations and palates with such dishes as: Crêpes Suzette, Scotch Scones, Russian Borsch, Italian Spaghetti, Gefüllte Fish, Wienerschniztel, Danish Applecake, Cornish Pastries, English Steak and Kidney Pie, Armenian Shish-Kebabs, Chinese Tea and Rice Cakes, Swedish Fattigmansbakelser, Tamales and Tortillas, Scandinavian Smorgasbord, Indian Curry, Banbury Tart," and more.[49] Although largely European fare, which reflected the heritage of most YWCA women, international festivals introduced foods from a variety of regions and continents. Through the adventurous eating of representative dishes, the citizen of the world extended her sense of knowledge and her tolerance for others.

Themed parties paired international lessons with friendship and make-believe travel. Girls' magazines and organizations recommended dinners at which different courses were served at different homes in the style of a "globe-trotting" progressive dinner.[50] Two teens from Clayton and St. Louis, Missouri, wrote in *Seventeen* about the foreign food party given by their high school committee of the National Council of Christians and Jews. As a "mixed group" themselves, they thought a foreign food party was a good way to learn about each other and the world. They researched the history of barbecue in Spanish, Chinese, and the West Indian cultures and kashrut (Jewish dietary laws for keeping kosher), capping the evening off with "Hungarian *strudel* and Cokes."[51]

"International flavors" might lead to "new adventures," but recipes and plans for international dinners in *Seventeen* and *American Girl* also provided advice to would-be homemakers. They were a way to care for family and friends through home-cooked meals. Girls also read that because the recipes originated in peasant villages, they were easy on the budget.[52] And for the weight-conscious teenager who might need further convincing, magazines hyped Chinese food as a "hearty," "good-tasting," but "not fattening" menu choice to broaden a girl's cultural perspective.[53]

Girls' institutions touted international cooking as a way to increase the enjoyment of the family meal, subtly underlining the point that international-ism was connected to girls' basic duties to their families and making it consistent with the homemaker training prevalent in girls' organizations. *Camp Fire Girl* staff writer Dorothea Love urged girls to plan a family meal based on the country of their Camp Fire friendship group, their sister-club affiliate abroad. Rather than merely preparing food, Love suggested, girls should make family meals "festive" and full of international significance. Indeed the meal itself might take place as part of an international-themed evening complete with foreign family games. Overall, the idea was to integrate international tolerance into domestic training so it became part of girls' civic identity via the addition of creative planning to her family chores. A girl could be a kind of international ambassador, bringing information and experiences from other countries into her own home and onto her family's dinner table.[54]

The International Content in Girls' Magazines

Reading was another way girls consumed international themes. Magazines such as *Seventeen, American Girl*, and *Bookshelf* published stories about girls from around the world. Articles discussed the lives of girls—especially their education and families—in other nations, including Great Britain, Russia, China, India, Sweden, Greece, Iran, Turkey, and asked U.S. girls to compare their own lives with those of others. Printed letters to the editors in *Seventeen* praised articles about girls abroad and asked for more. One *Seventeen* reader wrote in 1951, "Could you run stories about girls in other countries? I am very hopeful. I think this helps in promoting world peace and better understanding which is so badly needed at this time."[55]

Articles on girls around the world were of several types. Reading could encourage sympathy for girls abroad even as it offered the grist for self-congratulatory comparisons of political, economic, and cultural experiences. Like the *Seventeen* article that showed kimono-clad tourists, many articles featured American girls who traveled or lived abroad. These daughters of military officers, diplomats, and businessmen reported on customs and sights in their new locales. Girls' magazines also published monthly columns about girls around the world. The *American Girl* carried a number of stories, such as "Teen-Ager . . . Hindu Style" and "Teen-Ager . . . Colombian Style" that compared American girls' lives to those of their peers abroad. The *Bookshelf* introduced individual Y-girls around the world through their own words in their Friendship by Mail column. The girls' magazines also recommended further intercultural reading through book lists and reviews. At the same time as the magazines portrayed foreign life to American girls, they used the lens of American teenage culture to promote U.S. life to girls abroad, which allowed others to measure their own nation's economic well-being against that of the United States.

One clear component of teenage life was substantial leisure time to attend dances, go to movies, read, and listen to records. About the girl in Greece, the *Bookshelf* noted, "So you see that teen-agers in Greece lead similar lives to those you know. Customs may differ slightly, but young people everywhere are busy with studies, home duties, and recreational activities."[56] Girls' literature depicted girls around the world as enjoying leisure time, suggesting it was a universal teenage desire to have fun, but these same media indicated that American girls were especially fortunate in their leisure activities. The *Bookshelf* mentioned the leisure activities of teen girls elsewhere in the world, and American girls could then compare. Whereas Japanese teens loved to watch and play baseball, view movies from the United States, France, Italy, and Japan, and listen to hit tunes on the radio, a Chilean Y-Teen enjoyed church groups but only attended school dances when her father permitted. A girl from Uganda had little time away from tending poultry to supplement her family's income, though she was active in the YWCA. The attention to leisure and recreation made them markers of girlhood in the Cold War period. And American teens were especially fortunate, according to *Seventeen* and girls' organization magazines, to enjoy many club activities, dances, and parties that their peers did not enjoy. In France, for example, girls were described as so busy with intense study programs that they "didn't have time . . . for school clubs or societies."[57]

Magazines began depicting girls around the world during World War II with articles that highlighted Allied girls' wartime contributions, extolled female heroism, and reminded girls how different their lives in the United States were from the lives of those who lived in theaters of war. *Seventeen* spotlighted the war work of Indian girls and women, telling of girls who rode elephants sixty miles through jungles and gunfire to save the animals from being commandeered by the Japanese army.[58] Prior to the rise of Cold War tensions, *Seventeen* featured Russian girls, too, as patriotic heroines who, not unlike American pioneer women, "face situations that are rarely demanded of women and certainly not of young girls in America today."[59] Although some American readers may have viewed such articles as describing a signally foreign and unfamiliar experience, other girls may have read these articles as endorsing the abilities of girls like themselves to act and shape their world.

Following the war, the magazines presented stories about the increasing rights, especially to education, of women and girls in other countries. *American Girl* subscribers read that their peers in India might attend missionary schools and be raised in "the modern age of Hindu India" where "girls are free to study and play and choose their own husbands," even if those girls still could not "go out unchaperoned with young men."[60] In a story about the changing customs in Iran, *Seventeen*, with surprising sympathy for traditional Muslim culture and with remarkable insight into how culture constructs social views about feminine beauty and propriety, compared the Shah Reza-Pahlavi's decree to bar the *chaddar* and the veil to an American girl's being forced to give up her hairpins and combs. Nonetheless, *Seventeen* marveled, women and girls had "adjusted to a whole new world in twelve years" as lost customs were replaced by education, choice in marriage, and access to health care and even careers.[61]

Adopting heteronormative standards, magazine editors included information about dating practices around the world. Girls read in *Seventeen* that the "respectable, middle-class French schoolgirl leads a rather different life from that of her American sister." The French girl "uses no make-up," *Seventeen* explained. "No parties, no dates, no boys," *Seventeen* exaggerated as it announced that since boys and girls attended separate schools, "boys are creatures from another world."[62] Depictions of American girls as fortunate in their freedom to meet boys and marry for love were accompanied by narratives about how customs in the rest of the world were coming to look more like their own. *American Girl*'s "international-date-line tour," which examined dating customs around the world, allowed girls to compare their relative freedom of choice on the dating scene. One article characterized a few countries as similar to the United States in that boys and girls met each other in shared schools and enjoyed dances and other parties, often as two-somes. But marriages were still arranged in many countries. Many also separated adolescent boys and girls in schools. Most countries, however, were described as progressing toward a freer life for women. Girls in Morocco, for example, were "rebelling against the old idea that their place, after high school, is in the home." American girls read that just as they "hoped their college experience—academically as well as socially—would foster their domestic aspirations," often marrying right after graduation or quitting school to get married, U.S. girls read that Moroccan girls were going to college in increasing numbers to "be intellectual mates as well as homemakers and mothers."[63] Thus, girls' magazines taught international citizenship by including information about girls around the world. The materials editors selected suggested that there were universal themes in girls' cultures around the world and that girls' freedoms were progressing toward American models.

Sending Consumer Culture across Borders

In addition to learning about those in other countries, U.S. girls shared American consumer culture, especially that pertaining to teenage girls, with their counterparts abroad. When girls' organizations exported consumer goods, they were in part making gestures of generosity and in part, whether wittingly or not, providing evidence of the success of American democratic capitalism. This generosity served U.S. diplomatic interests. When girls sent their magazines, play kits, books, school supplies, and toys, they supported a model of childhood like their own, one marked by educational opportunities and free from labor and adult responsibilities. These things were as important as blankets and food in establishing "freedom from want."

Seventeen and the *American Girl* encouraged readers to think of the magazines as ambassadors they could send to their pen pals abroad to showcase their own style and opportunities. American girls did, in fact, share their magazines with pen pals and friendship groups in other countries, and editors published letters from abroad in the letters section that further encouraged the practice. One, from J. W. of Airdrie, Scotland, expressed this older teen's dismay that her American relatives had stopped sending the magazine, which she credited with her "reputation for the originality of the parties" she gave. A girl in Holland said that her friend was receiving *Seventeen* and that they read it cover to cover. A

Norwegian teenager called it "the best magazine I have ever read" and wished she had a magazine like it in Norway.[64] The Girl Scouts urged members to send the *American Girl* to pen pals abroad. One fourteen-year-old from Rottingdean, England, who received the magazine from her pen pal, called it "wizard," a British slang term for *cool*, because, she said, she liked the stories and found the fashions "smashing."[65]

The magazines' attempts to show what the American girl teenager was like were not always successful ambassadorship, however. A letter from a British girl complained about the shallowness of American values. The advertisements left her envious and she criticized girls in the United States for not taking greater advantage of their good fortune. She "compared some of the fashions in *Seventeen* with the few things I have and almost wept" over the "gray gloom of Europe" with its expensive meat and the "poor quality and high price of clothes." Her tone turned critical, however, as she asserted that based on what she had seen in *Seventeen*, she felt "a little closer to life and reality than the average American girl." Although many American girls could not afford what was advertised in *Seventeen*, she believed that Americans had so many choices of clothes but all wanted to look alike. Although she hated that British women were still getting paid less than men as laborers and girls less than women (a comment that implied, incorrectly, that pay was equal in the United States), she seemed to think that American girls did not work at all, for she concluded that British girls thought for themselves and worked for themselves, whereas American girls had everything done for them.[66]

Other foreign girls liked what they learned. Although she did not say how she gained access to the magazine in Prague, a girl in Czechoslovakia wrote in 1949 to say that she and her friends were "*Seventeen* gluttons," devouring the magazine whenever they could. She longed for the "heaps of food and pretty dresses and pretty things [that] don't exist in reality here."[67] A letter from M. M. in Lahore, Pakistan, spoke to the dissemination of U.S. girls' culture through fashion. She asked her personal tailors to make all her clothing using *Seventeen* patterns.[68] Similar letters came from Holland, where a seventeen-year-old had copied a dress from a picture in *Seventeen*, and from Germany, where a girl from Nuremberg explained, "When I want a new dress, hair style, or perfume, I always look first in *Seventeen*." These and other letters from a variety of countries expressed gratitude for the American fashion and beauty lessons they picked up from *Seventeen* and the *American Girl*, which the German understood to be "knowledge . . . of American teenagers."[69]

In fact, American girls worried that *Seventeen* did not always put them in the best light. One American teen criticized a short story in *Seventeen* because it depicted American girls as narrow-minded. She worried about what her pen friends in Germany and Switzerland would think when they read it.[70] *Seventeen*, then, despite the assertions of its more political articles, sometimes created the impression that American girls were entitled and overindulged, leading to expressions of envy of American prosperity along with resentment that undermined whatever mutual understanding *Seventeen* claimed to advance.

Seventeen and the *American Girl* were not alone in trying to share the American story through magazines but supported a larger business and government collaboration intended to tell America's story abroad. Magazines for Friendship, an organization supported by the USIA, wanted to combat communist propaganda abroad and tell the "true" story of the United States through magazines. It advertised that ordinary Americans could help win the Cold War by sending "our better U.S. magazines" abroad through local organizations affiliated with Magazines for Friendship. In addition to asking Americans never to send pulp, comics, or sensationalism, the group provided a list of periodicals that were desired. These included the *American Girl* and *Boys' Life*, as well as other favorites such as the *Saturday Evening Post, Newsweek, Life, Business Week*, and *Good Housekeeping*.[71] By the end of 1957, the A&P's Stores Publishing Company shipped six thousand copies of *Woman's Day* abroad each month.[72] The Girl Scouts recommended the program to its leaders, and in 1958, Eisenhower's People-to-People program recommended American citizens share books and magazines such as *Life, Good Housekeeping*, and *National Geographic* with people in other countries.[73] A USIA report urging advertisers' cooperation in shaping the American image abroad explained that pictures, magazines, and catalogs "present a picture to large audiences on all levels of what we are doing and how we are living."[74] Sending magazines to pen pals in other nations fostered the association of American capitalism with the good life.

Magazine shipments reflected the U.S. government's promotion of democratic capitalism abroad. To counter communism's appeal to those who might be susceptible to its promises of a better life, President Eisenhower resolved to show that the American capitalist system better provided for a high standard of living for all its citizens. The emphasis was not on luxury goods but on "the common man's yearning for food, shelter and a decent standard of living." He had earlier argued before the House Subcommittee to Study the U.S. Information Act of 1947 that ordinary items such as "ice boxes, radios, [and] cars," as well as "how much [Americans had] to eat, what they wear, when they get to go to sports spectacles, and what they have available in the way of art galleries" were easily comprehended by people abroad.[75] When girls sent magazines abroad, these were the same kinds of consumer items—though ones that appealed to girls—that were showcased in their pages. Along with fashion spreads were advertisements for Gorham sterling silver, Ipana toothpaste, Lane Cedar Chests, and Swans Down cake mixes, implying that these were items ordinary American girls and their families could afford.

Consumer Activism and the International Impulse

Despite championing free enterprise and American prosperity as the deserved results of the country's particular blend of capitalism and democracy, many Americans were not entirely comfortable with either wealth or global power. Material prosperity, however welcome, nourished simultaneous and sometimes contradictory anxieties about a greedy, shallow culture, and led girls' organizations to weave into their programs consumer education that connected to larger issues of social justice. Thus, although both the *American Girl* and *Seventeen* offered glamour through glossy fashion spreads, interior decorating advice, and advertisements for makeup and beauty products, information they encouraged American girls to share, girls' institutions simultaneously criticized materialism and offered consumer education.

Messages about consumption could be contradictory, demonstrating adults' underlying ambivalence about increased material comforts in U.S. girls' culture. Indeed, adults' concerns about materialism led often to sharp criticisms of the consumer economy, even as leaders put their faith in the notion that American abundance derived from the United States' own distinct democratic capitalism. These anxieties extended to worrying about how those abroad saw the United States and found expression in advice to girls to downplay American prosperity in their pen pal letters and their relief packages.[76]

Girl Scout publications also urged caution regarding consumer advertising and warned girls about how advertisers played upon consumers' desires, offering girls advice on decoding advertisements in what must have been some of the organization's first media literacy projects. The 1953 handbook recommended that girls study advertisements to "see how companies make you want to buy their products" and asked girls to think about the emotional appeals.[77] Not falling into marketers' traps, as well as modesty and manners, were a global girl's responsibilities.

Travelers who bragged would "lose friends for yourself and your country." One *Seventeen* article recounted the sad tale of an American girl who lost the opportunity of romance with a French boy because, in the shadow of the Eiffel Tower, she failed to remark on its beauty, noting instead how small it was compared to the Empire State Building. Similarly, *Seventeen* assured readers that Europeans were grateful for the Marshall Plan and other sources of reconstruction funds but lectured that it was impolite to remind them of U.S. aid. *Seventeen*'s author ended by reminding her readers that Europe's "young people your age knew war and the battlefield on their land while we, a strong and youthful nation, were able to take time to get ready to save ourselves."[78] Thus, even as *Seventeen* celebrated American abundance, its copy exhibited adult discomfort with the narrative of American wealth, reminding its American readers, many of whom were only six or seven at the war's end, that they had been spared much of the war's suffering and that American abundance was a result of this fortunate U.S. position in the war.

Deep concern that materialism sapped spiritual and political values rested uneasily next to official declarations that economic prosperity and democratic values reinforced each other. The program director of the Camp Fire Girls, Ruth Teichmann, urged that "children and young people" be helped to develop "a real conviction about human dignity and worth. . . . They must be helped to a clearer intellectual understanding of what democracy means, and just what it is that must survive." She compared genuine democratic living to the false symbol of choice in consumer goods that was often held up as emblematic of American democracy: "Too many times at home and abroad, we translate democracy into materialistic terms: the fifteen-cent soda and the car in every garage. Conceivably these things *might* one day prevail in a totalitarian country. The valuing of every human being as having worth in himself, could not."[79] Like Teichmann, Martha F. Allen, the director of the Camp Fire Girls, worried about the stifling cultural impact of materialism. She was apprehensive, for example, "about the conforming teen-ager; about his parent, 'the organization man'; about robot societies in which human individuality is discouraged and all men march as one in the interest of the State." To defend democracy, she sought the means to help girls relate to the group while retaining their individuality.[80] For Allen, materialism ran counter to the human dignity and the free development of one's personality proclaimed in the Universal Declaration of Human Rights and threatened to produce the very conformity that she associated with communist societies. Girls needed to balance their high standards of living, or social security, which the Declaration of Human Rights had called necessary for cultural and individual expression, with a commitment to ameliorate want among others.

Likewise, the YWCA turned girls' attention not only to consumption for personal desires but also toward consumer advocacy. The YWCA's consumer education mixed budgeting advice and product research with discussions of consumer empowerment and social justice. Such efforts tied girls' international citizenship responsibilities to progressive political movements that understood "consumers as arbiters of the public interest."[81] Indeed, the consumer movement drew its ranks from the same middle-class women that joined the YWCA with its liberal Christian reform values.

Beginning in the 1920s, the movement argued that the "purchasing power of poor and working-class Americans was essential to the health of the economy, as well as to the health of those groups."[82] The National Association of Consumers and other organizations (including the American Association of University Women, the American Veterans Committee, and the League of Women Shoppers) advocated standby price controls, rationing, reciprocal trade agreements, rent control, and public housing, all issues raised in the pages of the YWCA *Bookshelf*.[83] For a time, girls' citizenship duties included awareness of consumer issues in relation to other social concerns, demonstrating those issues' broad acceptance by mainstream American educational and youth organizations.

After the war, the YWCA worked for social justice along economic and racial lines through consumer advocacy. One lesson suggested that members figure out "What is the Score on Cost of Living?" by tracking prices, creating their own "market baskets," or holding a mock trial of poor housing, job discrimination, or restrictive covenants—"any evil your group is particularly concerned about."[84] Such lessons were intertwined with international awareness as Y-Teens learned how price increases in the United States had negatively affected European recovery, since nations wanting to buy food and steel could purchase less than they had planned.[85]

The YWCA concern about material excess intertwined with its recognition of the need for consumer knowledge to produce a consumer activism that would enable girls and women to spend their money in progressive ways. YWCA prefaced its consumer awareness campaigns with the suggestion that girls save money in order to serve others. A 1948 YWCA program packet explained, "In the United States today there is a great deal of 'ready' money. Wages are higher than they have ever been—but so are prices. We have in this country a higher standard of living than we have ever had—while the people of many countries eke out a miserable existence. We know, many of us, that we waste our money or do not spend it wisely. It is often money we should have liked to put toward a CARE package, or money we might have sent to the Round-the-World Reconstruction Fund." To help, the YWCA printed three articles from the National Consumer-Retailer Council, all advising girls and women how to save when buying interior decoration and clothes.[86] These savings ensured that girls were poised to contribute to international relief and cultivate a new relation to the world.

Y-Teen leaders also coached girls to think of others, using the language of consumer desire as well as that of the freedom from want concept outlined in the Atlantic Charter. One program guide interchanged "want" and "need," directing groups to "have a discussion on 'What People Want'" and then asking, "What can be done in your YWCA to help meet the needs of people?" The needs and wants were deeper than consumer goods, extending to "food, clothing, health, peace, spiritual strength, justice and fair dealing." The United States had both "the resources and responsibilities . . . in building a world of free peoples" through material aid, YWCA materials insisted.[87]

Other girls' organizations also promoted savings and savvy consumption. The Camp Fire Girls savings lessons directed girls' attention beyond their own personal purchasing desires. At the outset of the Korean War girls were reminded of war's effects on the U.S. and global economies. Camp Fire Girls saved to buy anticipated U.S. savings stamps and discussed the importance of likely rationing.[88]

One young author, teenager Virginia Weyman of Saegerstown, Pennsylvania, demonstrated girls' understanding of the complex connections between the threat of war, internationalism, and consumer rights. Her 1952 prize-winning essay on the topic "How Differently I Would Plan My Future If I Knew World Peace Were Assured for the Next Fifty Years" appeared in *Seventeen*. A prominent businessman sponsored the contest, and Alice Thompson and other distinguished figures served as judges. After "confessing" that she had "no desire for a career other than that of homemaker," Virginia detailed how fifty years of peace would bring material as well as spiritual blessings to her domestic scheme. She was not, however, a girl who wanted to buy fashions and the latest home appliances. Rather, she explained, "A world without war would not have to face up to the problems of inflation due to shortages, overproduction, war scares and general instability. I could count on family income and our savings to have a stable purchasing power." She not only ended by claiming her female role as teacher and moral compass to her future children but also added a stinging criticism of militarized democratic politics: "While I was teaching my children the meaning and practice of brotherhood, I would not be forced to justify the untenable position that war is necessary to preserve the American way of life."[89] Virginia's view shows that at least some American girls who read *Seventeen* were politicized beyond the role of "playing foreign shopper." Virginia might have understood peace as a product of mutual understanding and friendship, what she called "brotherhood," but she also understood that her ability to function as a homemaker and a member of her community and a citizen of the world depended on some as-yet-unarticulated means of challenging militarization.

Conclusion

Girls' new global responsibilities extended familiar feminine responsibilities of consumption as well as service from the home and local community to the nation and the world. Literature from the Camp Fire Girls, the Girl Scouts, the YWCA, and *Seventeen* magazine encouraged girls to bring their feminine natures to bear on world affairs by building relationships with girls around the world through understanding and sharing.

Girls who played foreign shopper were consumer citizens who bought into an internationalist identity in which they consumed information about their global peers and cooked the food of allies for their families. Moreover, as girls learned to turn their privileged position in the world into a duty to help those abroad, they shared their way of life, especially their consumer, leisure, and fashion choices, with girls abroad. U.S. girls participated in the global spread of American culture and in the construction of the view that the Untied States was a benevolent global power. As they shipped gifts of magazines, pencils, and Kool-Aid abroad, they shared American abundance and were believed to build U.S. moral authority. The images they sent to their peers depicted American teen culture as a symbol of American prosperity and the success of democratic capitalism. Despite how well the girls' role meshed with government projects during the Cold War, the more radical aspects of the girls' programs—consumer advocacy, antiracism, and internationalism—led right-wing anticommunists to target the YWCA and the Girl Scouts in the mid-1950s.

5

"We Hand the Communists Powerful Propaganda Weapons to Use against Us"

Defending Global Citizenship during the Post–World War II Red Scare

In early 1952, a Girl Scout Council in Orange County, California, threatened to bar Costa Mesa's lone troop because of the town's reputation as a hotbed of subversive groups. By early 1953, trouble was also brewing in Santa Ana. In the *Santa Ana Register*, the Pro America organization and Freedom Clubs there accused the Girl Scouts' Thinking Day of advancing UNESCO's vision of world government, something that was neither on UNESCO's agenda nor served by its programs. There were whispers in the Detroit area that the Girl Scouts was a communist organization because of its interracial activities and because the Girl Scout Council displayed a UN flag.[1] Rumblings also occurred in Houston, Texas, as the Minute Maids, an offshoot of the conservative women's group the Minute Women, suggested in their fall 1953 recruitment materials that their counterpart, the Girl Scouts, included communists. Officials of the Daughters of the American Revolution (DAR) questioned whether wearing a World Pin was unpatriotic.[2]

In this context, girls' organizations maintained their democratic-training efforts, but linked messages of internationalism and antiprejudice to anticommunism. The director of the Camp Fire Girls, Martha Allen, asserted the need to counter racism within the organization's ranks, asserting, "If democracy could be made 100% effective in the United States I don't believe it would be possible to convert a single American citizen to communism. Whenever we fail to practice democracy we hand the communists powerful propaganda weapons to use against us and we dim the faith of people in the goodness of our way of life." The Camp Fire Girls, then, could fight communism by making "friends for democracy" and by "making democracy work at least in our own organization" through efforts to fight prejudice and teach girls about the dignity of all human beings.[3]

Youth organizations were not always able to define the terms of the anticommunist battle. The Camp Fire Girls avoided being incriminated, but others became targets during the post–World War II red scare precisely because of their stress on internationalism and antiprejudice. Anticommunists viewed children and youth as particularly vulnerable to so-called un-American influences and saw educational institutions as especially corruptible. Conservatives resisted U.S. involvement in multilateral institutions and were suspicious that the United Nations was dominated by communists. Many conservative women believed that internationalist foreign policy led to cycles of war. As communism surged in Eastern Europe and Asia, anguish about liberal expressions of internationalism found expression in a small but vocal and well-connected right-wing network.[4] The right-wing anticommunists argued that the female "do-gooders" allowed their organizations to be hijacked in their hopes for peace.

Superpatriots in the American Legion, DAR, Pro America, and within the YWCA and the Girl Scouts alleged that the two organizations had been infiltrated by communists.[5] They challenged the groups' internationalist programs, which had until then been accepted as mainstream and nonpolitical. Although the public and their own memberships generally supported both organizations, damage had been inflicted. The YWCA's model of liberal Christian civic engagement was eroded as the Right assumed the moral authority to speak for Christian women. In response, the Girl Scouts tried to avoid witch hunts. Still it modified its handbook to limit material that had been labeled political and increased its patriotic content. In this way, leaders bound girls' world citizen responsibilities. Although girls' organizations continued their internationalist message into the late 1950s, they sought greater legitimacy through collaboration with the government's People-to-People program.

"World-Mindedness" and the Attack on Education

The attacks on the Girl Scout and Y-Teens were part of a larger assault on education. Public educators' embrace of intercultural education and internationalism also drew criticism as Cold War tensions intensified in the 1950s. Anticommunists regularly accused the White House, UNESCO, the National Citizens Commission for the Public Schools, the National Education Association, the Ford Foundation, and teachers' unions of collaborating to "turn your children into socialist world-citizens." One editorial warned that the schools were "turning out alarmingly increasing numbers of illiterate juvenile delinquents" who "knew nothing about American history, [and] laughed at patriotism." The critics claimed that "progressive" education indoctrinated the "whole child" with "world-mindedness" through "group dynamics" to "surrender our sovereignty."[6]

Such charges repeated those of the anticommunist Allen Zoll, whose 1949 pamphlet argued that progressive education increased juvenile delinquency and prepped children for the "Soviet slave state . . . [where] 'truth' is mere utility, morality is a vestige of superstition." Zoll singled out social studies for allegedly teaching history with "subtle derision of 'nationalism' and 'patriotism'" as further evidence of the communist infiltration of U.S. education. The character-building youth organizations, originally inspired by the progressive education movement, were also suspect.[7] Criticizing the Girl Scouts for world-mindedness, the Fullerton, California, *Educational News Service* complained in 1954 that the organization's internationalism reflected "a pattern that covers the whole field of education."[8]

The United Nations, and especially UNESCO, with its "bold statements against racism, [and] its employment of many professional women," became special targets of anticommunists.[9] Under the influence of conservative groups, the Los Angeles City School Board voted 6–0 to ban the UNESCO bulletin series Toward World Understanding from its schools in 1953 for the same sentiments that were so widespread in children's educational materials after the war. Toward World Understanding advocated teaching children about "world citizenship," arguing that "one world or none is the choice given us by military reality." The DAR distributed circulars across the country that criticized UNESCO for inspiring fear in order to force Americans to give over control to its own "international communists."[10] An Orange County group complained that the United Nations had designed UNESCO to "pervert public education" and called it "the greatest subversive plot in history."[11] The Santa Ana Freedom Club, an anti-UNESCO organization, and Pro America, a conservative women's organization, spread rumors that UNESCO brainwashing had led the Girl Scouts to change "Girl Scout Thinking Day" to "International Thinking Day."[12] Despite these complaints, girls' groups trick-or-treated for UNICEF, sponsored the folk dancing that UNESCO endorsed for world understanding, and reprinted the UNESCO constitution's phrase that "since wars begin in the minds of men, it is in the minds of men that the defenses of peace must be constructed" as inspiration. In 1951, the *Camp Fire Girl* magazine instructed members to make little UN flags to top cupcakes for Flag Day parties.[13]

Women, especially, were thought to be susceptible to emotional responses to world tragedies and so prey to communist ideas. Reactionaries targeted girls' organizations because their activities struck the Right as "do-goodism," the kind of emotional response that could lead to dangerous thought. Altruistic efforts to send CARE packages and party kits might heighten U.S. moral authority, but they were also associated with what was decried as the "bleeding heart" liberalism typical of women "enamored of idealistic social policies and malleable enough to be controlled by Communists." Moreover, wealthy society women, such as those who supported many local YWCA groups, were thought to be susceptible to communist influence because of their supposed guilt about their wealth, their boredom, and their past exposure to liberal college professors.[14]

Indeed, when a young Phyllis Schlafly criticized the YWCA in 1953 for its harboring of communist influences, she used this rationale to explain why women's groups were susceptible to communism. Schlafly contended that YWCA women were easily duped by their "dedication to improve social and economic conditions." She added that wanting to tax the rich was an "emotional" response for women, but it made them a "mouthpiece for the [Communist] Party line."[15]

Feminist gestures were also taken as evidence of communism because of the communists' stated commitment to gender equality and because "'proper' femininity was more difficult to reconcile with wielding authority." Even though the Girl Scouts and YWCA were not generally regarded as feminist organizations, both were run by women for girls and women, and both advocated, in modest ways, social justice. Moreover, the Girl Scouts' national office had repeatedly clashed with the masculine sense of entitlement. In the 1920s and 1930s, Girl Scout officials defended the organization against the threat of a patent violation lawsuit by Boy Scouts officials who opposed girls' use of the "Scout" moniker, which they deemed masculine.[16] By contrast, the Camp Fire Girls' origins among early twentieth-century youth workers as the girls' corollary to the Boy Scouts of America, but offering a program that emphasized beauty, symbolism, and ritual, may have seemed more appropriately feminine. Camp Fire's history as a more traditional organization that pushed the boundaries of female respectability less than did the Girl Scouts may also have insulated the organization from attack.[17] Moreover, although the Girl Scouts pledged to do their duty to God and their country and the YWCA was clearly religious, Camp Fire's addition of the phrase "worship God" to the Law of the Camp Fire Girls in 1942 may have offered some protection, as did the Boy Scouts' regular avowal of religion as a marker of what distinguished the organization from "godless communists."[18]

In addition, the Girl Scouts' prominence likely brought the attention of the American Legion and others. The Girl Scouts' strong sense of international sisterhood and its World Association provided the organization with extranational relationships that might have made them more threatening to U.S. conservatives who did not attack other groups as vehemently.[19] The Girl Scouts' pronouncement of world friendship likely threatened those who wanted to preserve American sovereignty at all costs and to diminish the participation of the United States in the United Nations. The Camp Fire Girls, with its smaller membership, may simply have been a less significant target for anticommunists wanting to score political points in politicizing childhood.

The Boy Scouts of America's exemption from attack is easier to understand. Although it established a World Brotherhood badge in 1952, and although boys participated in World Scouting jamborees, these programs only expanded as the red scare was waning in the late 1950s and early 1960s. Then the organization actively cultivated the image of the antiprejudiced internationalist boy citizen as a "testament to American benevolence."[20] In addition, the organization stressed patriotism and loyalty to the nation-state in a way that placed it above conservative reproach. Although *Boys' Life* did not regularly discuss communism, themes of American heritage, including military history, were common. Articles about the history of Valley Forge and stories about the frontier reminded readers of the Americanness of the organization.

The Boy Scouts of American also closely guarded its American identity through tight membership rules. Scouts from other countries were not automatically members of the American organization. Its federal charter and bylaws required American citizenship of members. According to the organization bylaws of 1946, adults had to be citizens of the United States or at least to have begun naturalization proceedings to be eligible to serve on the National Council. Youth members could register as "visiting" Scouts with existing U.S. clubs for the duration of their stay. "Adult aliens," however, were forbidden to register or be enrolled "in any capacity."[21] The narrow membership considerably limited the international brotherhood the Scouts espoused. By contrast, the Girl Scouts restricted only National Council (governing body) membership to U.S. citizens, and Camp Fire had no such limit on membership.

Moreover, despite the existence of world associations, each nation's organization established its own take on national goals.[22] Although autonomy characterized girls' organizations, too, the Boy Scouts of America saw itself as strengthening American liberty through patriotism much more than the girls' organizations did.[23]

Nor was the organization ever rumored to be a special target of the Communist Party USA (CPUSA) in the same that the YWCA and YMCA were. Rather, the CPUSA actively targeted Boy Scouts of America for derision. Although the Special House Committee for the Investigation of Un-American Activities (the Dies Committee) reported in 1938 that a communist front group had sought to distribute a socialist document at a Boy Scout jamboree, the communists had sought to slander the Boy Scouts, and undermine its membership recruitment, as "a capitalist and not a poor man's boy organization." The group was not accused of trying to infiltrate the Boy Scouts. Similarly, the Young Pioneers of America, a communist youth group that ran summer camps, said the Boy Scouts was an organization "for capitalist wars" and accused the organization of militarizing children for the bosses.[24]

Such charges suggested that the Boy Scouts of America avoided activities that might be accused of being popular-front collaborations and likely endeared the organization to American conservatives. Moreover, women's international peace groups that were denounced in the committee hearings as having been manipulated by socialists were criticized in part for condemning the Boy Scouts' militarism.[25]

The suspect Japanese Americans in internment camps, too, could prove their loyalty through youth organization membership, but among affiliations Boy Scouts was most strongly associated with patriotism. The director of the War Relocation Authority submitted to the Dies Committee what he claimed to be proof of Japanese American loyalty: "They have joined organizations like the Boy Scouts, the Girl Scouts, the Young Men's Christian Association, the Young Women's Christian Association, and the Campfire Girls." He argued that to deny that these organizations had shaped Japanese American minds was to say that American institutions "have no real strength or cogency." Boy Scouts, however, were most commonly identified with patriotism. In a 1943 Dies Committee investigation of Japanese American loyalty, Japanese American Boy Scouts were lauded for defending the American flag during a riot at Manzanar War Relocation Center the previous year.[26] Gender and a clear patriotic identity helped guard the Boys Scouts from the microscope of right-wing anticommunists.

Anticommunism and the Y-Teens

In the postwar years, both the YWCA and the Girl Scouts were accused of being under communistic influence. Several YWCA women were named in Dies Committee and House Un-American Activities Committee (HUAC) hearings, and both organizations experienced a broad right-wing smear campaign. As a result of the YWCA's refusal to remove particular women from office and its support for labor, racial integration, and internationalism, the association faced attacks from conservatives within the organization and without. Recycling prior accusations and citing each other, anticommunist crusaders attempted to end YWCA women's political influence using the vulnerability of girlhood as a reason for their interference. In response, the YWCA stood by its liberal Christian mission as it worked for the needs of its constituents, girls, women, and their families. Both the YWCA and the Girl Scouts called their organizations apolitical, but the YWCA passed resolutions supporting congressional legislation and maintained that "our interest in legislation is a living, vital interest" founded in the YWCA's Christian commitment.[27]

Anti-leftist pressure and smears were not new for the YWCA. In the 1920s and 1930s, the YWCA had been criticized for its support of pacifism and industrial-labor organizations. The infamous spiderweb chart created by the U.S. War Department in 1923 listed the YWCA, as well as the Girls' Friendly Society, the League of Women Voters, and other liberal and leftist women's organizations, denouncing it as part of a "socialist-pacifist movement," and in 1934 Elizabeth Dilling's *The Red Network: A "Who's Who" and Handbook of Radicalism for Patriots* repeated these charges, calling the YWCA and the YMCA communist or communist infiltrated. Such charges had originated in part from a CPUSA resolution in 1934 to "start mass work in the youth organizations controlled by the bourgeoisie, that is especially the industrial Y's," or the industrial branches of the YWCA and YMCA.[28]

In the 1930s, when the CPUSA sought to work with progressives and liberals in a popular, or united, front against fascism, the YWCA's collegiate, industrial, and business and professional groups worked with organizations like the American Youth Congress (AYC), a national federation of progressive youth organizations interested in economic issues. It brought together groups as diverse as the Women's Christian Temperance Union and the Young Communists League (YCL), which soon came to dominate it. YWCA president Theresa Paist explained the affiliation: "We have not selected a few harmless questions for study and discussion but have endeavored to face squarely all those circumstances in our common life which condition the lives of women and girls in our membership." To do anything less was to abdicate the "Christian liberalism of the organization," which had been under fire at least since the creation of the spiderweb chart. Popular-front connections, which, according to YWCA scholar Amanda Izzo, were "the touch-stone for red-baiting from the 1930s through the 1950s," were consistent with the "fairly leftist public affairs agenda" of the YWCA national board.[29] Still the YWCA maintained its AYC affiliation longer than most mainstream organizations did, disaffiliating in 1941, two years after the AYC supported the Nazi-Soviet nonaggression pact.

Moreover, during the 1940s, the YWCA national office refused to remove members "on the basis of 'guilt by association,'" declaring purges a "weapon of old-world tyrannies" and a danger to the "heart of the democratic principle in our organization and in the country as a whole."[30] The YWCA provided its membership with updates on YCL conventions and regarded the membership of individual members of American Youth for Democracy, as the YCL was renamed in 1943, as an individual choice.[31]

When anticommunist attacks intensified after the war, the YWCA largely abided by its earlier resolve to avoid ousting members and to support those accused. They refused to purge their leadership and largely rejected the concept of loyalty oaths. In 1948, the national YWCA hired a private investigator, however, to review the relationships of all members of the national board and its professional staff "because we realized that our personal belief in the persons who make up the Board and staff would not answer our critics and because in the minds of the public such relationships have become a kind of evidence, at the least, of communist leanings." Still the YWCA's interpretation of the evidence was that although some had had ties to organizations on the Attorney General's List of Subversive Organizations, there was no proof "that there was a single communist in the group." Moreover, the staff then in place did not have current relationships with the listed groups.[32] The YWCA refused to implement screening beyond the already standard "commitment to the Christian purpose of the organization," which members had already pledged.[33]

Soon after President Truman's March 1947 announcement of the Federal Loyalty Program, which subjected all federal employees to investigation, the national YWCA became the target of media attention. Marian M. Strack, speaking at a dinner for the DAR and SAR (Sons of the American Revolution), denounced the YWCA as a leftist political outfit and established a list of allegations that hounded the YWCA for years. The YWCA, Strack contended, supported "cooperation with Russia and increased immigration of Jewish refugees," included works by Paul Robeson and the Congress of Industrial Organizations in a songbook, and recommended books that included Lillian Smith's *Strange Fruit* and Richard Wright's *Black Boy*. It also supported leftist goals like the Office of Price Administration's rent-control program, free school lunches, and national health care—aims that had been taken up by numerous women's groups in the 1940s.[34] Similar rumblings spread through the right-wing press and conservative women's organizations, whose newsletters cited each other, along with references from before the war. In 1948, the federal government's pamphlet *100 Things You Should Know about Communism and Religion* argued that communists were infiltrating religious clubs and organizations. Writing that communists had targeted the YWCA and the YMCA, it explained, "If you want to keep your own organization fit for your own family's membership, you had better stay on the alert."[35]

In late 1947, three local association officers from the YWCA of the New York City borough of Queens resigned; two publicly cited infiltration of the national offices by communists as their reason for leaving. At first, press coverage was limited to local newspapers. As the former local president continued to make accusations, however, she found the ears of more powerful civic leaders willing to listen and publicize her claims. In January 1948, she presented her evidence to congressional investigators and in March, the former YWCA officers, along with several American Legion men, gathered as a self-appointed committee instituted to force the YWCA to purge its board and staff.[36]

Much of the attention to the YWCA emphasized the organization's work with girls. During the resignation crisis, headlines emphasized the YWCA's teenaged constituency and the perceived vulnerability of girls. When the committee declared, "Communists are attempting to propagandize 3,000,000 teenaged girls through the Young Women's Christian Association," the story made national news. Beside the point was that the figure of three million grossly overstated Y-Teen membership. (In 1949, there were 350,000 Y-Teens in the United States; three million represented the reach of the entire YWCA organization across the globe.) National papers such as the *New York Times* and *Chicago*

Tribune carried the story and local dailies screamed the same headline offered by the committee's statement. The *Post* of Birmingham, Alabama, changed it a little with its headline "Reds Charged with Using YWCA to Communize Girls."[37] Girls' vulnerability made news across the nation.

Attention centered on specific aspects of traditional girls' programming such as teaching "song to girls in local 'chapters'" to build community and for entertainment. During the interwar and postwar periods, folk songs of peasant origin were common, as were work songs. Accusations that the YWCA songbooks were communistic, first made by Dilling, reemerged as the former Queens president derided the work songs "Drill Ye Tarriers" and "Sing Along the Way" as communistic and charged that the two songs appeared in the "official songbook of the Communist party." Other folk songs, especially those from Russia, also came under fire. ("The Star Spangled Banner" appeared in both as one tongue-in-cheek report from the *Forest Hills Post* noted, but anticommunists did not publicize that.)[38]

Although American girls' vulnerability to communism made startling headlines, anticommunists also warned that youth around the world had already been infected and so internationalism was dangerous. Further accusations claimed that, through its internationalism, the YWCA had been overrun by "red youths" and that "young reds" were just as dangerous to the organization as the older women in the national office: "These young people are under direct and indirect Communist influence," one of the resigning Queens officials exclaimed. She saw the influence of young communists in the YWCA's ties to the World Federation of Democratic Youth.[39]

The WFDY, whose members pledged to "build a deep and sincere international friendship among the peoples of the world [and] to keep a just lasting peace," formed in 1945 at the London World Youth Conference of youth organizations.[40] Headquartered in Paris, it held biennial international youth festivals that were routinely denounced as Soviet propaganda. A State Department memo warned that "Communist international front groups seized upon the world's desire for peace and for reduction of tensions to promote 'popular front' efforts of their own. . . . In plain terms, this means that the Communist fronts are trying to merge with non-Communist groups that have been antagonistic towards them before." The State Department singled out the YMCA and YWCA among the groups it believed the WFDY representatives were targeting with "repeated offers of cooperation and conciliation."[41]

The YWCA's relationship to the WFDY was complicated. The national YWCA had no formal affiliation with the WFDY, but the business and professional group and the industrial constituency-group, separate YWCA units organized according to their unique concerns, had voted to affiliate. Several YWCA representatives had attended the London conference at which the WFDY was established.

Elsa Graves, of the YWCA's National Industrial Council, gave a speech to the conference emphasizing the organization's hope to extend the New Deal to the world and supporting the United Nations, labor unions, and expanded access to housing and education.[42]

Charges related to the YWCA's affiliation with the WFDY continued. In 1948 came the publication of *Behind the Lace Curtains of the YWCA*, an exposé of communist infiltration that pointed particularly to the WFDY. It called attention to Graves's election as a WFDY council member, a role the YWCA said she filled as an individual and not as a YWCA representative. Joseph Kamp, the book's author, argued that activities she recommended, such standard internationalist fare as writing to pen pals and holding local world youth festivals, mimicked those of the WFDY and were especially suspect.[43]

In fact, the YWCA's early interest in the WFDY and its world festivals quickly waned. In 1947, YWCA officials explained, they had "begun to smell a rat" and sent delegations neither from "the National Board nor from the Industrial or Business or Professional Councils of the YWCA" to the controversial 1947 Prague World Youth Festival, which had heavy Soviet control. In October 1947, the national board and councils delayed by resolution direct affiliation with the WFDY, although only after the State Department refused to sponsor a delegation. The YWCA industrial council representatives had applied for naval transport, but they were turned down; the State Department would not use its exchange programs to aid students gathering for political purposes. Mainstream newspapers still reported as late as October 1947 that only a "minority" of the American delegation to Prague complained that the meeting was communist dominated. It was not, therefore, surprising that YWCA women concerned about peace would have been interested in participating.[44]

Although much attention surrounded the YWCA's work with girls, conservatives addressed the YWCA's adult program as well, circulating information about the supposed infiltration of the YWCA so as to protect other, unknowing organizations that might seek to work with it. *Counterattack*, the right-wing organ published by former FBI agents, disseminated accusations broadly, including to the Boy and Girl Scouts councils, so that they might protect themselves from infiltration.[45]

Counterattack dredged up prewar Dies Committee hearings tying Rose Terlin, chief editor of the YWCA's Woman's Press (the YWCA publication department) and a member of the public affairs department of the national board, to "communist circles." *Counterattack* had no new information, and Terlin might well have considered these older accusations to have become irrelevant, since the War Labor Board had hired her during World War II to a position that required an FBI clearance. *Counterattack* also misidentified Terlin as a national

council member of the AYC.[46] Although the YWCA repeatedly defended Terlin, it ended its political education news services at the end of 1950, and she
resigned from the national board. In 1952, the YWCA also sold the Woman's
Press. No records suggest that her departure or these changes resulted from
right-wing attacks, but "it seems likely that the pressure either directly or indirectly influenced these decisions." A combination of political pressures and
concern over finances likely resulted in these shifts.[47]

The attacks on the YWCA were also a part of the articulation of a broad
new conservative Christian platform that, in the second half of the twentieth
century, replaced the liberal Christian outlook of the YWCA as the most visible
element of Christian women's political engagement. At the same time that she
was running her 1952 congressional campaign, Phyllis Schlafly, then a member
of the Alton, Illinois, YWCA's board, confronted the association from within. At
first YWCA leaders referred to Schlafly as possessing "many fine qualities" and
believed she "will prove to be an excellent volunteer after she has had more
experience and developed a little more tolerance." Yet Alton leaders also spoke
of "outbursts" that they hoped might be kept "within the family."[48]

In 1951, Schlafly, suspicious of communist influence in the YWCA, sought
to implement a loyalty oath that would commit YWCA staff to "the American
system of individual opportunity, private property and an economy free from
governmental control and ownership" as well as to Christian values. A revised
oath made it into two Alton contracts, but the sworn declaration was dropped
because of criticism, especially within the Y-Teen and Young Adult Program.
Schlafly had established herself as a conservative wave maker.[49]

The next spring she compiled a fifteen-page letter of complaint outlining
the "red" influences in the organization. Much of Schlafly's critique recycled earlier materials. She took up the accusations against Terlin, for example, despite
her recent resignation. Schlafly turned new attention to the educational purposes of the YWCA, questioning the fitness of the publications to teach "young
Christian women." She criticized books recommended in the *YWCA Magazine*
(formerly the *Woman's Press*) as being leftist. Even after Terlin was no longer editor, Schlafly said other YWCA professionals were still "infected with the Marxian
philosophy."[50]

Schlafly also turned attention to young adults, arguing that YWCA college
campus speaker Vera Micheles Dean and others who addressed a YWCA meeting at Miami College in Ohio were associated with communist front groups.
Although Dean addressed college students, Schlafly referred to them as "teenagers," playing up their vulnerability and indirectly connecting them to the
Y-Teen program for junior and high school girls. When the student YWCA meeting passed a resolution calling for U.S. recognition of the People's Republic of

China, Schlafly argued that the vulnerable "students were deluded into calling on the UN and the U.S. to welcome Red China as a 'peace-loving' democracy" even as they "had our Marines trapped at the Chosen Reservoir."[51]

Schlafly's China critique overlapped with others'. In 1952, *Counterattack* made accusations against the YWCA's Talitha Gerlach, pointing to her position as a director of YWCA operations in China to claim she served as chair of the China Welfare Appeal, which *Counterattack* called a "front set up to collect 'Friendship Cargoes' for [the] Communist government." The meaning of gift exchanges and supplies changed from being a sign of moral authority to becoming a reason for suspicion. The YWCA had sent aid to China from 1937 to 1946, and the Y-Teens had a friendship project with China in 1948. Such gifts became suspect, however, when China turned communist and yet continued to be an affiliate of the World YWCA.[52]

Schlafly singled out the YWCA's support of the United Nations for special criticism. She counted forty-nine "separate glowing references" in *YWCA Magazine* over an eighteen-month period. Calling attention to the YWCA's Christian mission, she wondered why it supported an organization that did not mention "the name of God" in its charter "or any official publication" and disallowed prayer at the start of Security Council and Assembly meetings. Schlafly also argued that the United Nations was a tax burden to the nation, wasting money through development projects and placing nearly the entire burden of the Korean conflict on the shoulders of American soldiers. Anticipating the arguments used against the Girl Scouts, she charged that the UN Declaration of Human Rights was a Marxist and atheistic document that omitted the right to private property at the insistence of communist delegates.[53]

Although the YWCA made adjustments that revealed its leaders' anxiety about anticommunism, the loss of donations (the Y struggled after the 1950s to stay solvent), and disaffiliating branches, it did not back down.[54] YWCA officials maintained that members could not be atheistic communists—and often expressed surprise at the labeling—because of their Christian commitments. The national board believed that its resolve to continue "in these critical times the constant and constructive struggle for the Christian way of life and for the democratic principles upon which our country has been built" provided evidence of its "concrete expressions" of "Christian purpose" and how "firmly the YWCA stands against the Communism conspiracy."[55]

At a time when government officials shied away from particular words, such as *democracy*, that they believed had been co-opted by communist propagandists, the YWCA refused to adopt the right-wing definition of such terms. It declared that "attention needs to be called to the extent to which principles and convictions and phrases as old as Christianity itself have spuriously been identified by many people with the Communist Party Line. To class those who speak of 'a better world' or 'a new society' as communistic, is to be historically and currently illiterate."[56]

In 1954, Dorothy Groeling, author of numerous articles on the United Nations and Y-Teen internationalism, reported in the pages of the *Bookshelf* on what anticommunist distortion was doing to teens. Just as the Girl Scout crisis began, she emphasized that youth organizations should teach "individual freedom and dignity" as a way to combat not only communism but the extremes of anti-communism as well. "Teen-agers don't need to be 'indoctrinated' in what our country stands for," she explained, "but they must be helped to develop their own convictions. . . . The fear of differing in opinions from the majority of people is affecting young as well as older citizens." Rather than using purges and kowtowing to those on its right, Groeling called for "wise guidance and open discussion . . . to counteract this fear." She then emphasized the links between "the three R's of citizenship . . . rights, responsibilities, and relationships," to which she tied the need for more intensive action for human rights, antiracism, and internationalism. "Being convinced of the dignity and worth of each person is essential for good human relations in a democracy," she concluded.[57]

The Girl Scouts Confront Anti–United Nations Politics

At the time of the post–World War II red scare, the U.S. Girl Scouts had maintained a strong program in international friendship for decades. WAGGGS, which linked the Girl Guides and Girl Scouts around the world by facilitating "friendships between the girls of all nations" through international exchanges and encampments, had its own pin and flag. It was designed as a nonpolitical body open to girls across race, nationality, religion, and class.[58]

The American Girl Scouts also had an intensive international friendship program that promoted pen pals, scrapbook exchanges, and more. Girls contributed regularly to the Juliette Low World Friendship Fund, which funded camp scholarships for girls from different countries, encampments, and international conferences. After World War II, it helped reestablish Girl Guiding in other countries.[59] In 1945, the Girl Scouts' board took an "affirmative stand on the United Nations" and the national organization became an accredited national organization with a UN observer. Girl Scout representatives attended briefing sessions of the Department of Public Information, U.S. Mission to the United Nations, and the Conference Group of U.S. National Organizations on the United Nations.[60] For the Scouts, international friendship was generally understood to boost the moral authority of the United States and its foreign policy. Girls, who were not generally called upon to defend the nation, carried responsibility for developing global relationships.

In the early 1950s, however, anticommunist crusaders looking to end U.S. membership in the United Nations attacked the Girl Scouts. They saw no moral authority in support for the United Nations and labeled it communist propaganda. Criticism came not only from outside the Scouting community but also from within the organization and its Community Chests, institutions that reflected America's political diversity.[61] One adult member of the Northwest Cook Council wrote to the national office to ask if the officials there "didn't . . . know that the U.N. was drawn up by the Communists."[62] Outside organizations, including the DAR; the American Legion; and Pro America, a conservative women's organization, also tried to affect Girl Scout programming.[63] In 1954, a DAR member from Hinsdale, Illinois, complained that local Girl Scouts planned to use a UN pledge at an international program. Officials at Girl Scout headquarters advised against it, but the Macomb Girl Scouts used it anyway, prompting the local DAR member to wonder why Girl Scout national headquarters did not "force a council to do what we say."[64]

The overall effect on the Girl Scouts was to narrow its focus on both peace and girls' opportunities. In *Freedom Is as Freedom Does*, philosopher Corliss Lamont wrote that the Girl Scout controversy was part of broader efforts at censorship and concluded that "this absurd episode" regarding the Girl Scouts, a mainstream organization that had adopted liberal ideals, demonstrated "the objectives of the American witch-hunters," not merely to stop communist propaganda but to stop "facts and views which tended to support a liberal attitude in international relations."[65]

The Girl Scouts avoided instituting political litmus tests for its members and leaders, arguing that its own internal requirements for volunteers were adequate. Trying to place the organization beyond ideological controversy, officials asserted in 1949 that "it is not our business to define Communism, but it is our business to define Girl Scouting and to interpret it."[66] Girl Scout officials resisted broad witch hunts and investigations of their staff or members, refusing to purge members as some unions and political organizations had done. On a case-by-case basis, however, they allowed memberships to lapse and refused to enroll groups that might bring further attacks. By the end of 1951, the national office kept a file on rumors and reports of suspected communists, gamblers, and others who were likely to "cause a stir locally."[67]

National headquarters also pushed out controversial adult members. In 1951, the national office backed a local council's decision to ask a leader who was secretary of the New York Civil Liberties Union not to reregister when she was involved in a suit charging that the American Legion had wrongfully blocked the Westchester County Civil Liberties Union in New York from use of a public building. Girl Scout officials worried that "the troop will be disturbed by impending controversy" and deemed her reenrollment in that Girl Scout council too troubling for children and for the organization.[68] In 1954, the national headquarters backed the decision of the Seattle council to hold up registration of a troop because its assistant leader was married to a man who had been called before HUAC.[69] That same year, it asked a Dayton, Ohio, leader who had herself been investigated by HUAC to "suspend her Girl Scout activities during this period of investigation." Yet the Girl Scouts also refused to distribute the anticommunist pamphlet that the General Federation of Women's Clubs distributed because it advanced a "witch hunt" atmosphere and kept close tabs on extremist outbreaks in its own ranks.[70] Navigating the controversy clearly evoked contradictory values and actions.

Although most often controversy centered on leaders, girls sometimes were brought into the fray. Girl Scout officials stood by the two for whom records exist. When a Camp Fire group pushed out a local girl when her father was accused of communist sympathies in 1951, the local Girl Scout troop sought to extend Scouting membership to her because the "child should not be penalized."[71] Similarly, in 1953, the daughter of a reporter for the Telegrafnoje Agentstvo Sovietskovo Soïuza (TASS), a Soviet news agency, was allowed to maintain her membership even though her mother was an atheist and the American Legion had declared the agency "an espionage center and station in this country."[72] Although adult leaders might be encouraged to resign, Girl Scout standards supported these girls despite the politics of their parents.

Indeed, as an organization that saw itself as crucial to citizen training but nonpolitical, the Girl Scouts tried to walk a thin line and appeal to the Right, Left, and center. In Silver City, New Mexico, during the early 1953 production of the film *Salt of the Earth*, which was decried in Congress as communist inspired and likely to induce racial hatred because of its portrayal of the poor treatment of miners of Mexican heritage by white owners, this was increasingly difficult to do. Girl Scout headquarters urged the local council to keep its anticommunist activities "strong and positive." Amid violence and threats in nearby Bayard and Central, the Girl Scouts tried to rein in its own anticommunists and requested that the local group change its slogan from "Girl Scouts of Silver City—Help Fight Communism through the Girl Scouts" to "Girl Scouts—A Force for Freedom." The council was in no place, Girl Scout officials believed, "to sit in judgment on whether the movie-making union is communist." But national leaders also believed that the girls should not be prevented from "participation in an important community issue in which children are already involved through their schools and their families."[73] The Girl Scouts understood the protest against the film as civic engagement but also wanted to ensure that they were not seen to be choosing the side of extremism.

Despite the efforts of the Scouts to avoid political controversy, right-wing extremist attacks, which began as isolated events, continued. They mirrored larger questions about the United Nations as an overall institution, about UNESCO, and about civil rights. Also in 1953, accusations swirled when the Girl

Scouts backed the work of individual civil rights leaders whom federal authorities had flagged in loyalty programs. The attacks never addressed the content of materials the Girl Scouts recommended or used but mirrored much of the red scare by going after the presumed political backgrounds of the creators. In early 1953, the *Girl Scout Leader* recommended Langston Hughes's *First Book of Negroes*, a history and survey of contemporary African Americans written for children and endorsed by the American Library Association and prominent newspapers. The Girl Scouts also recommended Dorothy Canfield Fisher's *A Fair World for All*, a children's book explaining the Universal Declaration of Human Rights. Hughes's book assiduously avoided mentioning those prominent African Americans like Paul Robeson and W.E.B. Du Bois who were associated with the Left and instead made clear that American democracy could fix the United States' racial problems. Although this was the position promulgated by the USIA, the review in the *Girl Scout Leader* came only a month before Hughes was called before Senator Joseph McCarthy's Senate Permanent Subcommittee on Investigations to testify about the inclusion of supposed communist authors in the State Department's overseas library program.

Later that year, the Girl Scouts asked Ethel Alpenfels, author of *Sense and Nonsense about Race*, a book written for young people and popular in school libraries, to speak at the Girl Scout national convention. Alpenfels, a well-respected anthropologist, had been named in a 1949 HUAC report as a sponsor of the Cultural and Scientific Conference for World Peace, as was Hughes. The conference was decried by the Right as a gathering of communist front organizations interested in promoting Soviet foreign policy and discrediting American culture. This had led Alpenfels to be rejected as a speaker in the Los Angeles schools, and the right-wing press described her as subversive. The Girl Scouts did not cancel or apologize for her speech. In fact, officials supported her, replying to inquiries from the Wheeling Area Girl Scout Council that her speech about how to "bring *all* girls into a harmonious working relationship in the Girl Scouts" was relevant and proved to be immensely popular with conference attendees.[74]

After the inclusion of Hughes's history book in the *Leader*, right-wing attention to the Girl Scouts grew steadily and culminated in the *Girl Scout Handbook* crisis of 1954. At the center of the controversy was the 1953 new edition of the handbook for the nine- to fourteen-year-olds who made up the group specifically titled Girl Scouts, the volume understood as the *Girl Scout Handbook*.[75] Although an interim revision had been published in 1947 and was slightly updated ten times, the last major rewrite of the handbook had been in 1940, when the Girl Scouts consulted a group of sociologists and educators about the scope of program activities.[76] The lead researcher and author of the new edition, Margarite Hall, was a longtime Girl Scout administrator who took interest in international issues.

The Girl Scouts did due diligence to ensure a mainstream, informative handbook that advanced the goal of teaching girls about their citizenship roles in the postwar world. Before the new handbook was cleared by the director of the program department and by the national executive director, drafts made the rounds of the national program committee, program development staff, council volunteers, and national staff members, as well as outside educators and consultants. Feedback on the UN sections, which were "essentially the same" as those written for the 1947 edition, came from the Girl Scouts' international division and the United Nations. But controversy raged nonetheless.[77]

In March 1954, conservative political organizer and news editor Robert LeFevre published specific complaints about the *Girl Scout Handbook* in the conservative magazine *Human Events*. It was an attack that grew out of personal pique. The Fort Lauderdale Girl Scouts had invited LeFevre to speak at a regional meeting, but when officials learned about his strongly anti–United Nations speeches, they asked for assurance that he would not give a political talk. He canceled his appearance, citing what he referred to as the Girl Scout leaders' attempts to squelch his freedom of speech, and set about to discover why the Girl Scouts had, in his view, censored him.

True to his anti-UN politics, LeFevre's biggest complaint, and the focus of his article, was the Universal Declaration of Human Rights and the Girl Scouts' "unqualified recommendation" of it.[78] He provided lengthy critiques of the various articles in the declaration, none of which the *Girl Scout Handbook* actually elaborated on, followed by an examination of what he believed to be the Girl Scouts' emphasis on world over U.S. citizenship. The handbook, he complained, devoted four pages to the United Nations, asked girls to memorize a portion of the UN Charter, no longer included a hard-to-make-out photostat of the Bill of Rights, and merely referred briefly to the Constitution and the Bill of Rights without assigning girls specific phrases of those documents to memorize. In addition, LeFevre thought the Girl Scouts ridiculed free enterprise and promoted cross-race associations.[79]

LeFevre's article made the circuit of right-wing organizations and began to pop up in Community Chest discussions, threatening the financial livelihood of the organization. Various newspapers reprinted LeFevre's charges over the next several months. In Europe, the Sojourners, a Masonic organization, circulated the LeFevre article to U.S. troops stationed in England.[80] One regional board member heard the rumor that the "Girl Scouts are Communistic from top to bottom and that the Handbook has been banned in Eastern cities."[81]

Meanwhile, letters from Girl Scout insiders, including at least one major donor, offered similar critiques. The Board of Directors of the Racine Council of Girl Scouts appointed a special committee to peruse the handbook in light of LeFevre's article. The Racine board approved its committee's recommendation to delete content praising the United Nations. It agreed that the phrase "We the People of the United Nations" should be deleted because it implied that "every citizen of the United States is included in the United Nations because the United States is a member." The board members also wanted to get rid of a positive comparison between the Bill of Rights and the Declaration of Human Rights because such an endorsement was "a political matter" and to cut the listing of the League of Women Voters as a civic organization with which girls might work, since no other organizations were named. They wanted the One World badge to be renamed the My World badge to coincide with the My Country and My Government titles and to change the requirements for earning it to include earning the My Country and My Government proficiency badges as prerequisites. This would serve to foreground U.S. citizenship rather than world connection. The various recommendations provided the Girl Scouts the opportunity to follow internal counsel rather than LeFevre's.[82]

The Girl Scouts created a committee to review the handbook. Within two months of LeFevre's exposé, the Girl Scout program committee and the National Executive Committee had authorized over sixty revisions, about two-thirds relating to the charges of communist subversion or UN propaganda. Meanwhile, the organization undertook a review of all its publications for "questionable" material. Even the general interpretive leaflet, *These Are the Girl Scouts*, which had a circulation of over 150,000 in 1953, stressed international friendship and the Scouts' "work for peace and world understanding."[83] The Scouts also delayed at least one publication. *Hands around the World* was scheduled for revision in 1955, but the U.S. organization turned the booklet over to the World Association, which finally put out a revised edition in 1958, published in London, and without UN references.[84]

Meanwhile, in July 1954, members of the U.S. House of Representatives entered articles and also their own thoughts into the appendixes of the *Congressional Record*. Timothy Sheehan, an Illinois Republican described by the *Chicago Tribune* as a defender of Joseph McCarthy and a critic of the United Nations, began this debate when he entered LeFevre's article into the *Record* on July 2, 1954. Later that month, Republican congressman Robert Kean of New Jersey countered by entering an article by industrial engineer, psychologist, former Girl Scout national board member, and mother of twelve children Lillian Moller Gilbreth, arguing the Girl Scouts were an "antidote to communism." A Republican representative from Indiana included an unpublished essay refuting the LeFevre piece. Several others also entered the debate. By the end of July, the back and forth seemed to have abated, and Sheehan himself entered Girl Scout national president Olivia Layton's comments about how the 1954 revised, fifth impression of the current handbook would reinsert the Bill of Rights and take other measures to clarify the Scouts' citizenship goals for girls.[85]

But as the revisions were headed to the printer, another shoe dropped. The American Legion Department of Illinois, at a convention that also "overwhelmingly" endorsed Senator McCarthy, voted a resolution of censure and condemnation of the Girl Scouts for "un-American" literature. The resolution cited FBI director J. Edgar Hoover's warning that "subversive and un-American influences are attempting to capture the minds of our youth" and denounced the Girl Scouts for recommending "the writings of certain pro-Communist authors, so identified by government agencies," in its official publications and for promoting the "United Nations and one-world citizenship." The Illinois legion urged all "parents of our American youth keep a close watch on all organized youth activities in which their children are engaged."[86] Although Girl Scout fathers at the convention fought the resolution on floor, they lost when a "very oratorical minister rose to his feet and read the [Hughes poem] 'Goodbye, Christ.'" Many regarded the poem, written in the early 1930s, as a rejection of religion and commitment to communism.[87] The Girl Scouts had never recommended or reprinted the poem, but the taint of an author who might question religion was enough to sway the convention.

A press storm followed and sometimes mocked the knee-jerk superpatriotism of the American Legion men. Although some coverage disparaged the Girl Scouts and many newspapers reprinted quotations from American Legion men lambasting Girl Scout officials, many articles "literally laughed the Illinois resolution out of court."[88] The *Chicago Daily Sun-Times* asked, "How screwy can we get?" in quoting an American Legion member with two daughters who were Girl Scouts and who had opposed the resolution. The *Charlotte News* depicted the American Legion members as "tired men anxious to adjourn and resume the less boring aspects of convention life" and described veterans organizations as uncritically supporting all anticommunist resolutions. The *Chicago Daily News* assured parents that they need not "worry for fear they have been rearing little subversives, of deceptively attractive appearance, who have been selling cookies to help finance a plot to overthrow the government." In her My Day column, Eleanor Roosevelt held that Girl Scouts "have always emphasized the value of getting to know young people in other areas of the world" and added that it might not be a "bad thing to indoctrinate members of the Girl Scouts with an interest in the UN." The cartoonist Herbert Block (Herblock) provided a visual—a group of aging McCarthy-supporting legionnaires preparing to ambush a Girl Scout troop sitting around a bonfire. One commands, "Stand fast, men—they're armed with marshmallows."[89]

The Girl Scouts found many supporters. Some legionnaires noted publicly that they were keeping their daughters in the Scouts. Even some local DAR chapters went on record supporting the organization. Church and religious groups, Kiwanis, Rotary, Zonta, the Anti-Defamation League, the Boy Scouts of America, and others expressed support in various ways.[90]

IMAGE 7. "Stand Fast, Men—They Are Armed with Marshmallows."
A 1954 Herblock cartoon, published August 11, 1954. © The Herb Block Foundation.

Even in the face of bad press, the American Legion brought a modified resolution to the floor of the national convention in September; it tempered the original denunciations by congratulating the Girl Scouts for "educating the girlhood of America to an appreciation of the responsibilities of U.S. Citizenship" but still urged "the leadership go further" to check and report if "those responsible for inserting [into the handbook] the recognized un-American propaganda," namely, the favorable references to the United Nations and One World, "are still directing policies of the Girl Scouts."[91] Layton was livid and wrote a press release defending the Girl Scouts as thoroughly American, but the Girl Scouts' national office could not afford to ignore the American Legion, whose membership over-lapped with other civic organizations such as Rotary, Kiwanis, and others that regularly offered financial sponsorship for camps and other expenses of the Girl and Boy Scouts.[92]

Meanwhile, retail outlets began to return handbooks to Girl Scout head-quarters. National executive director Dorothy Stratton and Layton agreed to distribute a free supplement to retailers with still-unsold copies, to councils, and to individual girls who had bought the 1953 edition. Although the move pre-vented loss of revenue on the unsold copies and prevented the Girl Scouts from having to recall the old text, as some were calling for it to do, the issuance of the insert appeared to respond to the American Legion. It also directed attention to the specific changes and to the absurdity of many of them.

Although critics would come to charge the Girl Scouts with simply alter-ing the handbook in response to the attacks, the story was more complex. The Girl Scouts maintained that there were no changes to actual programming and policies, and an entire chapter on international friendship, copious detail on the WAGGGS, and numerous mentions of the United Nations remained in the book. Moreover, the changes were a response not only to LeFevre and the American Legion but also to a changing political climate and demands from within the organization. In fact, edits had begun with the initial imprint of the 1953 tenth edition. Rather than keep the 1947 edition's language noting that "Scouts and Guides all over the world are known for their willingness to help other people," the 1953 text had dropped, even before the controversy began, "all over the world" with its reminder that girls were part of an international community.[93]

The Girl Scouts were not alone. Other children's books were also revised to avoid misinterpretation. The 1958 edition of Lois Fisher's *You and the United Nations* featured similar changes. Although a cartoon calling on readers to take responsibil-ity for the United Nations remained, references to "one world" and "world citizen-ship" duties were not as frequent, and the revised book read more like a report and less of an endorsement. In 1951, Fisher told her juvenile readers that after the travesty of World War II, "people began to think seriously about how they could live together as world citizens, and that is how the United Nations began." In 1958, how-ever, the phrase *world citizens* was dropped. A description of the United Nations as the old woman in the shoe who responded to social welfare issues was replaced by a less poignant description of the UN commissions and specialized agencies working to "help people help themselves," although oddly, the picture of the shoe remained. A picture of children on the page with the preamble to the Declaration of Human Rights was Americanized, although multiple races remained.[94]

The insert and the fifth impression shifted girls' citizen roles back toward nation and home. Girl Scout officials claimed the changes had two purposes.

First, revisions "point[ed] up the emphasis on training for good U.S. citizen-ship." Second, the changes would "clarify the part of our program that is directed toward building friendships between Girl Scouts and children of other nations." To these ends, the handbook included enhanced patriotic content such as three stanzas of "The Star Spangled Banner." It also printed the text of the Bill of Rights along with an obligatory requirement to study it. The new handbook reminded readers that George Washington's birthday was the same as Lord Baden-Powell's. The Girl Scouts eliminated "statements that might be interpreted as having political implications." Hence the One World badge became My World, as the Racine council had suggested. Sometimes the United States was added to a world activity. "Present a patrol skit showing what it means to be good neighbors in your community and in the world" became "Present a patrol skit showing what it means to be good neighbors in your community, your country, and in the world."[95]

In programming, as well as in the handbook, the Girl Scouts played up "duty to God and country." When the All-States Encampment met, the campers were offered a deluge of patriotism. The closing banquet celebrated Betsy Ross, had performances of the signing of the Declaration of Independence and the Bill of Rights, and included the song "I Sing America." Whereas Four Freedoms tableaux had been popular in the 1940s to portray the freedom of religion and speech, the new program used the Bill of Rights to show the importance of freedom of reli-gion and suggested the Bible as a prop.[96] Similarly, Layton's press release cited the Girl Scouts' forty-two years of proud service to the nation, "training girls to be reverent to God and to be loyal, patriotic citizens of the United Sates."[97] National headquarters advised leaders and directors to emphasize the organiza-tion's spiritual values and patriotic activities, the "development of individuals in relation to the group," homemaking, and local service activities.[98] The girls' walls narrowed from the world to the personal, domestic, and local.

To avoid what Girl Scout officials called misinterpretations, the Girl Scouts took out of the handbook all overt praise for the United Nations, including a description of the Universal Declaration of Human Rights as "one of the finest pieces of work accomplished by the United Nations." The section with UN back-ground was renamed "My World" from "One World" and a page of material was deleted, leaving a completely blank page at the end of the section. The insert's instructions to cross out seemingly innocuous activities such as "Arrange a choral speaking piece from parts of the United Nations Charter" and "Make a calendar of important Girl Scout and United Nations dates," must have made girls wonder. In addition, "You are preparing yourself for world citizenship" became "you are preparing yourself to be an active citizen and a 'friend to all.'"[99]

Instead of learning about the broad work of the United Nations, girls were given a more narrow focus on women and children. They no longer needed to

memorize the statement on neighborliness in the UN Charter to gain a proficiency badge, though they still read and discussed it. They read that "Girl Scouts
are particularly concerned with that part of the United Nations work which
deals with the welfare of children and youth," and their projects were designed
accordingly. Juliette Low was no longer referred to as "one of the first true internationalists" or credited with "one world" thinking.[100]

In addition to internationalism, the Girl Scouts altered language about
social justice. LeFevre had attacked references to government assistance by calling public health services "socialized medicine," and in response, the Scouts
reversed the order of government agencies to begin with the local. Housing was
removed entirely from a list of "large government project[s] which helps people" because critics said it was not clear if housing subsidies helped or harmed
the poor.[101]

The revisions diluted the directness with which the handbook had
approached antiprejudice. "How do you rate as a friend to all? Do I use such
expressions as 'dago,' 'nigger,' 'chink?'" became "Do I call names that might
hurt people's feelings?"[102] Complaints from a parent who believed the phrasing
encouraged prejudice and might be a "bad influence on girls" likely persuaded
the Girl Scouts to remove the words.[103] They were eliminated, but doing so also
cut out the specific statement about American racism. Similarly, the advice to
"start now by making new friends with those you think you do not like" was
made easier. The revision read, "Start now by making new friends," without the
direct challenge to prejudice.[104]

The Board of Directors of the Richmond (Virginia) Area Girl Scout Council unanimously opposed many revisions, "particularly those concerning the
United Nations." The Richmond public relations chair complained that "the
substitution of that one short paragraph on the United Nations which says
absolutely nothing but that there is such an organization and the U.S.A. is a
member, and the paragraph on the World Association of Girl Scouts and Girl
Guides . . . [instead of] four pages . . . devoted to that alone, is a disavowal of the
only organization wherein lies a hope for world peace. Our country *is* a member
of the 'only World organization set up to iron out the different viewpoints of
nations, and that has the authority to do so,' so what is wrong with saying it? We
should back the United Nations, not repudiate it," she insisted.[105] The *Girl Scout
Handbook* did not, however, purge all mentions of international friendship, and
the Girl Scouts remained a supporter of international friendships for girls. The
handbook retained basic information on the United Nations even though the
encomia were gone.

So, too, did other important contents about world amity remain. A
twenty-two-page chapter that centered on international friendship still
reminded girls of the concentric circles of civic responsibility: "Friendship

among people of many nations . . . begins within your own heart and in your own home. It spreads from home to home, community to community, and country to country. . . . It brings with it peace among all people of one nation and all peoples of the world."[106] Headings such as "World Gifts" for products from around the world were retained, although the revised handbook introduced tea as a product of noncommunist India rather than China. The "World Neighbor" section continued to encourage American Scouts to learn about girls in other countries. It maintained the commitment to WAGGGS and to the world pin and

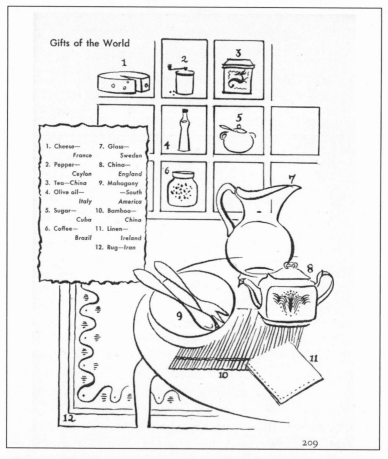

IMAGE 8. The Girl Scouts encouraged international awareness with an illustration of "gifts of the world," or products from different countries. Anticommunists questioned references to communist China. The revised imprint listed India as a producer of tea and the Philippines as a producer of bamboo.

Girl Scout Handbook: Intermediate Program, 1953, 1st impression, 209. Collection of National Historic Preservation Center, Girl Scouts of the USA.

world flag flown at international encampments. The Girl Scouts tried to clarify and sweep away the more politically controversial statements in the handbook while retaining the global girl's relationships to others, especially other Girl Scouts and Guides around the world.

Deletions certainly struck some leaders and girls as odd. Leaders in the Texas and Oklahoma region reported, "The girls themselves have talked about what they can do to help people understand us better."[107] Others voiced frustration. One leader wrote that an eleven-year-old in her troop was working on the Citizens Here and Abroad badge when the changes came down. She "has found a real change in her 'program,'" despite official claims to the contrary, as she "laboriously erased the now forbidden references, and written in the 'my World' for One World,' [sic] 'the pin' for 'World Pin' etc." The leader noted the girl seemed "confused," perhaps because "I could only tell her that these changes were made because Mr. LeFevre, who did not like the United Nations or people to be concerned with other parts of the World than our own, made such a fuss that the leaders in New York made the changes to quiet him."[108] Another leader, addressing the alteration of "Service is your way of making this a better world in which to live" to "Service is your way of making a contribution to your community," challenged national board members to sit down with a girl, as she had done, and tell her to cross out the commitment to make the world better.[109]

As during the YWCA controversy, much of the attack was based on gendered assertions of girls' and women's naïveté regarding political matters and therefore served to silence their organized voices on behalf of peace and social welfare. Girl Scout staff saw this immediately and noted that although women's groups had sent critiques, "as of this date no individual woman has written a letter of the LeFevre genre nor has any women's organization criticized us. *Rather Interesting.*"[110] When the California Federation of Republican Women (CFRW) reviewed the handbook, their commentary was much more measured. The CFRW reviewers took time to count references to the U.S. Constitution in the 1940 and 1953 editions, finding that the 1953 edition, with the addition of the My Government badge, had more. They praised the addition of the My Government merit badge. They agreed that the photostat of the Bill of Rights was of poor quality and needed to be replaced, and they were not bothered by the comparison of the Girl Scouts to the United Nations, saying that "we have to remember that the Girl Scouts are part of an International Organization, and have been from the beginning."[111]

Still, the CFRW believed the Girl Scouts had politicized its program in left-leaning ways and urged mothers of Girl Scouts, Scout leaders, and others to write to Girl Scout headquarters with suggested revisions. The CFRW complained that the Universal Declaration of Human Rights was presented as "like our own Declaration of Independence" and as "one of the finest pieces of work accomplished by the United Nations." They were, CFRW members insisted, "in complete disagreement on this point. Republican women have opposed the Declaration of Human Rights from the very beginning." The CFRW thought LeFevre's reference to socialized medicine had "no basis in fact," noting that the section was purely informational, but as to the large government projects that help people, CFRW reviewers wrote, "the Girl Scout Council advocates Government Housing. We may not agree that 'helps' is the right word to use in this connection." Although the CFRW preferred less "worldmindedness," they recognized that this emphasis was not unique to the Girl Scouts and therefore deserved no special condemnation. Rather, on the whole, CFRW saw the Girl Scouts as "patriotic."[112] Girl Scout officials found the review, which had much in common with the Racine recommendations that were incorporated into the changes, helpful and objective.

By contrast, one Scout official commented that male critics belittled Girl Scout officials as "nice, sincere girls unable to face the fact that subversives were at work in our organization."[113] Once the label of "dupe" or "naive do-gooder" was applied, and their concept of citizenship was labeled "political," it was difficult to recover the authority to expand girls' relation to the world. Even supposed friends attacked Scout officials supposed naïveté.

Mark M. Jones, a management consultant who worked for the Boy Scouts and Girl Scouts in the 1930s, had written privately to Girl Scout headquarters during the American Legion controversy and had expressed gendered assumptions about women's political aptitude. He warned that a concerted effort by "advocates of Internationalism had stepped up their campaign for the penetration of Girl Scouting," resulting in the organization's recent "one world, internationalist, United Nations propaganda." The "fine women, the very best," however, were not to be blamed, for they "substitute sentimentality for sensibility and, in many instances cannot get at the facts." Continuing his attack on Girl Scout staff members' intelligence, he wrote, "Probably the employed head of the Program Division, through whom this was put over, did not ever realize what was taking place right over her own desk," though "she is a very nice lady." Jones conceded that three or four unnamed leftist Girl Scout officials might have acted with intent, but the rest, he believed, were clueless.[114]

Ross Roy, advisory board member of the Detroit (Michigan) Area Girl Scout Council as well as a member of the Boy Scouts executive board, Detroit Area Council, probably saw himself as a helpful insider, but demanded change in absolute terms and even complained of Girl Scouts' revisions.[115] Roy's letters urged the Girl Scouts' national board to "go in the Boy Scout direction" and create an apolitical "*United States* citizenship book."[116] He repeatedly lauded the Boy Scout's patriotism and removal of UN references.[117] And he charged the Girl

Scouts with violating its own policy of remaining nonpolitical because of the women officials' "emotionalism" with regard to the United Nations, international friendship, the World Association, and the World Pin. A former national Girl Scout director found his confrontational approach "sickening and infuriating" and wondered that Roy "doesn't think that people live in a world, but only in their own country."[118] Clearly Ross Roy and Girl Scout officers did not agree on what constituted the "political." To make the handbook politically neutral, Roy urged the Girl Scouts to purge all the UN content and not just the editorializing that the revisions had already deleted.[119] He further advised omitting the One World badge for the Girl Scouts, explaining that "the Boy Scouts have no such badge." He rejected the World Association Pin and Flag on the same grounds.[120]

The revisions bothered Roy: "It will still contain United Nations propaganda."[121] He wanted to lessen the focus on girls' civic responsibilities, remarking that the "Girl Scout could be asked to do something individually for her 'family's comfort and protection' rather than to 'learn about government officials who direct special services.'" Roy held the Girl Scout citizen, rather than government programs, responsible for the "*individual* well-being" and the emotional maintenance of American families.[122] He disagreed with the revised and narrowed emphasis on specialized UN agencies, declaring that "the welfare of children and youth in the United States is a *family* responsibility first."[123] Roy sought to narrow girls' citizenship duties to support of nation and family.

In response, Edith Conant of the Program Department asked Ely Maxwell, the publications advisor, to compare the *Girl Scout Handbook* to materials from the Camp Fire Girls and the Boy Scouts of America. Hall had reviewed the Boy Scout, Camp Fire Girl, and the Y-junior high program books when preparing the 1953 edition, and she stayed in contact with Camp Fire's program department on overlapping concerns. Maxwell found much political content in the Boy Scout publications; only it tended toward conservatism. Boys read, for example:

> It may seem desirable to add more and more services to those the government performs for us. But there are drawbacks to such a trend. One is that more services mean more government; and the bigger our government becomes the harder it is for the people to control, and the more power it has over the lives of the citizens. This can and does lead to loss of individual liberties and freedom of opportunities. It leads to our dependence upon the government for "security"—an unwillingness to accept personal responsibility for our own welfare. . . . Eventually, it leads to a situation in which the government also *decides* everything for them—what kinds of food farmers will raise, what goods the stores may sell, how much people must pay for the things they buy—even what jobs people must do and where they must live. This, certainly is not the American way, our way.

To Roy's contention that the Boy Scouts of America was devoid of political content, Conant wrote that maybe he thought this an "incontrovertible fact," but "to many people it is one side of a political issue."[124]

The *Girl Scout Handbook* had much in common with the *Book of the Camp Fire Girls*. Although the Camp Fire Girls "lean[ed] toward individualism" with its less structured program, it placed a similar "strong, overt emphasis on international friendship as does the Girl Scout program."[125] Maxwell observed, "The Book of the Camp Fire Girls would appear to be, if anything, more vulnerable than the Girl Scout Handbook to the charge that it 'gives United Nations and One World citizenship precedence over American citizenship.'" The Camp Fire Girls' highest rank, the Torchbearer in Social Leadership, omitted specific requirements with respect to the U.S. flag, Constitution, and Bill of Rights, but offered several optional UN activities. As the Girl Scouts did, "the ideal of good U.S. citizenship is expressed, throughout all the Camp Fire rank requirements, in terms of service to the community." Camp Fire did not describe the U.S. flag ceremony, but it did describe its own ceremonies. Camp Fire's "My World" section was roughly equivalent to the Girl Scouts' information in the international friendship chapter. Conant meant no criticism of the Camp Fire Girls, emphasizing that "it is merely evidence that the Camp Fire Girls share the Girl Scouts' belief that it is important to understand the people and cultures of other nations."[126] Despite the similar construction of girls' new relationship to the world in the two organizations, the Girl Scouts, with its higher profile, found itself under scrutiny.

The final round came in the fall of 1954, shortly after McCarthy's overreaching Senate committee confronted the army and the anticommunist hysteria began to diminish. The Girl Scouts was again briefly in the news. This time, moderate and liberal reporters criticized the organization for "retreat" and "appeasement." In a radio broadcast, journalist Louis Lyons expressed disappointment that the Girl Scouts altered its ideals and purged its handbook. Reporter Ben Bagdikian's articles in the *Providence Journal, Christian Register*, and the *Atlantic Monthly* increased the circulation of Lyons's criticism, and these articles perhaps had a greater impact than the right-wing attacks had on public opinion.[127]

For the first time during the controversy, a majority of the letters the Girl Scouts received (58 percent) was unfavorable.[128] Jane E. Romeyn, from East Hartford, Connecticut, wrote that as a former Girl Scout and troop leader, she was not disturbed by the original charges, ascribing them to "narrow-minded bigots," but she was disturbed that "Girl Scouts would bow down before men of this low type and actually change the Handbook to suit them!"[129] Former members said they were disheartened after reading Bagdikian's *Providence Journal* article. One wrote, "I am distressed that a respected National organization of such age and strength, which has for years taken a straight and fearless position in favor of world understanding, friendship among nations and fellowship among individuals of all races, colors and creeds should have allowed itself to qualify this position by changing the wording in its handbook on such subjects as the United Nations, international friendship and even simple friendship itself."[130] Girl Scout followers and much of the public had accepted a global role for girls. They agreed that cultivating international understanding was an acceptable role for American girls.

By late spring of 1955, the worst of the red scare had passed. The Girl Scouts continued to print new impressions of the tenth edition—twenty-nine of them—primarily as a result of growth in the organization. In 1956, the American Legion Savannah (Georgia) Post made amends by helping to restore the Juliette Gordon Low Birthplace as a memorial and national center for Girl Scouts. The American Legion's national council even commended the Girl Scouts for "American ideas."[131] Meanwhile, when LeFevre's new organization, the Congress of Freedom, met in San Francisco, the Girl Scouts undercover representative was "pleasantly disappointed" that the conference was poorly attended and that little attention was paid to the organization.[132] Congress authorized the Department of Defense to "give material assistance" to the 1956 senior Girl Scout roundup.[133]

Into the 1960s, John Birchers and other extremists invoked the Girl Scout controversy in anticommunist attacks on church groups and schools.[134] The controversies, however, stayed primarily local. The Girl Scouts believed the organization to be safe enough to suggest to the State Department that Khrushchev visit a Girl Scout encampment during his visit in 1959.[135] Yet the organization also sent its regional directors and leaders three thousand copies of an FBI pamphlet that reported on how world communist strategy targeted youth agencies "to control for its own evil purposes the explosive force which youth represents" as well as explaining how its own screening of affiliations with other organizations made it safer.[136]

Girl Scout officials and staff members expended enormous energy and postponed numerous summer vacations as a result of the anticommunism attacks. To some extent the extremists lost. Girl Scout membership numbers remained strong.[137] The Girl Scouts kept much of its international friendship program, stood by its participation in WAGGGS, and continued to gradually adopt policies to become more interracial. The national board of directors restated its support for the "principles of the United Nations" at its October 1954 meeting in Detroit.[138] The Girl Scouts had, however, grown cautious about political content for girls and therefore, as director Dorothy Stratton said, "learned . . . [to] look with a weather eye at any of the 'causes' which Girl Scouts take up."[139] The crisis created a greater need overall for public and government legitimization.

People-to-People and Government Legitimacy

In the wake of the red scare, the Girl Scouts aligned its activities with the federal government's cultural and visitor exchange programs. President Eisenhower's People-to-People program, which sought to advance U.S. moral authority and world friendship through the cultural exchange practices already prevalent in private organizations such as girls' organizations, was especially significant. Through forty-one separate committees representing such interests as youth, sports, business, letter writing, and cartoonists, People-to-People turned ordinary Americans into goodwill ambassadors.

Girls' organizations were members of the initial People-to-People Youth Activities Committee in 1956 and they quickly refashioned their international programs as People-to-People exchanges. In the late 1950s, the Girl Scouts referred to its Scout and Guide exchange as a "People-to-People Ranger Exchange."[140] Through People-to-People, girls' organizations once again asserted aspirations to shape a climate conducive to world peace. When Stratton accepted membership on the Youth Committee, she wrote, "In view of the serious crises in various parts of the world at the present time, the Girl Scout organization is more than

IMAGE 9. "I'm Going to Report You *All* to the A.S.P.C.A.!" hollers an older American woman, but the girl says, "By Golly, That's Why We Go Abroad—Because Things Are Different!" Jimmy Hatlo portrayed American girls as proponents of cultural tolerance.

Cartoonists Committee of the People-to-People Program, "You Don't See These Sights on the Regular Tours," New York, 1958, James M. Lambie Records, Box 57, People-to-People Partnerships 1960, Eisenhower Library. © 1958 King Features Syndicate.

ever committed to helping in every way possible to enhance understanding and agreement between Americans and other people. I feel that the Youth Committee offers a means of integrating the efforts of the various youth agencies."[141]

People-to-People also built on the expertise of youth leaders and educators, giving them a voice in the People-to-People program.[142] The 1958 Youth Activities Committee's resource book for youth groups was written by youth organizers and it channeled the People-to-People message to youth organizations throughout the nation.[143] It included examples of activities long a part of girls' organizations such as raising funds through the Girl Scouts' Juliette Low World Friendship Fund, observing International Thinking Day, learning the folk dances and games of other countries, and hosting foreign guests, speakers, progressive dinners, and international food fairs. The guide directed leaders to collaborate with familiar agencies such as CARE; Magazines for Friendship; UNESCO; UNICEF; Seeds for Democracy through the Asia Foundation; Share Your Birthday Foundation, which encouraged young Americans to bring gifts for an overseas recipient to parties; the Foster Parents' Plan; and Art for World Friendship. It highlighted special days like "U.N. Day" and "Pan American Day" for building world-mindedness into the regular youth program.[144]

When the Girl Scouts of the USA hosted an international-themed roundup in Colorado Springs in 1959, planners proclaimed it "the people-to-people program on a young adult level," but it fit squarely within typical Girl Scout programming. Approximately ten thousand Girl Scouts and Guides from the United States and twenty-seven other democracies camped together in troops blending girls from different countries. The visitors spent another three weeks after the roundup in U.S. homes. With assistance from the Foreign Service Institute of the Department of State and Berlitz, Girl Scout officials prepared a "Say It" card, or language crib sheet, which was later made available to other youth groups through the People-to-People program, to help girls greet and get to know one another. Instead of being the target of subversion accusations, Voice of America broadcast interviews of Girl Scouts at the roundup, a sign of renewed legitimacy.[145]

After the worst of the red scare passed, the Girl Scouts still felt the need to compare the encampment to the Soviet-dominated World Youth Festival scheduled for July of the same year, which promised to bring girls and boys from one hundred countries to Vienna. The Girl Scout roundup, without "ominous" communists wandering around, provided "every camper with the chance to get to know girls from different parts of their own and other countries and to appreciate their different backgrounds, thinking, and aspirations." Stressing the individualism the right wing had called for, the Girl Scouts promised that the encampment would help girls develop "individual ideas and self-determined activities" while providing one answer to juvenile delinquency.[146] The Girl Scouts had learned to balance international and American themes. A flag-raising ceremony each morning included all the national flags of WAGGGS members, but an all-American frontier theme (complete with a rodeo and Boy Scouts performing American Indian dances) invoked America's pioneer story of self-reliance and pervaded the nine-day roundup. Even the roundup's international friendship was framed as "world frontiers," a phrase that invoked American pioneer history even as it internationalized the theme.[147]

As the internationalist activities fell in line with government efforts, Girl Scout officials reaffirmed that internationalism had long been a core part of the Girl Scout and Guide identity. The Girl Scout report to the 1960 White House Conference on Children and Youth drew attention to Girl Scout international exchanges dating back to 1926 and explained, "Girl Scouts of the U.S.A. has always used the people-to-people approach in fostering international friendship and understanding."[148] Girl Scout reports made explicit the organization's service to the nation, noting that because our government believed "friendly Americans win American friends," the Girl Scouts did its part to "work with the government" on exchanges and other international friendship activities.[149]

Conclusion

After the criticism from outside groups, Girl Scout official Vaal Stark noted that the upshot of the crisis might be to "help many leaders take their jobs even more seriously."[150] Youth organizations that thought of themselves as outside the realm of politics had been targeted by political groups, and girlhood itself was politicized to reflect the growing anticommunism of the era. Ruth Hunger, first vice president and chair of the national executive committee, deplored how "the training, the faith, the fun and friendship of nearly two million little girls should be put in jeopardy by a controversy that is basically a conflict of grown-up ideas" and charged that the "people who criticize the Girl Scout organization and the Girl Scout Handbook on political grounds are more interested in creating a political furor than in the welfare of American girls."[151]

The girl citizens' political roles had been exposed, diminished, and rechanneled to fit a more cautious agenda. Because the mood following World War II was conducive to experimentation, the Girl Scouts and other girls' institutions had carved out new roles for girls to build peace through their relationships with their families and communities and their peers in other countries. Although girls' institutions had portrayed these actions as commonsensical, right-wing commentators were pointing to them as political and seeking to roll them back to preserve the fragility of girlhood and advance conservative policies of their own. As Lyons correctly pointed out in his broadcast, when the Girl Scouts asked girls to give service "to your community" instead of giving service to make "this a better world," they "put the Scouts back to their community."[152]

Epilogue

The "Watchers of the Skies"

Youth organizations revised their programs after World War II in recognition of U.S. global power and in order to counter the dangers of atomic war. They embraced world citizenship. Girls became ambassadors of goodwill, sending CARE packages, pen pal letters, and other symbols of global friendship as the United States and Soviet Union competed for moral authority around the world. At a time when the dominant boys' organization became more closely wedded to concerns about national security, girls' organizations served as reservoirs for the language of peace and stressed the principles of common humanity and girls' responsibility to help shape the peace. A commitment to pacifism, international control of nuclear armaments, antiprejudice, and economic justice were undercurrents in girls' organizations throughout the 1950s. Girls' organizations provide evidence of the ongoing contributions of liberal women during this era.

A recitation written and used by Iowa Y-Teens in 1948 to explain their program illuminates how many women and girls saw their new relation to the world: "As members of Y-Teens, we are the future. We are all the future there is—our faith, our love, our understanding, our courage." The atomic bomb made their expanded role imperative: "Now we live in the New Age; The atomic age! We may use our power to become children of God—Or to destroy us."[1]

In addition, the Y-Teen recitation rejected materialism, committed girls to promote racial equality and social welfare, and praised American freedoms in "a world united!" To create this world, Y-Teens called on the YWCA, Congress, the United Nations, and God. They believed they were assured of moral credibility and responsibility: "We are members of the oldest and largest woman's organization in the world. We ought to be watchers of the skies; With the widest vision;

The deepest sympathy; The most sensitive outreach; The longest look ahead; And the most limitless courage!"[2] The commitment to watch the skies—an allusion to civil defense as much as to John Keats's poem about the excitement of discovery—offered a model of girls' citizenship to the generation of girls who came of age in the first decade and a half after the end of World War II.

Their stories belie a popular misperception that young people's internationalism began with the Peace Corps. In fact, work for peace shifted to a slightly older group as the government-sponsored overseas volunteer program recruited college graduates. Those who went abroad came from the generation that had come of age with their country's new relationship to the world, felt deeply the era's aspirations for mutual understanding, and many had already worked for peace through youth organizations. Twenty-five thousand young people wanted to know how to join before John F. Kennedy took office and polls showed that 71 percent of Americans favored the enterprise.[3] The Peace Corps answered a need for a humanitarian function in U.S. foreign policy, one that youth organizations had pushed for since World War II had ended.

In terms of gender, the Peace Corps departed somewhat from the model put forth by girls' organizations of peace built through relationships. Although its volunteers got to know the people in their host countries, the Peace Corps officials in Washington, DC, had a vision that volunteers might act in the traditions of a masculine pioneer lore of toughness and self-reliance as they helped the pioneers of other countries develop their frontiers. Some staffers believed that women were not up to the hard work they had in mind. Still, 40 percent of volunteers in the 1960s were women.[4]

When women volunteered they sometimes met the limits of the new relation to the world. Although men too were placed as teachers, staffers viewed teaching, home economics, and nursing as especially suitable for female volunteers, though many did hard manual labor as well. Peace Corps historian Fritz Fischer writes, "In 1960s America, women had certain roles to fulfill, and female volunteers were supposed to show the women of the third world how to fill those roles." Moreover, the relationships that they developed with men abroad (both American and foreign) were perceived as problematic, and pregnancy was punished with removal from the field (even when it was not medically called for).[5]

Ideologically, the Peace Corps and girls' global relationships served the same purpose—to legitimize and provide a moral framework to the expansion of U.S. power. Young women fit awkwardly into the Peace Corps because Cold War girls symbolized a protected childhood, material privileges, nonsexual human relationships, and the domestic center of the United States. Still they were drawn to participation because, like the girls' programs of the 1940s and 1950s, the Peace Corps offered them a chance to help others and create new friendships. They might help ensure peace.

In the next several decades, girls' organizations and the nation faced new challenges. There evolved new opportunities for young people of which the Peace Corps was just one example. The number of opportunities that required travel abroad and face-to-face interaction increased in the 1960s in girls' organizations as well as through government programs. In 1966, the Camp Fire Girls hosted the Horizon Club Conference Afloat, the last major program planned by Martha Allen, who retired that year, and her staff. Over one thousand American Camp Fire Girls went to Puerto Rico, Colombia, and Jamaica by ship, spending twenty days traveling and staying with host families. Aboard the ship, they attended five sessions a day covering Camp Fire programming and socioeconomic, political, and cultural life in the United States and Latin America, especially the countries scheduled for visits. They also studied conversational Spanish. At each port, about four hundred girls from the host countries joined them as overnight guests on board while an equivalent number of Camp Fire Girls lodged with families on shore. In Columbia, the American girls visited local children in a kindergarten, a normal school, an intermediate school, and local "barrios." In Jamaica, they attended lectures, shopped, and met with local youth groups. According to a report on the trip in the *Camp Fire Girl*, American girls found "adventure, independence, new friends, expanded views of the world, new concepts of service, and a comprehension of the basic similarities of all people."[6]

Camp Fire's Conference Afloat extended the international-exchange work of the Girl Scouts, though it was shorter lived. After a decade in the planning, the Girl Scouts' Our Cabaña opened in 1957 in Cuernavaca, Mexico, adding a Latin American destination to the WAGGGS list of world centers that already included Our Chalet in Switzerland, which opened in 1932, and Our Ark, a London hostel that opened in 1939 and has since been replaced by the Pax Lodge. The world centers served as sites for recreation, training, and workshops for girl and adult Scouts and Guides from around the world. In 1966, WAGGGS opened its fourth world center, Sangam, in Pune, India. The Kusafiri African world center was conceived differently. It began in 2010 as a center without a central location. Instead, conferences and gatherings are held at different sites in Africa to provide a centerlike experience. In all the countries, the goal has been to create global meeting places for girls and women in Scouts and Guides.[7]

The world centers have extended WAGGGS international mission, but they have not been without challenges. Problems that Girl Scout officials faced in Cuernavaca showed how difficult it can be to bring the aspirational ideals of mutual understanding into practice. In the late 1950s, rowdy behavior by the American girls at the site, especially their flirting with Mexican boys and using foul language, hastened a shift in Girl Scout planning. Instead of focusing on rules and manners, they adopted more comprehensive multicultural training that encouraged girls to learn from local people and develop long-lasting friendships.[8] These themes, already present in girls' literature and projects, became more pressing.

American girls' organizations continued to address issues of social justice, and still do. But in the 1960s and early 1970s, the era of Vietnam War protests, girls' organizations were not the place where young people's voices for peace, which had grown louder, turned. At a time when bumper stickers and buttons proclaimed "Question Authority," joining what many viewed as a bourgeois character-building organization like the Scouts grew increasingly less popular. In addition, U.S. foreign and military policy in Vietnam and especially covert action in Cambodia went against the ideal of openness and sharing that People-to-People and the ideals of integration and cooperation expressed. Awareness of these foreign policy realities stifled any volunteerism that appeared tied to the state or appeared too nationalistic. In 1969, young people reported a decreasing sense of connection to church, school, family, and civic institutions, and even the number of Peace Corps volunteers dropped after 1966.[9] The membership of the Camp Fire Girls, the Girl Scouts of the USA (though not internationally), and Y-Teens dropped in the mid-1960s.[10]

Still, many who participated in the protest movements of the 1960s had been members of the girls' organizations in the 1950s and expected to shape America and the future. They simply changed the venues in which they acted as they got older. Moreover, girls who remained or became members raised questions within their organizations about Vietnam, women's liberation, and flag burning.[11]

Many perceived youth organizations to be out of date, even as soul searching and member surveys produced change. Expanding opportunities for girls in sports and other activities and also the draw of home-based entertainment (television and then computers) took girls away from organizations and volunteering. At the same time, the increase in the percentage of mothers who worked outside the home meant fewer women available to run activities for the organizations. Questions about the potential longevity of girls' organizations arose. The baby boomers were reaching their twenties, and organizations could not count on the growth of the youth population to boost its numbers.

Responding to the challenges, girls' organizations retooled their age groupings, introduced a broader range of activities beyond those considered feminine (Camp Fire Girls learned to hammer), and experimented with coeducational programs. The Camp Fire Girls began admitting boys in 1975, declaring the goal of working toward equal partnerships between the genders. The Girl Scouts took the other route, introducing more coeducational activities but maintaining the overall space devoted to girls. The Boy Scouts of America started special "Venture" troops that included girls at the older levels but left its main programs for boys alone. On the international stage, however, the World Organization of the Scout Movement officially admitted girls in 1977, even though many national

Scouting organizations remained closed to them. Different nations have grappled with the problem of coeducation differently. Sweden combined its organizations in 1960. WAGGGS, however, has resisted opening its membership beyond admitting a few boys and men who were members of Guide programs in countries that were experimenting with coeducational programs.[12]

In the 1970s and 1980s, membership stabilized and began to rebound. Internationalism remained a theme in girls' organizations, although it was often dwarfed by domestic social justice concerns, teenage-pregnancy awareness, and antidrug campaigns. Camp Fire Girls continued to earn citizenship awards for learning about people from other countries and different ethnic groups, touring the United Nations and learning about other peacekeeping organizations, reading the United Nations Charter, and explaining how the Camp Fire Girls carries out its purposes through world friendship and writing to pen pals.

More advanced projects for middle school girls were introduced. One focused on peace and asked girls to keep a book of peace ideas, art, and other mementos that demonstrate peace at home, in the community, and beyond. The project guidelines adapted a line from a Carl Sandburg poem to urge leaders and girls to consider a scenario: "Suppose they gave a war and nobody came." Girls were also asked to interview religious leaders and elderly people about war.[13] The Girl Scouts, too, continued to run their international post to pair pen pals. Its guidebook for Senior Girl Scouts suggested preparing an international meal and advised girls to learn about exports, diversity, and international relations.[14]

Girls today unknowingly draw on the legacy of these organizations' work in earlier decades. Among them are part-time aid workers like Jordana Confino of Westfield, New York, who learned about the struggles for girls around the world from her mother's stories and news updates. In the eighth grade, she started a club to address world problems, and the group attended a UN conference on women and girls. The club became Girls Learn International, which raises money for girls' education. U.S. chapters, based in schools, have partner chapters in poor countries. Although the "ostensible aim is to empower girls in countries like Pakistan, some of the major beneficiaries are the American girls" who—just as girls did in the 1950s through the Girl Scouts and *Seventeen* magazine—learn to serve others, and about human rights and the world beyond their own doors.[15]

Girls' organizations today remain an important source of international awareness. A Girl Scout leader group on Facebook provides advice on Education First tours to places like the South Pacific and India and has a thread for connecting girls to pen pals in the United States and abroad. (Girl Scouts still write letters, but they also now use e-mail and exchange digital videos.) Troops celebrate Malala Yousafzai's achievements and her ongoing work to protect girls' access to education around the world. They hold vigils for Syrian refugee children and seek ways to help UNICEF address the crisis. Moreover, the Girl Scouts of the USA website boasts not only WAGGGS and its 146 member countries but also its own UN affiliation and Global Action Awards to encourage local troops to work on the eight United Nations Millennium Development Goals, particularly education. The Girl Scouts partners with the Peace Corps and Michelle Obama's Let Girls Learn initiative.[16] On Thinking Day, Girl Scouts of all ages and across the nation learn about and celebrate different cultures, ignoring once again the 1950s anticommunists' demands that George Washington's birthday receive equal acclamation.

Just as American girls were once encouraged to assume responsibility in the world, today's girl may join a mission or temporary vacation project overseas. There has been a recent increase in short-term mission trips in youth ministries. Many go and forge genuine human connections and work with local people to build stronger communities locally and transnationally. As there were problems at Our Cabaña, today's global girl citizen brings her own set of cultural baggage. A couple that hosts mission trips in Guatemala notes that many young people exhibit cultural superiority and naïveté.[17] Many bring consumer and tourist values with them, "serving the hungry a meal before shopping for souvenirs." They may merge tourism and consumption with their experiences of the world abroad.[18]

One Christian theologian argues that failure to recognize the historical connection between colonialism and mission work leads to, at best, shallow relationships between Christians and, at worst, to neocolonial relationships.[19] Girls on today's missions may fail to question the power relations that they encounter. One former mission trip worker calls it the "white savior" complex, describing her mission trip to Tanzania:

> Our mission while at the orphanage was to build a library. Turns out that we, a group of highly educated private boarding school students, were so bad at the most basic construction work that each night the men had to take down the structurally unsound bricks we had laid and rebuild the structure so that, when we woke up in the morning, we would be unaware of our failure. It is likely that this was a daily ritual. . . . Basically, we failed at the sole purpose of our being there. It would have been more cost effective, stimulative of the local economy, and efficient for the orphanage to take our money and hire locals to do the work, but there we were trying to build straight walls without a level.[20]

As *Seventeen* did in the 1940s and 1950s, girls' media promotes international engagement for today's girls. In the 2006 and 2008 Disney films, *Cheetah Girls 2* and *Cheetah Girls: One World*, a multicultural band travels to Spain and India, showcasing girl empowerment through travel and friendship. While both films encourage a cosmopolitan identity for young women, the film set in India encourages friendships with peers not from North America and Europe. The Cheetah Girls unite with girls in other countries through their shared interest in fashion, music, and dance and see themselves as empowering "less-fortunate 'global' girl sisters." Global inequalities and the real differences between girls in the films are obscured by the supposed friendships that develop as the stars dress in the brightly colored saris that *Seventeen* would have proudly printed in the 1950s and sing about sharing "One World."[21] There is danger in these examples that girls' internationalism is a product of but fails to contend with America's power.

Girls' organizations have advanced internationalism and antiprejudice as twin efforts. Peace studies research indicates that educating children about human rights can alter cultural norms about violence in the process.[22] The Girl Scouts currently admits any child who is "recognized by the family and school/community as a girl and lives culturally as a girl," and *Seventeen* magazine currently educates young people about expanding transgender rights, providing space for teens to tell their own stories. Camp Fire was one of the first youth institutions to officially include sexual orientation in its inclusion statement, and the YWCA runs rape crisis centers as part of its mission of "eliminating racism, empowering women and promoting peace, justice, freedom and dignity for all."[23] The World Scout Organization launched Messengers of Peace in 2011, "a global initiative designed to inspire millions of young men and women in more than 220 countries and territories to work toward peace." Using social media, Scouts from around the world share their peace efforts and try to inspire others to create security and peace in their homes, communities, and the world.[24] Young people's institutions clearly have other agendas as well, but helping girls create peace and security is one of them.

As in the 1950s when the patriarchal social structure allowed girls to assume the role of advancing world peace through human relationships, this remains a position with little power. When conservatives disagreed with the expanded role of girls in the world and the latter's association with social justice and human rights claims, girls were contained. Americans spoke more loudly of peace through strength. Deterrence—guaranteeing the absence of American lives lost in battle or attack through the presence of overwhelming deterrent force, ready to be deployed at a moment's notice—focused on the threat of force over collaboration. Today the war on terror again threatens to subsume conversations about human relationships and caring under a defensive national security posture. While it is unlikely that youth organizations' attention to peace will transform this situation, it cannot hurt to have children around the world learn more about and interact with one another. We can also learn from the past efforts of girls' organizations to apply broad definitions of peace and security that are more than the absence of war, ones that include rights, dignity, and mutual understanding.

ACKNOWLEDGMENTS

This book has benefited from the advice and support of many colleagues, institutions, friends, and family members.

I want to thank first the women who shared pen pal letters or talked to me about their girlhoods: Lore Bachhuber, Elizabeth Frank, Mary Alice Sanguinetti, Ann Chenall, Barb Kubik, Gail Oblinger, and Julie Hillman. Several generously shared letters they had written as teenagers, something many of us would be terrified to do with a near stranger. (All interview recordings are in the possession of the author and were completed with Internal Review Board approval, University of the Pacific.)

I am grateful for the wisdom, advice, and help of many colleagues and friends who read chapters at various stages, critiqued and congratulated me, and pushed me to think about the material in new ways. Their insights have made this a better book. My particular thanks to Amy E. Davis and Naoko Shibusawa, who both read the manuscript in its entirety, as well as to Mischa Honeck, Michael Holm, Edith Sparks, Donna Alvah, and Janet Farrell Brodie, who read portions of the manuscript. My writing group, especially Traci Roberts-Camps and Marcia Hernandez, provided interdisciplinary feedback on drafts as well as company and support. I am also grateful for the early conversations that helped me decide to position the book as a girls' history with Nancy Hewitt, as well as Judith L. Bishop and Marta Robertson, with whom I connected through the National Center for Faculty Development and Diversity (an incredible institution that insists on daily writing).

Also instrumental in the project are the institutions and sponsors that have supported my work. Although this project is not my dissertation, part of its research developed out of that research generously supported by a Schlesinger

Library Dissertation Support Grant, Harvard University. More recent financial support included an Eisenhower Presidential Library Abilene Travel Grant; a Sophia Smith Collections, Travel-to-Collections Grant, Smith College; and a Scholarly/Artistic Activities Grant from the University of the Pacific. In addition, the research on this project was made possible by openness and helpfulness of staff, librarians, and archivists: Mike Wurtz at the Holt Atherton Collections, University of the Pacific; Yevgeniya Gribov at the National Historic Preservation Center, Girl Scouts of the USA; Kevin M. Bailey at the Dwight D. Eisenhower Presidential Library; and Jeff Randolph at Camp Fire National Headquarters. This project also benefited from materials consulted at the Harry S. Truman Library and Museum; the San Francisco History Center, San Francisco Public Library; the Sallie Bingham Center for Women's History and Culture at the David M. Rubenstein Rare Book and Manuscript Library, Duke University; and the local Camp Fire Councils of Mt. San Antonio, Montclair, California; San Andreas, San Bernardino, California; Oklahoma City; Roganunda, Yakima, Washington; and San Diego, California. Phyllis Raines also opened her private Camp Fire collection to me. My thanks also to Katie Keeran and Kimberly Guinta, at Rutgers University Press.

Last, but certainly not least, I give my heartfelt appreciation to my husband, Erik Helgren, whose support of my work and devoted partnership in our family life helps me attain whatever balance is possible in academic life. My boys, Thomas and Stephen, are constant reminders of the fact that children shape our everyday lives and our worlds and that the historians' job must be to tell stories that might make all of our children's futures more secure. Thanks must also go to my mother, Julie Hillman, who was a Girl Scout in the 1950s and my first Camp Fire leader in the 1970s. She had little knowledge that I would someday write about those institutions but she inspired me to be curious about what and why we were learning the things we were. My father, Charles Hillman, too, always placed high standards in learning and inquiry.

NOTES

ABBREVIATIONS USED IN THE NOTES

ALC   American Legion Controversy Files, National Historic Preservation Center, Girl Scouts of the United States of America, New York, NY

CFEMC Records Camp Fire for Eastern Massachusetts Council Records, Schlesinger Library, Radcliffe Institute for Advanced Study, Harvard University, Cambridge, MA

Camp Fire Girl *Camp Fire Girl: A Bulletin of News and Suggestions for Leaders of Camp Fire Girls*

CFNH   Camp Fire National Headquarters, Kansas City, MO

DDEPAP   Dwight D. Eisenhower Papers as President, Dwight D. Eisenhower Presidential Library, Abilene, KS

EL   Dwight D. Eisenhower Presidential Library, Abilene, KS

GSUSA   National Historic Preservation Center, Girl Scouts of the United States of America, New York, NY

JML Records   James M. Lambie Records, Dwight D. Eisenhower Presidential Library, Abilene, KS

OKC   Camp Fire, Oklahoma City Council, Oklahoma City, OK

HST Papers   Harry S. Truman Papers

San Andreas   Camp Fire, San Andreas Council, San Bernardino, CA

San Diego   Camp Fire, San Diego County Council, San Diego, CA.

SFUSD Records San Francisco Unified School District Records, 1854–2005, San Francisco History Center, San Francisco Public Library

Smith   Sophia Smith Collection, Smith College Archives, Northampton, MA

TL   Harry S. Truman Library and Museum, Independence, MO

USIA   United States Information Agency

WHCOCY Records White House Conference on Children and Youth Records, 1930–1970, Dwight D. Eisenhower Presidential Library, Abilene, KS

INTRODUCTION

1. M. M., Excelsior Springs, MO, Letters to the Editor, *Seventeen*, July 1948, 4.
2. Truman quoted in "Miss Kempthorne in America," radio broadcast, BBC London to USA, ca. 1950, Transcript in CFEMC Records, carton 1, folder 9. See also "Message from Truman: Camp Fire Girls Make Public Anniversary Congratulations," *New York Times*, March 16, 1950, 39.

3. "Girl Scout Week Dedicated to World Citizenship," *New York Age*, November 3, 1945, 4.

4. Dorothy B. Robins, *Experiment in Democracy: The Story of U.S. Citizen Organizations in Forging the Charter of the United Nations* (New York: Parkside Press, 1971), xii.

5. On postwar girls' culture, see Rachel Devlin, *Relative Intimacy: Fathers, Adolescent Daughters, and Postwar American Culture* (Chapel Hill: University of North Carolina Press, 2005); Wini Breines, *Young, White, and Miserable: Growing Up Female in the Fifties* (Boston: Beacon Press, 1992); Joanne Meyerowitz, "Beyond the Feminine Mystique: A Reassessment of Postwar Mass Culture, 1946–1958," in *Not June Cleaver: Women and Gender in Postwar America, 1945–1960*, ed. Joanne Meyerowitz (Philadelphia: Temple University Press, 1994), 229–262.

6. See the 2014 special forum in *Diplomatic History*, "Transnational Generations: Organizing Youth in the Cold War West, 1945–1980," about children and international politics, especially Mischa Honeck and Gabriel Rosenberg, "Transnational Generations: Organizing Youth in the Cold War," *Diplomatic History* 38, no. 2 (2014): 233–239; and Paula S. Fass, "Intersecting Agendas: Children in History and Diplomacy," *Diplomatic History* 38, no. 2 (2014): 294–298.

7. Lesley J. Pruitt, *Youth Peacebuilding: Music, Gender, and Change* (Albany: State University of New York Press, 2013), 6.

8. Naoko Shibusawa, *America's Geisha Ally: Re-imagining the Japanese Enemy* (Cambridge, MA: Harvard University Press, 2006), 5; Sara Fieldston, *Raising the World: Child Welfare in the American Century* (Cambridge, MA: Harvard University Press, 2015); and Fieldston, "Little Cold Warriors: Child Sponsorship and International Affairs," *Diplomatic History* 38, no. 2 (2014): 240–250. See also Tara Zahra, *The Lost Children: Reconstructing Europe's Families after World War II* (Cambridge, MA: Harvard University Press, 2011). For a discussion of adults' deploying children's representations as tools of foreign diplomacy, see Anita Casavantes Bradford, *The Revolution Is for the Children: The Politics of Childhood in Havana and Miami, 1959–1962* (Chapel Hill: University of North Carolina Press, 2014).

9. Tammy M. Proctor, *Scouting for Girls: A Century of Girl Guides and Girl Scouts* (Santa Barbara, CA: Praeger, 2009); Marcia Chatelain, "International Sisterhood: Cold War Girl Scouts Encounter the World," *Diplomatic History* 38, no. 2 (2014): 261–270; and Mary Logan Rothschild, "Girl Scouting, Internationalism, and the Communist Menace" (paper presented at the Berkshire Conference on the History of Women, Claremont, CA, June 2005).

10. Elizabeth Cobbs Hoffman, *All You Need Is Love: The Peace Corps and the Spirit of the 1960s* (Cambridge, MA: Harvard University Press, 1998).

11. Margaret Peacock, *Innocent Weapons: The Soviet and American Politics of Childhood in the Cold War* (Chapel Hill: University of North Carolina Press, 2014), 95–96.

12. For a discussion of the State Department and cultural exchange, see Penny M. Von Eschen, *Satchmo Blows Up the World: Jazz Ambassadors Play the Cold War* (Cambridge, MA: Harvard University Press, 2004); Mary L. Dudziak, *Cold War Civil Rights: Race and the Image of American Democracy* (Princeton, NJ: Princeton University Press, 2000). For a discussion of how, in the 1940s and 1950s, the field of children's literature maintained prevalent 1930s themes—intercultural awareness, antiauthoritarianism, and workers' rights—see Julia L. Mickenberg, *Learning from the Left: Children's Literature, the Cold War, and Radical Politics in the United States* (New York: Oxford University Press, 2006).

13. Robert Coles acknowledges that children receive much of their political outlook, moral judgments, and understanding of history from their environment and the

adults in their lives, but he asserts that children also ask questions and create their own meanings. See Robert Coles, *The Political Life of Children* (Boston: Atlantic Monthly Press, 1986), 25, 137–138.

14. Susan Zeiger, *Entangling Alliances: Foreign War Brides and American Soldiers in the Twentieth Century* (New York: New York University Press, 2010), 7.

15. Landon R. Y. Storrs, *The Second Red Scare and the Unmaking of the New Deal Left* (Princeton, NJ: Princeton University Press, 2013), 206; and Elizabeth Borgwardt, *A New Deal for the World: America's Vision for Human Rights* (Cambridge, MA: Harvard University Press, 2007).

16. Proctor, *Scouting for Girls*, 126.

17. One survey showed that 26 percent of high school students were in a club or organization that dealt with world affairs. See Michael Scheibach, *Atomic Narratives and American Youth: Coming of Age with the Atom, 1945–1955* (Jefferson, NC: McFarland, 2003), 38, 206.

18. Proctor, *Scouting for Girls*, 118; Steven Mintz, *Huck's Raft: A History of American Childhood* (Cambridge, MA: Harvard University Press, 2006), 282. Camp Fire Girls, *Annual Report of the Camp Fire Girls*, 1944, CFNH; and Camp Fire Girls, *Annual Report of the Camp Fire Girls, 1964–1965*, CFNH. The estimation is made using the 1950 U.S. census data on age and sex at http://www2.census.gov/prod2/decennial/documents/21983999v2p1ch3 .pdf. As journalist William Harlan Hale noted at the time, girls were not alone in joining groups: "Never, in fact, has the American predilection for 'grouping' in multitudes of bodies been so pronounced" (Hale, "Every Man an Ambassador," *Reporter*, March 21, 1957, U.S. President's Committee on Information Activities Abroad [Sprague Committee] Records, box 9, People-to-People Activities 29 [1], EL). See also Robert D. Putnam, *Bowling Alone: The Collapse and Revival of American Community* (New York: Simon & Schuster, 2000), 57, 72, 254–255.

19. For a discussion of prolonged childhood, see John Demos and Virginia Demos, "Adolescence in Historical Perspective," in *Childhood in America*, ed. Paula S. Fass and Mary Ann Mason (New York: New York University Press, 2000), 132–138; and Viviana A. Zelizer, *Pricing the Priceless Child: The Changing Social Value of Children* (1985; repr., Princeton, NJ: Princeton University Press, 1994), 56–72.

20. Susan A. Miller, *Growing Girls: The Natural Origins of Girls' Organizations in America* (New Brunswick, NJ: Rutgers University Press, 2007), 80.

21. Ibid., 3; and Minutes of a Conference between Representatives of the Girl Scouts of America, the Girl Guides of America, and the Camp Fire Girls of America, New York, June 6–7, 1911, Board Minutes, 1911–1912, 21, CFNH.

22. See Laureen Tedesco, "Making a Girl into a Scout: Americanizing Scouting for Girls," in *Delinquents and Debutantes: Twentieth-Century American Girls' Cultures*, ed. Sherrie A. Inness (New York: New York University Press, 1998), 22; and Mary Aickin Rothschild, "To Scout or to Guide? The Girl Scout–Boy Scout Controversy, 1912–1941," *Frontiers: A Journal of Women's Studies* 6, no. 3 (1981): 115–121.

23. Amanda Lee Izzo, "The Commandment of Love: Liberal Christianity and Global Activism in the Young Women's Christian Association of the USA and the Maryknoll Sisters, 1907–80" (PhD diss., Yale University, 2010), 5, 8. See also "Historical Note," YWCA of the U.S.A. Records Finding Aid, Smith, 2007, http://asteria.fivecolleges.edu/findaids/ sophiasmith/mnsss292_bioghist.html.

24. Proctor, *Scouting for Girls*, 9, 12.

25. Ibid., 43. Eduard Vallory, "Status Quo Keeper or Social Change Promoter? The Double Side of World Scouting's Citizenship Education," in *Scouting Frontiers: Youth and the*

Scout Movement's First Century, ed. Nelson R. Block and Tammy M. Proctor (Newcastle, UK: Cambridge Scholars, 2009), 207–222. Robert Baden-Powell, "Address to the International Girl Guide Conference by the Founder," quoted in Proctor, *Scouting for Girls*, 43.

26. Vallory, "Status Quo Keeper or Social Change Promoter?," 217.

27. David I. Macleod, "Original Intent: Establishing the Creed and Control of Boy Scouting in the United States," in *Scouting Frontiers*, 17. For further discussion of gender and boys' organizations, see Jeffrey P. Hantover, "The Boy Scouts and the Validation of Masculinity," in *The American Man*, ed. Elizabeth H. Pleck and Joseph H. Pleck (Englewood Cliffs, NJ: Prentice Hall, 1980), 285–301; David I. Macleod, *Building Character in the American Boy: The Boy Scouts, YMCA, and Their Forerunners, 1870–1920* (Madison: University of Wisconsin Press, 1983); Jay Mechling, *On My Honor: Boy Scouts and the Making of American Youth* (Chicago: University of Chicago Press, 2001); and Benjamin René Jordan, *Modern Manhood and the Boy Scouts of America: Citizenship, Race, and the Environment, 1910–1930* (Chapel Hill: University of North Carolina Press, 2016).

28. Arthur A. Schuck, "A Friend to All," *Boys' Life*, April 1960, 34.

29. Girl Scouts of the USA, *Hands around the World: International Friendship for Girl Scouts* (New York: Girl Scouts of the USA, 1949), 12.

30. Proctor, *Scouting for Girls*, 8–11, 51–52.

31. Kristine Alexander, "Similarity and Difference at Girl Guide Camps in England, Canada, and India," in *Scouting Frontiers*, 108, 114–117; see also Kristine Alexander, "The Girl Guide Movement and Imperial Internationalism in the 1920s and 1930s," *Journal of the History of Childhood and Youth* 2, no. 1 (2009): 37–63.

32. Jennifer Helgren, "Native American and White Camp Fire Girls Enact Modern Girlhood, 1910–39," *American Quarterly* 66, no. 2 (2014): 333–360; Philip J. Deloria, *Playing Indian* (New Haven: Yale University Press, 1998); and Shari M. Huhndorf, *Going Native: Indians in the American Cultural Imagination* (Ithaca, NY: Cornell University Press, 2001).

33. Kelley Massoni, *Fashioning Teenagers: A Cultural History of Seventeen Magazine* (Walnut Creek, CA: Left Coast Press, 2010), 58–59.

34. Ibid., 168–169.

35. Benson and Benson, Inc., *Life with Teena: A Seventeen Magazine Survey* (New York: Triangle, 1945); and Massoni, *Fashioning Teenagers*, 89–93.

36. For insight into the complex messages of girls' fiction, see Sherrie A. Inness, ed., *Nancy Drew and Company: Culture, Gender, and Girls' Series* (Bowling Green, OH: Bowling Green State University Popular Press, 1997). For a discussion of the international dissemination of girls' fiction and of international themes in Nancy Drew, see Elizabeth Marshall, "Global Girls and Strangers: Marketing Transnational Girlhood through the Nancy Drew Series," *Children's Literature Association Quarterly* 37, no. 2 (2012): 210–227.

37. Mintz, *Huck's Raft*, 284, 285; Peter N. Stearns, "Girls, Boys, and Emotions: Redefinitions and Historical Change," *Journal of American History* 80, no. 1 (1993): 39; and Breines, *Young, White, and Miserable*, 50, 78.

38. See Paul Boyer, *By the Bomb's Early Light: American Thought and Culture at the Dawn of the Atomic Age* (Chapel Hill: University of North Carolina Press, 1994); and Robert A. Jacobs, *The Dragon's Tail: Americans Face the Atomic Age* (Amherst: University of Massachusetts Press, 2010).

39. For further discussion of how the mood in America had shifted toward resignation to Cold War conflict with the Soviet Union and away from hope that world government or collaboration through the United Nations could create peace, see Boyer, *By*

the Bomb's Early Light, 40, 43; Scheibach, *Atomic Narratives and American Youth,* 20; and Lisle A. Rose, *The Cold War Comes to Main Street* (Lawrence: University Press of Kansas, 1999), 3–4. For a discussion of American foreign policy commitment to a Cold War strategy, see Walter LaFeber, *America, Russia, and the Cold War, 1945–2006,* 10th ed. (Boston: McGraw Hill, 2008), 45–49, 57.

40. Christina Klein, *Cold War Orientalism: Asia in the Middlebrow Imagination, 1945–1961* (Berkeley: University of California Press, 2003), 23.

41. Klein, *Cold War Orientalism,* 23–24.

42. See Elaine Tyler May, *Homeward Bound: American Families in the Cold War Era,* rev. ed. (New York: Basic Books, 1999); and Peacock, *Innocent Weapons,* 40.

43. Borgwardt, *A New Deal for the World,* 76–77.

44. Abbott Washburn, Brief Presentation of People-to-People Program, Prepared for June 8, 1956, Cabinet Meeting, Abbott Washburn Papers, box 18, People-to-People (6), EL. Girl Scouts of the USA, "Evaluation Report Prepared for the 1960 White House Conference on Children and Youth," 1959, WHCOCY, 1930–1970, box 188, Evaluative Report Girl Scouts of the USA, EL.

45. Hale, "Every Man an Ambassador."

46. For a discussion of the history of foreign student migration as U.S. geopolitical history, see Paul A. Kramer, "Is the World Our Campus? International Students and U.S. Global Power in the Long Twentieth Century," *Diplomatic History* 33, no. 5 (2009): 775–806. See also Liping Bu, *Making the World Like Us: Education, Cultural Expansion, and the American Century* (Westport, CT: Praeger, 2003); and Jennifer Leigh Gold, "Color and Conscience: Student Internationalism in the United States and the Challenges of Race and Nationality, 1886–1965" (PhD diss., University of California, Berkeley, 2002).

47. For further discussion of women's roles in World War II, see William H. Chafe, *The American Woman: Her Changing Social, Economic, and Political Roles, 1920–1970* (New York: Oxford University Press, 1972); and Karen Tucker Anderson, *Wartime Women: Sex Roles, Family Relations, and the Status of Women during World War II* (Westport, CT: Praeger, 1981). For further discussion of Cold War roles, see May, *Homeward Bound;* and Laura McEnaney, *Civil Defense Begins at Home: Militarization Meets Everyday Life in the Fifties* (Princeton, NJ: Princeton University Press, 2000).

48. On young people's generational identities, see William M. Tuttle Jr., *"Daddy's Gone to War": The Second World War in the Lives of America's Children* (New York: Oxford University Press, 1993), 242–249; and Kelly Schrum, "'That Cosmopolitan Feeling': Teenage Girls and Literacy, 1920–1970," in *Girls and Literacy in America: Historical Perspectives to the Present,* ed. Jane Greer (Santa Barbara, CA: ABC-CLIO, 2003), 103–120. On girlhood as a social construct, see Miriam Forman-Brunell, *Babysitter: An American History* (New York: New York University Press, 2009), 11; and Marcia Chatelain, *South Side Girls: Growing Up in the Great Migration* (Durham, NC: Duke University Press, 2015), 14–15. For a discussion of children's roles in the nation, see Martha Saxton, "Introduction to the First Volume of the Journal of the History of Childhood and Youth," in *The Global History of Childhood Reader,* ed. Heidi Morrison (New York: Routledge, 2012), 103.

49. Henry W. Bragdon and Samuel P. McCutchen, *History of a Free People* (New York: Macmillan, 1954), x.

50. Tuttle, *"Daddy's Gone to War,"* 115–116.

51. Scheibach, *Atomic Narratives and American Youth,* 16–17.

52. Rebecca de Schweinitz, *If We Could Change the World: Young People and America's Long Struggle for Racial Equality* (Chapel Hill: University of North Carolina Press, 2011), 62.

53. Grace Palladino, *Teenagers: An American History* (New York: Basic Books, 1996), 112–113. For a discussion of how media led to the perception that delinquency was on the rise, see James Burkhart Gilbert, *A Cycle of Outrage: America's Reaction to the Juvenile Delinquent in the 1950s* (New York: Oxford University Press, 1986); and Mintz, *Huck's Raft*, 291–292. For girls and delinquency, see Devlin, *Relative Intimacy*, 55–60. A 1952 study in Maryland found the problem of "maladjustment" occurred four times as often in boys than in girls. "More Maladjusted Boys Found Than Girls, in High School Survey," *Personnel and Guidance Journal* 31 (November 1952): 130.

54. "Camp Fire Girls Postwar Program," *Camp Fire Girl: A Bulletin of News and Suggestions for Leaders of Camp Fire Girls* 24, no. 7 (1945): 1–2.

55. Lou B. Paine, "Characteristics of Camp Fire" (address delivered at Region I Annual Conference, Boston, April 6–7, 1956), CFEMC Records, carton 1, folder 6.

56. Camp Fire Girls, *The Book of the Camp Fire Girls*, new ed. (New York: Camp Fire Girls, 1962), 86–87.

57. Tarah Brookfield, *Cold War Comforts: Canadian Women, Child Safety, and Global Insecurity* (Waterloo, ON: Wilfrid Laurier University Press, 2012), 75.

58. Diana Selig, *Americans All: The Cultural Gifts Movement* (Cambridge, MA: Harvard University Press, 2008).

59. Spencer quoted in Harriet Hyman Alonso, *Peace as a Women's Issue: A History of the U.S. Movement for World Peace and Women's Rights* (Syracuse, NY: Syracuse University Press, 1993), 84, see also 86–91, 165; Erika Kuhlman, *Reconstructing Patriarchy after the Great War: Women, Gender, and Postwar Reconciliation between Nations* (New York: Palgrave Macmillan, 2008), 118–121; Marian Mollin, *Radical Pacifism in Modern America: Egalitarianism and Protest* (Philadelphia: University of Pennsylvania Press, 2006); and Gertrude Carman Bussey and Margaret Tims, *Pioneers for Peace: Women's International League for Peace and Freedom, 1915–1965* (Oxford: Alden Press, 1980).

60. Amy Swerdlow, *Women Strike for Peace: Traditional Motherhood and Radical Politics in the 1960s* (Chicago: University of Chicago Press, 1993). In Canada too, Cold War peace activists declared that "masculine qualities such as individuality, aggression and competitiveness fostered war. [It] could be avoided by following feminine qualities" (Brookfield, *Cold War Comforts*, 73).

61. Cynthia Enloe, "Taking Women's Lives Seriously: An Interview with Cynthia Enloe," by Stephanie van Hook, September 12, 2012, http://wagingnonviolence.org/feature/taking-womens-lives-seriously-an-interview-with-cynthia-enloe/; and Jacqueline Castledine, *Cold War Progressives: Women's Interracial Organizing for Peace And Freedom* (Urbana: University of Illinois Press, 2012).

62. On female friendships in the twentieth-century United States, see Linda W. Rosenzweig, *Another Self: Middle-Class American Women and Their Friends in the Twentieth Century* (New York: New York University Press, 1999). For a discussion of friendship as an alternate foundation for women entering politics, see Sarah C. Chambers, "Republican Friendship: Manuela Sáenz Writes Women into the Nation, 1835–1856," *Hispanic American Historical Review* 81, no. 2 (2001): 225–257; and Sharon Marcus, *Between Women: Friendship, Desire, and Marriage in Victorian England* (Princeton, NJ: Princeton University Press, 2007). For a discussion of building networks through friendships, see Amanda E. Herbert, *Female Alliances: Gender, Identity, and Friendship in Early Modern Britain* (New Haven, CT: Yale University Press, 2014); and Leila J. Rupp, *Worlds of Women: The Making of an International Women's Movement* (Princeton, NJ: Princeton University Press, 1997), 11, 199–202. Aristotelian concepts of friendship and democracy excluded the feminine. The husband-wife relationship was once understood as

existing between a master and an inferior, not a "friendship" as signified by "brotherhood" or fraternity. See Jacques Derrida, *Politics of Friendship*, trans. George Collins (New York: Verso, 2005), 206.

63. Virginia Woolf, *Three Guineas* (London: Hogarth Press, 1937; repr., Matrino, 2013), 109; page number from the reprint. Eleana J. Kim uses the phrase "intimate diplomacy" to describe the politics of international adoptions. See Kim, *Adopted Territory: Transnational Korean Adoptees and the Politics of Belonging* (Durham, NC: Duke University Press, 2010), 76. For a discussion of women's transnational identities, see Leela Gandhi, *Affective Communities: Anticolonial Thought, Fin-de-Siècle Radicalism, and the Politics of Friendship* (Durham, NC: Duke University Press, 2006) and Katherine M. Marino, "Transnational Pan-American Feminism: The Friendship of Bertha Lutz and Mary Wilhelmine Williams, 1926–1944," *Journal of Women's History* 26, no. 2 (2014): 63–87. On women's citizenship, see Martha Gardner, *The Qualities of a Citizen: Women, Immigration, and Citizenship, 1870–1965* (Princeton, NJ: Princeton University Press, 2005), 146.

64. For a discussion of how girls learned about the United States to share about their nation abroad, see Jennifer Helgren, "'Homemaker Can Include the World': Internationalism and the Post World War II Camp Fire Girls," in *Girlhood: A Global History*, ed. Jennifer Helgren and Colleen Vasconcellos (New Brunswick, NJ: Rutgers University Press, 2010), 304–322.

65. Harry S. Truman to the Boy Scouts of America, February 7, 1946, and Harry S. Truman to the Girl Scouts, February 25, 1946, both in HST Papers: White House Office of the President's Correspondence Secretary Files, box 5, Youth Groups, TL. See also Harry S. Truman to Bernice Baxter, October 25, 1946, HST Papers: White House Office of the President's Correspondence Secretary Files, box 5, Youth Groups, TL.

66. Sophie Wittemans, "The Double Concept of Citizen and Subject at the Heart of Guiding and Scouting," in *Scouting Frontiers*, 63.

67. For a discussion of gender and militarization, see J. Ann Tickner, *Gendering World Politics: Issues and Approaches in the Post–Cold War Era* (New York: Columbia University Press, 2001); Tickner, *Gender in International Relations: Feminist Perspectives on Achieving Global Security* (New York: Columbia University Press, 1992); Cynthia Enloe, *Maneuvers: The International Politics of Militarizing Women's Lives* (Berkeley: University of California Press, 2000); and Donna Pankhurst, "The 'Sex War' and Other Wars: Toward a Feminist Approach to Peace Building," *Development in Practice* 13, no. 2 (2003): 154–177.

68. "Strengthen the Arm of Liberty," *Boys' Life*, February 1949, 3; and "Liberty's Challenge," *Boys' Life*, March 1949, 9.

69. "Sisters in Uniform," *American Girl* 42, no. 3 (1959): 51.

CHAPTER 1 "WHAT KIND OF WORLD DO YOU WANT?"

1. V. R., Altona, Illinois, Letters to the Editor, *Seventeen*, February 1948, 4. Altona's reference to bacteria is especially interesting because American authorities tried to suppress information on radiation for fear that atomic weapons would be labeled chemical or biological weapons, which were banned by the Geneva Protocol. Nonetheless, movies and comic books presented dark themes of mutation and horror resulting from atomic radiation, and children were aware of these motifs. For a discussion of the suppression of information about radiation, see Janet Farrell Brodie, "Radiation Secrecy and Censorship after Hiroshima and Nagasaki," *Journal of Social History* 48, no. 4 (2015): 842–864.

2. Dorothy W. Baruch, *How to Live with Your Teen-Ager* (New York: McGraw-Hill, 1953), 4.

3. JoAnne Brown, "'A Is for Atom, B Is for Bomb': Civil Defense in American Public Education, 1948–1963," *Journal of American History* 75 (1988): 68–90; Robert A. Jacobs, "Curing the Atomic Bomb Within: The Relationship of American Social Scientists to Nuclear Weapons in the Early Cold War," *Peace and Change* 35, no. 3 (2010): 434–463; Robert A. Jacobs, *The Dragon's Tail: Americans Face the Atomic Age* (Amherst: University of Massachusetts Press, 2010), 3; and Sybil K. Escalona, "Children and the Threat of Nuclear War," in *Behavioral Science and Human Survival*, ed. Milton Schwebel (Palo Alto, CA: Science and Behavior Books, 1965), 201–209.

4. Michael Scheibach, *Atomic Narratives and American Youth: Coming of Age with the Atom, 1945–1955* (Jefferson, NC: McFarland, 2013), 133.

5. Camp Fire Girls, Inc., Report of the Camp Fire Girls, Inc., to the 1960 White House Conference on Children and Youth, 7, WHCOCY Records, box 141, Camp Fire Girls, Inc., EL. Rachel Devlin, *Relative Intimacy: Fathers, Adolescent Daughters, and Postwar American Culture* (Chapel Hill: University of North Carolina Press, 2005), 53, 55–61; Marilyn Irvin Holt, *Cold War Kids: Politics and Childhood in Postwar America, 1945–1960* (Lawrence: University Press of Kansas, 2014), 87; and Margaret Peacock, *Innocent Weapons: The Soviet and American Politics of Childhood in the Cold War* (Chapel Hill: University of North Carolina Press, 2014), 85–86. Devlin says that the delinquency rates for girls were increasing faster than they were for boys, but that most of the girls' delinquent behaviors were "status violations" rather than "penal violations," meaning that they involved engaging in activities, such as underage drinking, sexual activity, or curfew violations that were illegal only for young people. For a discussion of social disruptions within the family, see Robert L. Griswold, *Fatherhood in America: A History* (New York: Basic Books, 1993), 167–172. For further discussion of domestic disunity in wartime society, see Arthur A. Stein, *The Nation at War* (Baltimore, MD: John Hopkins University Press, 1980), 38–53.

6. Kenneth Osgood, *Total Cold War: Eisenhower's Secret Propaganda Battle at Home and Abroad* (Lawrence: University Press of Kansas, 2006), 1.

7. Marcia Elaine Cottom to President Truman, April 10, 1950, HST Papers, Official File, box 339, OF 57 Girl Scouts of America, TL.

8. Survey Research Center, University of Michigan, "Public Attitudes Toward American Foreign Policy: A Nation-wide Survey," July 1947, HST Papers, Staff Member and Office Files: Charles W. Jackson Files, box 12, Public Attitudes Toward American Foreign Policy [2 of 2], TL.

9. Kansas Council for Children and Youth, Summary Delegate Organizational Meeting, Executive Committee, December 19, 1952, 4–5, WHCOCY Records, box 6, Children and Youth—State Committees (2), EL; and "Unhappy Homes and Draft Lead Youth Problems," *Progress Bulletin* (January 1953): 1, WHCOCY Records, box 17, National Midcentury Committee for Children and Youth—Publications (2), EL.

10. Escalona, "Children and the Threat of Nuclear War," 205. See also, Milton Schwebel, "Nuclear Cold War: Student Opinions," in *Behavioral Science and Human Survival*, 211. Schwebel asked children directly if they thought there would be an atomic war and found them evenly split.

11. Baruch, *How to Live with Your Teenager*, 222.

12. Escalona, "Children and the Threat of Nuclear War," 201, 208, 209.

13. Schwebel, "Nuclear Cold War," 221.

14. Brown, "A Is for Atom," 78.

15. Schwebel, "Nuclear Cold War," 221.

16. "These Are the Homefront Ramparts," *Camp Fire Girl* 31, no. 8 (1952): 8.

17. "Psychologists Advise on the Atomic Bomb Peril," *School and Society* 63 (June 1946): 405–406.

18. Harry Truman, American Education Week Announcements, 1946 and 1949, HST Papers, Staff Member and Office Files: White House Office of the President's Correspondence Secretary Files, box 1, Education, TL.

19. Oveta Culp Hobby, "Education in an Age of Uneasiness," Address at Yale University, April 12, 1954, 10–11, Papers of Oveta Culp Hobby, box 39, Apr. 12, 1954—Spaulding Lecture, Yale University, "Education in an Age of Uneasiness," EL.

20. Ruth Teichmann, "Your Leadership Counts," *Camp Fire Girl* 30, no. 8 (1951): 1.

21. Martha F. Allen, "Camp Fire Girls in the Second Half Century," *Camp Fire Girl* 42, no. 3 (1963): 3–4.

22. Gladys Ryland, "A Step-by-Step Approach to Dealing with the Problems of Youth," *Bookshelf* 46, no. 1 (1962): 1–3.

23. "Camp Fire Girls in the Second Half Century," November 1962, 2, CFEMC Records, carton 1, folder 7.

24. Evelyn Goodenough Pitcher, "What Kind of Education for Girls?" November 15, 1963, San Francisco, Triennial Conference, National Council Meeting Minutes, 6–7, CFNH.

25. "Hear Your Heroes," *Seventeen*, January 1962, 74–77, 102–103; and "Youth Out for UNICEF," *Seventeen*, February 1962, 42.

26. "Characteristics of Camp Fire" (Address by Lou B. Paine, at Region I Annual Conference, Camp Fire Girls, Inc. Boston, Massachusetts, April 6–7, 1956), CFEMC Records, carton 1, folder 6. Camp Fire Girls, *Book of the Camp Fire Girls* (New York: Camp Fire Girls, 1946), 237–238.

27. Louise P. Cochran, "Girl Scouts at Home and Abroad," *Girl Scout Leader* 37 (December 1954): 5–6.

28. "A Family Council Meeting Discusses World Peace," *Bookshelf* 41, no. 3 (1958): 6–7.

29. "A Family Council Meeting Discusses World Peace," 6–7.

30. Girls Clubs of America, Inc., "Three Year Study of National and Local Girls Clubs of America, Inc. Citizenship Award Winners," August 3, 1959, 17, WHCOCY Records, box 142, Girls Clubs of America, Inc., EL.

31. Nancy Greider, "Interest in Life around Us," *Seventeen*, May 1949, 158–159.

32. Lisa L. Ossian, *The Home Fronts of Iowa, 1939–1945* (Columbia: University of Missouri Press, 2009), 36; Arnulf M. Pins, "Youth Participation in the Midcentury White House Conference on Children and Youth" (MA thesis, Columbia University, 1953), 8, WHCOCY Records, box 17, Pins, Arnulf A.—Report re Youth Participation in Midcentury White House Conference on Children and Youth, EL.

33. See Viviana A. Zelizer, *Pricing the Priceless Child: The Changing Social Value of Children* (repr., Princeton, NJ: Princeton University Press, 1994).

34. The National Committee for the Midcentury White House Conference on Children and Youth included five young people chosen from state and youth organizations. They served as a sounding board. Young people also served on the Advisory Council on Youth Participation, and over five hundred of the six thousand delegates were between the ages of twelve and twenty-three. See Pins, "Youth Participation," 16, 22.

35. "Recommendations Adopted by the Youth Section of the Second Governor's Conference for Children and Youth, Wisconsin," n.d., WHCOCY Records, box 6, Children and Youth—State Committees (1), EL. National organizations nominated three hundred young people to attend the 1960 White House Conference on Children and Youth. Young people had full delegate status, "taking their place beside adults in workgroups dealing with current problem [*sic*] facing American children and youth" (White House

Conference on Children and Youth, Press Release, July 28, 1959, WHCOCY Records, box 267, National organizations, EL).

36. National Council Meeting Minutes, St. Paul, MN, October 26–27, 1950, CFNH.

37. Helen M. Feeney, "Training Girls in Leadership," *Girl Scout Leader* 36, no. 7 (1959): 17, WHCOCY Records, box 188, Evaluative Report Girl Scouts of the USA, EL.

38. National Midcentury Committee for Children and Youth, Report on Children and Youth, 1950–1952, 1952, 13, WHCOCY Records, box 9, National Midcentury Committee for Children and Youth—Publications (2), EL.

39. Betty Booth, "Let's Have a Youth Council," *Seventeen*, May 1948, 88–89, 128, 130, 132.

40. Twenty-five states had youth councils or clubs organized to raise awareness and consider political solutions to the atomic threat. The *New York Herald Tribune* hosted a highly publicized youth forum in 1950 that gathered thirty-four students. Young people from seventeen countries being helped by the Marshall Plan met with American high school students to discuss international affairs, atomic energy, music, housing, and more. The forum attempted both to create international friendships among the young people and to teach them about global politics. New York City's Municipal Broadcasting System carried the forum, and some speeches were broadcast on Voice of America. The 1950 youth forum was the fourth in a series. See Scheibach, *Atomic Narratives and American Youth*, 34; and *Working Together for the World We Want* (New York: New York Herald Tribune, 1949).

41. "San Francisco, Junior . . ." *Seventeen*, March 1946, 88–89, 234, 237. For an example of press questioning the categorization of delegates as "youth," see "Press Questions Age of Delegates to Youth Parley," *Harrisburg Telegraph*, November 6, 1945, 6.

42. "San Francisco, Junior . . . ," 234, 237.

43. Alice Beaton, "How Important Are You?" *Seventeen*, June 1946, 31, 33. Beaton was Alice's second married name. She also wrote under Alice Thompson, her first married name. Beaton was an original staff writer at *Seventeen*, and she shared founder Helen Valentine's progressive politics, especially concerning race and religious equality, issues with which her columns dealt. See Kelley Massoni, *Fashioning Teenagers: A Cultural History of Seventeen Magazine* (Walnut Creek, CA: Left Coast Press, 2010), 43.

44. Dexter Masters and Katharine Way, eds., *One World or None: A Report to the Public on the Full Meaning of the Atomic Bomb* (1946; repr., New York: The New Press, 2007).

45. Paul Boyer, *By the Bomb's Early Light: American Thought and Culture at the Dawn of the Atomic Age* (Chapel Hill: University of North Carolina Press, 1994), 291. The Reviewing Stand, *Seventeen*, May 1946, 12, 14.

46. Beaton, "How Important Are You?," 33.

47. Three years later, an injunction in *Seventeen*'s book review section stated, "Maybe you don't like to read about atom bombs, but you'd better pull your head out of the sand and look at this." The review recommended David Bradley's *No Place to Hide*, the doctor's account of his time as an army medic stationed on Bikini Atoll in the South Pacific during the atomic tests in 1946. Of this book, which made fallout known to the world, *Seventeen* reviewers said simply, yet boldly, "It tells things you must know" ("On the Book Beat," *Seventeen*, February 1949, 16).

48. Boyer, *By the Bomb's Early Light*, 294.

49. David E. Lilienthal, "Atomics for Teens," *American Girl* 32 (April 1949): 10.

50. See Nancy Potter, "You and the Atom," *Camp Fire Girl* 30, no. 3 (1950): 5. John Lewellen, with drawings by Lois Fisher, *You and Atomic Energy and Its Wonderful Uses* (Chicago: Children's Press, 1949). Although atomic science reached girls in their classrooms and clubs, materials directed specifically at girls assumed they were less interested

in science and less scientifically competent. Herman Schneider and Nina Schneider, juvenile science writers whose publications included articles in the *Camp Fire Girl*, contended that most girls would not choose scientific careers but should be comfortable, "emotionally at home," around the technological advances in homes and society (Herman Schneider and Nina Schneider, "Science for Young Ladies," *Camp Fire Girl* 26, no. 1 [1946]: 7). Children's science author Margaret Farrington Bartlett added that "new words" could replace the intimidating ones like "atom bombs, cures, and Einstein" that made science "forbidding and scary." Although texts for young people generally tried to portray atomic science in easily understood language accessible to the layperson, and although Bartlett's own children's books were written in age-appropriate language, simplification as a gender strategy put girls at a disadvantage and reduced the likelihood that they would be taken seriously as scientific or diplomatic leaders. Simplification as protection from fear replaced encouraging young women to take up a challenge (Margaret Farrington Bartlett, "New Words for Old," *Camp Fire Girl* 27, no. 3 [1947]: 11).

51. For a discussion of the National Defense Education Act's implications for different social groups, see Brown, "A Is for Atom," 68–69; Holt, *Cold War Kids*, 78–79, 152–153; and Susan J. Douglas, *Where the Girls Are: Growing Up Female with the Mass Media* (New York: Random House, 1994), 22.

52. See, for example, Have You Heard? *Seventeen*, May 1947, 166.

53. Dorothy McClure, "Social Studies Textbooks and Atomic Energy," *School Review* 57 (December 1949): 540–546.

54. Frank Abbott Magruder, *National Governments and International Relations* (Boston: Allyn and Bacon, 1955), 42, 614. Another Magruder text, *American Government*, became the target of the anticommunist group National Council for American Education for its "subversive" favorable coverage of the United Nation Charter and its description of the U.S. postal service as an example of an effective socialist structure (Magruder, *American Government* [Boston: Allyn and Bacon, 1944], 39. See also Peacock, *Innocent Weapons*, 75). Many U.S. history textbooks regarded the use of the atomic bomb in World War II as a military necessity, and especially after the invention of the hydrogen bomb in 1954, as a scientific triumph, even as the authors' tone and word-choices bespoke anxiety. See Kyle Ward, *History in the Making: An Absorbing Look at How American History Has Changed in the Telling over the Last 200 Years* (New York: New Press, 2006), 289–290. The popular Macmillan *History of a Free People* defended dropping the bomb on Japan by explaining that the military had predicted "a million American soldiers would be killed or wounded in overcoming the fanatical resistance of Japanese armies fighting on the sacred soil of their own county." The conclusion seemed obvious and acceptable: "The most terrible weapon the world had ever seen made it unnecessary to invade Japan or to count on the Russians for help" (Henry W. Bragdon and Samuel P. McCutchen, *History of a Free People* [New York: Macmillan, 1954], 633). Everett Augspurger and Richard Aubrey McLemore write simply, "[Truman] considered its use justifiable as a means of bringing about a rapid conclusion to the war" (Everett Augspurger and Richard Aubrey McLemore, *Our Nation's Story* [Chicago: Laidlaw Brothers, 1954], 737). As late as 1961, texts treated Hiroshima as a military decision of "last resort to force Japan to surrender and thus save the lives of hundreds of thousands of American fighting men" (Lewis Paul Todd and Merle Curti, *The Rise of the American Nation* [New York: Harcourt, Brace, 1961], 771).

55. Quoted in Scheibach, *Atomic Narratives and American Youth*, 108–114, 129.

56. Ibid., 176.

57. Ibid., 180, 190, 195, 200.

58. Founder Helen Valentine, who initially had a free hand with the content of *Seventeen*, was disappointed that girls were not more interested in citizenship. Media leader Walter H. Annenberg, who financed the magazine, pushed Valentine out over the issue of content and shifted the magazine toward more fashion and beauty in 1949. See Massoni, *Fashioning Teenagers*, 89–93, 184. The magazine continued to include citizenship content under Valentine's replacement, Thompson/Beaton, who shared many of Valentine's political outlooks, but the beauty and fashion content increased.

59. M. M., Brooklyn, NY, Letters to the Editor, *Seventeen*, April 1946, 4; Letters to the Editor, *Seventeen*, June 1946, 6.

60. H. G., Brooklyn, NY, Letters to the Editor, *Seventeen*, May 1951, 4.

61. The survey asked the members of a variety of national organizations what they believed to be America's most salient national purpose. Most regarded national security as the key priority. But the Boy Scouts and Girl Scouts—represented by senior members and their leaders in both instances—responded differently and youth organizations diverged from adult-only organizations. More Boy Scout members (80.9 percent) than Girl Scouts (74.7 percent) ranked "national security" first and members of adult organizations (most over 90 percent) were even more insistent that national security was the nation's first purpose. Adult organizations included the General Federation of Women's Clubs, Kiwanis, and the AFL-CIO. Most organizations reported that their members believed some national sacrifice would be involved. Least significant of all the purposes for the youth organizations were "maintenance of our system of government" and straightforward "material and economic gains." Later in the report, Girl Scout officials speculated that this was about "superficial" systems and not principles like freedom, which tended to rank high. Youth organizations ranked tolerance of extreme opinions as less important than did the adult organizations. Boy Scouts of America and Girl Scout members believed spreading the ideas of American democracy abroad was a close second priority, with the Girl Scouts slightly more in favor than the Boy Scouts (74.3 percent and 73 percent). See Report of Girl Scouts of the USA Participation in the National Purpose Project, with the National Recreation Association, Oct. 1962, WHCOCY Records, box 291, Girl Scouts of the USA (1), EL.

62. Girl Scouts of the USA, "International Friendship Begins at Home," Report for the National Program Committee by the 1959 Girls' Advisory Committee on International Friendship Activities, WHCOCY Records, box 166, Girl Scouts of the USA (2), EL.

63. Sharman Vaughn, "An Afternoon in Hiroshima," *Seventeen*, August 1951, 194, 260.

64. On women's participation in civil defense programs as a means of legitimating political participation and as an extension of maternalism, see Laura McEnaney, *Civil Defense Begins at Home: Militarization Meets Everyday Life in the Fifties* (Princeton: Princeton University Press, 2000); and Tarah Brookfield, *Cold War Comforts: Canadian Women, Child Safety, and Global Insecurity* (Waterloo, ON: Wilfrid Laurier University Press, 2012).

65. Oveta Culp Hobby, Statement before the Subcommittee on Civil Defense of the Senate Armed Services Committee, April 20, 1955, 13–14, Papers of Oveta Culp Hobby, box 58, EL; See also Brown, "A Is for Atom," 70.

66. Arline Broy, "Cooking for C. D.," *Camp Fire Girl* 33, no. 1 (1953): 7.

67. See McEnaney, *Civil Defense Begins at Home*, 7–8, 52–60.

68. Frances Loomis Wallace, "Here's How to Be Ready," *Camp Fire Girl* 33, no. 10 (1954): 4.

69. Esther R. Bien, "Be Prepared," *American Girl* 34 (April 1951): 14.

70. Nancy Haney, "Everybody's Job—Civil Defense," *Camp Fire Girl* 31, no. 2 (1951): 12.

71. "The Time Is Now," *Camp Fire Girl* 30, no. 5 (1951): 3.

72. Frankie Culpepper Georges, "Underground Shelters," *Camp Fire Girl* 31, no. 2 (1951): 14.

73. "The Time Is Now," *Camp Fire Girl*, 3; Haney, "Everybody's Job," 12; and "On the Map: Headline News in Girl Scouting," *American Girl* 34 (June 1951): 42.

74. "The Time Is Now," *Seventeen*, November 1954, 40.

75. Marie E. Gaudette, "World-Mindedness," *American Girl* 35 (February 1952): 16–17.

76. "The Time Is Now," *Camp Fire Girl*, 3.

77. Martha F. Allen, "You Can Contribute Courage," *Camp Fire Girl* 30, no. 4 (1950): 3.

78. Martha F. Allen, "The Future of Camp Fire," *Camp Fire Girl* 30, no. 7 (1951): 2.

79. "The World Federation Summer School in Geneva, Switzerland," *School and Society* 66 (July 1947): 54; and C. O. Arndt and Samuel Everett, "You Can Teach for World Citizenship," *Educational Leadership* 8, no. 1 (1950): 28–34. See, for example, Fisher quoted in Dorothy T. Groeling, "Teen-Age Citizens in Action: United Nations 'Know-How,'" *Bookshelf* 33, no. 4 (1950): 6. A Gallup poll in August 1946 found 54 percent of Americans in favor of "a world government with power to control the armed forces of all nations, including the United States." Another poll by Cottrell and Eberhart for the Social Science Research Council showed only 36 percent support for such a plan (Boyer, *By the Bomb's Early Light*, 37).

80. Lois Fisher, *You and the United Nations*, rev. ed. (Chicago: Children's Press, 1951).

81. Ibid.

82. "Highlights of the Y-Teen Pilot Conference," *Bookshelf* 36, no. 2 (1952): 11; and Eleanor Roosevelt and Helen Ferris, *Partners: The United Nations and Youth* (Garden City, NY: Doubleday, 1950), 41.

83. YWCA, "Week of Prayer and World Fellowship," 1951, November 11–17, 3, YWCA of the USA Records, box 320, folder 2, Smith.

84. Girl Scouts of the USA, *Hands around the World: International Friendship for Girl Scouts* (New York: Girl Scouts of the USA, 1949), 30.

85. In 1960, Girl Scout officials repeated such claims. Tisha Kunst Slote, member of the International Committee and the UN observer of the Girl Scouts of the USA, remarked, "The UN and its Specialized Agencies are concerned with aims and ideals that are but an extension of the very ones to which the Girl Scout organization is committed. The UN, like the Girl Scouts, seeks to achieve human dignity, peace and friendship, and to *help others* to achieve standards of living desired by all." Tisha Kunst Slote, "Report on the Work of the UN and Its Specialized Agencies," June 1960, Outside Organizations, International Groups, United Nations, General, 1946–1983, GSUSA.

86. Girl Scouts of the USA, *Girl Scout Handbook: Intermediate Program* (New York: Girl Scouts of the USA, 1947), 200.

87. Ibid., 198–200.

88. Groeling, "Teen-Age Citizens in Action," 6.

89. U.N. General Assembly, *Teaching of the Purposes and Principles, the Structure and Activities of the United Nations in the Schools of Member States*, November 17, 1947, A/RES/137, http://www.refworld.org/docid/3b00f0941f.html.

90. See, for example, Lucille Hein, "The Declaration of Human Rights," *Camp Fire Girl* 28, no. 7 (1949): 1. United Nations, "History of the Document," http://www.un.org/en/documents/udhr/history.shtml.

91. See, for example, "If We Are to Have Peace," *Bookshelf* 31, no. 4 (1948): 8. Program Packets were printed beginning in 1948. They had previously been mimeographed loose pages put into folders. Rose Terlin shared editorial responsibilities with guest editors with special expertise on the themes highlighted in the packets.

92. "Are Teen-Agers Responsible Citizens?" Survey, 1954, 1–3, YWCA of the USA Records, box 575, folder 1, Smith. Survey respondents included 50 percent more girls than boys.

93. Alva Bernheimer Gimbel, Report on United Nations Contacts, Minutes of the Executive Board of the Camp Fire Girls, ca. 1950, CFNH; Elizabeth Burns, Memo on Current International Developments in Our Work with the United Nations, February 19, 1954, Outside Organizations, International Groups, United Nations, General, 1946–1983, GSUSA; and Girl Scouts of the USA and World Association of Girl Guides and Girl Scouts Relationship with United Nations, October 1954, Outside Organizations, International Groups, United Nations, General, 1946–1983, GSUSA. In 1948, UNESCO approved WAGGGS consultative status (Girl Scouts of the USA, Appendix 88 attached to letter by Dorothy C. Stratton to Max McCullough, November 27, 1957, Outside Organizations, International Groups, United Nations, General, 1946–1983, GSUSA).

94. See, for example, "We Visited the UN," *Seventeen*, May 1950, 98–99, 162.

95. Dickey Meyer, "The Way for Nations," *Seventeen*, July 1946, 53–54, 120.

96. Girls' Friendly Society, USA, "Teen-Agers Build World Relationships," 1953, WHCOCY Records, box 167, Girls' Friendly Society (1), EL; Girls' Friendly Society, USA, "Major Program Emphases of GFS," 1953, WHCOCY Records, box 167, Girls' Friendly Society (1), EL.

97. Alice Thompson, "The Dumbarton Oaks Plan," *Seventeen*, March 1945, 80.

98. Review of *Nations and Peace*, by I. A. Richards, *Seventeen*, September 1947, 12.

99. See John Ashworth, "Blueprint for a Better World," *Seventeen*, September 1945, 89–90, 162, 164–165.

100. "The United Nations Is a Family Affair," *Seventeen*, November 1949, 86, 164.

101. Dorothy T. Groeling, "Postwar Planning—Now!" *Bookshelf* 26, no. 4 (1943): 7. Demonstrating the importance of class and labor policies, Groeling used the International Labour Organization as an example of an effective international treaty.

102. Girl Scouts of the USA, *Girl Scout Handbook*, 198.

103. Gimbel, Report on United Nations Contacts.

104. "Your United Nations," *Seventeen*, August 1951, 140.

105. "UN Day," *Seventeen*, October 1952, 108.

106. "How Far Down Can I Drink?" *Seventeen*, August 1950, 104.

107. Elizabeth Rowe, "From the Editor," *Camp Fire Girl* 31, no, 1 (1951): 1.

108. David Monod, *Settling Scores: German Music, Denazification, and the Americans, 1945–1953* (Chapel Hill: University of North Carolina Press, 2005), 66; William M. Tuttle Jr., *"Daddy's Gone to War": The Second World War in the Lives of America's Children* (New York: Oxford University Press, 1993), 115–116; Rebecca de Schweinitz, *If We Could Change the World: Young People and America's Long Struggle for Racial Equality* (Chapel Hill: University of North Carolina Press), 182; Zoë Burkholder, *Color in the Classroom: How American Schools Taught Race, 1900–1954* (New York: Oxford University Press, 2011); and Griswold, *Fatherhood in America*, 186, 208–209.

109. Katherine Glover, "Report on the Columbia Institute of Relations, under the Auspices of the National Conference of Christians and Jews and Columbia University," November 23, 1948, WHCOCY Records, box 6, Children's Bureau, Federal Security Agency—Reports on Trips by Katherine Glover, EL.

110. Robert Coles, *The Political Life of Children* (Boston: Atlantic Monthly Press, 1986), 24–25, 60–61.

111. De Schweinitz, *If We Could Change the World*, 194.

112. Minutes of Meeting of the National Committee Midcentury White House Conference on Children and Youth, September 8 and 9, 1949, WHCOCY Records, box 6, White House

Conference on Children and Youth—1950—Materials (1), EL; "Recommendations from the Work Session on Prejudice and Discrimination," 1950, WHCOCY Records, box 6, Midcentury White House Conference on Children and Youth—Advisory Council Summary of Minutes, 10/50, EL; and Advisory Council on Participation of National Organizations, Midcentury White House Conference on Children and Youth, "Report on the National Organizations' Programs and Services for Children and Youth," 7–8, 26, 1950, Midcentury White House Conference on Children and Youth, box 7, Midcentury White House Conference on Children and Youth—Advisory Council—Data for 10/50 Meetings, EL.

113. See Mary L. Dudziak, *Cold War Civil Rights: Race and the Image of American Democracy*, 2nd ed. (Princeton, NJ: Princeton University Press, 2011), 12; and Penny M. Von Eschen, *Satchmo Blows Up The World: Jazz Ambassadors Play the Cold War* (Cambridge, MA: Harvard University Press, 2004), 93, 121–122.

114. Quoted in de Schweinitz, *If We Could Change the World*, 82.

115. Peacock, *Innocent Weapons*, 46.

116. Allen, "The Future of Camp Fire," 1, 2.

117. In 1912, the Girl Scouts' constitution said the organization would "be open to all girls . . . who accept the Girl Scout Promise and Law" (Girl Scout Constitution, quoted in Lillian S. Williams, *A Bridge to the Future: The History of Diversity in Girl Scouting* [New York: Girl Scouts USA, 1996], 10). The Camp Fire Girls' certificate of incorporation pledged the organization "to make available to all girls" its educational-recreational program (Certificate of Incorporation of the Camp Fire Girls, New York, 1914, CFNH). See also Potente Susurro, "BHM: Black Girl Scouts and the Powerful Black Women Who Made It and Other Empowering Things Happen," February 19, 2010, http://likeawhisper.wordpress.com/2010/02/19/bhm-black-girl-scouts-and-the-powerful-black-women-who-make-it-and-other-empowering-things-happen/; and Elisabeth Israels Perry, "Josephine Groves Holloway," in *The Tennessee Encyclopedia of History and Culture*, December 25, 2009, updated January 1, 2010, http://tennesseeencyclopedia.net/entry.php?rec=641.

118. Benjamin René Jordan, *Modern Manhood and the Boy Scouts of America: Citizenship, Race, and the Environment, 1910–1930* (Chapel Hill: University of North Carolina Press, 2016), 200–201; "Scouts and NAACP Resolve Crisis," *Crisis*, March 1975, 100.

119. Camp Fire Girls, *Opportunity for All* (New York: Camp Fire Girls, 1955), 4, 16–18, CFNH.

120. Ron Schaumberg, *Wo-He-Lo: Book II, Camp Fire 1961–1979* (Kansas City, MO: Camp Fire, 1980), 299–305. Camp Fire received a Children's Bureau grant from the division of Health, Education, and Welfare in 1964 to promote outreach in Boston, Detroit, Washington, and eventually nine more cities.

121. For a discussion of the liberal Christian perspective, see Amanda Lee Izzo, "The Commandment of Love: Liberal Christianity and Global Activism in the Young Women's Christian Association of the USA and the Maryknoll Sisters, 1907–80" (PhD diss., Yale University, 2010), 41–48, 113–117. On racism and the YWCA, see also Nancy Marie Robertson, *Christian Sisterhood, Race Relations, and the YWCA, 1906–46* (Urbana: University of Illinois Press, 2007); Carole Stanford Bucy, *Women Helping Women: The YWCA of Nashville, 1898–1998* (Nashville: YWCA of Nashville, 1998); Judith Weisenfeld, *African American Women and Christian Activism: New York's Black YWCA, 1905–1945* (Cambridge, MA: Harvard University Press, 1998); and LaKisha Michelle Simmons, *Crescent City Girls: The Lives of Young Black Women in Segregated New Orleans* (Chapel Hill: University of North Carolina Press, 2015).

122. World's Young Women's Christian Association, "Prayer for Younger Membership," 1947, YWCA of the USA Records, box 352, folder 10, Smith. The Camp Fire Girls, by

contrast, in an effort to promote diversity, drew up three separate pamphlets for Catholic, Jewish, and Protestant Camp Fire Girls. Embracing the three major religions signaled alignment with the American consensus that religious diversity was to be tolerated as well as the narrow view of religious diversity that promoted American religiosity as a form of democratic exercise. To embrace American democratic values and, therefore, proper American citizenship meant including Catholics and Jews along with Protestants. See Camp Fire Girls, *Camp Fire and the Protestant Girl*, *Camp Fire and the Catholic Girl*, and *Camp Fire and the Jewish Girl*, all pamphlets (New York: Camp Fire Girls, ca. 1950) at CFNH.

123. Helen S. Wilbur, "What Say? The Book of Quiz Aids for Junior High Y-Teens" (New York: The Woman's Press, 1947), 24, YWCA of the USA Records, box 569, folder 7, Smith.

124. "Taking Hold of Words," *Bookshelf* 26, no. 6 (1943): 4.

125. *Camp Fire Girl* 25, no. 9 (1946): 2.

126. See, for example, "Camp Fire News and Views," *Camp Fire Girl* 33, no. 7 (1954): 8–9.

127. Boy Scouts of America, *Handbook for Boys*, 5th printing (New York: Boy Scouts of America, 1951), 313.

128. Gail Montgomery, "You Can Do Something about Prejudice," *Camp Fire Girl* 31, no. 4 (1951): 14; Camp Fire Girls, Draft of Pamphlet, *Opportunity for All*, 1955, 16, CFNH.

129. Camp Fire Girls, *Opportunity for All*, 5. Although councils in the Pacific Northwest, the Northeast, and the Midwest were, as would be expected, far ahead of southern councils in their degree of integration, de facto segregation was a reality in all of the locales. Buddhist and Protestant girls usually met in separate clubs in the Pacific Northwest, for example. In the South, African American participation increased, but also through segregated clubs. The Atlanta Council reached out to the African American community, and two of its best-functioning districts quickly served five hundred African American girls. The council boasted an African American field director who had been employed with Camp Fire since 1948. Still, this outreach brought segregated groups. In 1958, the Atlanta Council operated four girls' day camps, three for white girls and one for the black members. Regional Report, Minutes of the National Council of the Camp Fire Girls, Minneapolis, Minnesota, 11–12 November 1957, 56; Roll Call of the Regions, Minutes of the National Council of the Camp Fire Girls, Denver, Colorado, 10–11 November 1958, 17, CFNH.

130. *Bookshelf* 38, no. 3 (1955): 10; "Examining the Present: Study of Teenage Program," *Bookshelf* 44, no. 3 (1961): 2; and Report on Inquiry on Racial Inclusiveness in Student YMCAs, YWCAs, and SCAs, 1957–1958, Prepared by YWCA National Board, 1958, 3, YWCA of the USA Records, box 767, folder 15, Smith.

131. Constitution quoted in Elizabeth B. Burns to Arthur Darken, August 3, 1955, Outside Organizations, International Groups, United Nations, General, 1946–1983, GSUSA.

132. Girl Scouts of the USA, *Hands around the World*, 28.

133. Barbara Gair, "What Kind of World Do You Want?" *Seventeen*, February 1945, 60–61, 138, 158. The advice in Gair's article paraphrased Hortense Powdermaker's *Probing Our Prejudices* (Boston: Houghton Mifflin, 1944).

134. Elise F. Moller, *At Home with People: Ways of Banishing Prejudice* (New York: Woman's Press, 1945), 5–7, 9, 11.

135. Ethel J. Alpenfels, *Sense and Nonsense about Race* (New York: Friendship Press, 1946). Alpenfels served on the Education Policies Commission, a joint group of the National Education Association and the American Association of School Administrators. Her speaking to the 1953 Girl Scout National Convention brought charges that the Girl Scouts harbored communist sympathizers (see chapter 6). On Alpenfels, see

Madelaine Loeb, "Education Urged to Eradicate Fear," *New York Times*, June 22, 1948, 28; "Bunche and Three Others Named Members of Policy Body of Two Education Groups," *New York Times*, October 25, 1951, 12; "Sponsors of the World Peace Conference," *New York Times*, March 24, 1949, 4; and "Girl Scouts Begin Convention Today: 8,000 Expected at Cincinnati," *New York Times*, October 18, 1953, 71.

136. Ethel J. Alpenfels, "Let's Pack Up Our Prejudices," *Camp Fire Girl* 28, no. 7 (1949): 4–5.

137. Ibid.

138. Although she is best known for her anthropological treatment of Hollywood in the 1940s, Hortense Powdermaker also studied Melanesians, Rhodesians, and Mississippians. Her books include *Probing Our Prejudices: A Unit for High School Students* (New York: Harper, 1944) and *After Freedom, A Cultural Study in the Deep South* (New York: Viking Press, 1939). Powdermaker taught at Queens College, where she became a full professor in 1954.

139. "Book on Bias Endorsed: 'Probing Our Prejudices' Gets Backing of 111 Leaders," *New York Times*, October 23, 1944, 21.

140. Powdermaker, *Probing Our Prejudices*, 47.

141. Ibid., 15, 19, 33, 45, 59–60, 62, 63. For a discussion of microaggressions, see, for example, Derald Wing Sue, *Microaggressions in Everyday Life: Race, Gender, and Sexual Orientation* (Hoboken, NJ: Wiley, 2010).

142. Powdermaker, *Probing Our Prejudices*, 48.

143. Dorothy I. Height, "World Freedom in Our Hands: What Can We Do About Freedom in Our Town?" Program Packets, Fall 1948, YWCA of the USA Records, box 353, folder 6, Smith.

144. Ibid.

145. Ibid.

146. Girl Scouts of the USA, *Girl Scout Handbook* (1947), 189.

147. Roger Daniels, *Guarding the Golden Door: American Immigration Policy and Immigrants since 1882* (New York: Hill and Wang, 2005), 98–102.

148. "New Help for Displaced Persons," *Bookshelf* 32, no. 5 (1949): 10.

149. Ibid.

150. Dorothy I. Height, "Teen-Age Citizens in Action," *Bookshelf* 33, no. 3 (1950): 5–6.

151. Cordelia Cox and Annie Kate Gilbert, "World Friendship Begins at Home," *Bookshelf* 33, no. 5 (1950): 2, 4.

152. Daniels, *Guarding the Golden Door*, 105–109.

153. L. G., Dunkirk, New York, Letters to the Editor, *Seventeen*, February 1948, 7.

154. Maryann Higbee, "More Information," *Seventeen*, May 1949, 106.

155. The 1947 Resolution quoted in "If We Are to Have Peace," *Bookshelf* 31, no. 4 (1948): 7.

156. Newsletter for Teen-Age Program Directors, February 1952, 5–6, YWCA of the USA Records, box 572, folder 4, Smith.

157. "Highlights of the Y-Teen Pilot Conference," *Bookshelf* 36, no. 2 (1952): 10, 11.

158. Onda Jane McKeever, "What YWCA Membership Means to Me," *Bookshelf* 38, no. 5 (1955): 5.

159. Cynthia Rice, "What YWCA Membership Means to Me," *Bookshelf* 38, no. 5 (1955): 5.

160. J. W., Salt Lake City, Letters to the Editor, *Seventeen*, January 1946, 8.

161. Schoener quoted in "The Past Ten Years," *Camp Fire Girl* 34, no. 1 (1955): 12. See also "Youth, Adult Cooperation Is Topic for Discussion," *Memphis World* 20, no. 92 (1952): 2, http://www.crossroadstofreedom.org/view.player?pid=rds:70124.

162. "Are Teen-Agers Responsible Citizens?"

163. Beaton, "How Important Are You?," 31, 33.

CHAPTER 2 "HELLO, WORLD, LET'S GET TOGETHER"

1. Marie Kulova to Camp Fire Girls, July 7, 1947, in "Hello, World, Let's Get Together" Scrapbook of Doris E. V. Foster, Greater Boston Council, 1948, CFEMC Records, carton 1, folder 44.

2. For a discussion of moral legitimacy as important to foreign policy, see Elizabeth Borgwardt, *A New Deal for the World: America's Vision for Human Rights* (Cambridge, MA: Harvard University Press, 2007), 297; and Elizabeth Cobbs Hoffman, *All You Need Is Love: The Peace Corps and the Spirit of the 1960s* (Cambridge, MA: Harvard University Press, 1998), 1.

3. Lucille Hein, New York, to Heihachiro Suzuki, Tokyo, October 20, 1948, CFNH.

4. Julia F. Irwin, *Making the World Safe: The American Red Cross and a Nation's Humanitarian Awakening* (New York: Oxford University Press, 2013), 170.

5. Mary Degenhardt and Judith Kirsch, *Girl Scout Collector's Guide: A History of Uniforms, Insignia, Publications, and Memorabilia*, 2nd ed. (Lubbock: Texas Tech University Press, 2005), 158, 166; Tammy M. Proctor, *Scouting for Girls: A Century of Girl Guides and Girl Scouts* (Santa Barbara, CA: Praeger, 2009), xix, 125–126, 132; Susan Goldman Rubin, *Searching for Anne Frank: Letters from Amsterdam to Iowa* (New York: Abrams, 2003), 6–11, 47; and Sara Fieldston, *Raising the World: Child Welfare in the American Century* (Cambridge, MA: Harvard University Press, 2015), 58.

6. Emily Alice Katz, "Pen Pals, Pilgrims, and Pioneers: Reform Youth and Israel, 1948–1967," *American Jewish History* 95, no. 3 (2009): 258; and Bartow H. Underhill, Enclosures from letter of January 22, 1951, HST Papers, Staff Member and Official Files: Charles W. Jackson Files, box 30, folder U, TL. See also Russell M. Jones and John H. Swanson, eds., *Dear Helen: Wartime Letters from a Londoner to Her American Pen Pal* (Columbia: University of Missouri Press, 2009). The Camp Fire Girls' prewar handbook did not mention pen pals.

7. Abbott Washburn, Brief Presentation of People-to-People Program, Prepared for June 8, 1956, Cabinet Meeting, Abbott Washburn Papers, box 18, People-to-People (6), EL.

8. San Francisco Unified School District (SFUSD), *Building for World Understanding: To Live in Peace with One Another; San Francisco Elementary Schools' Report on Planned Study in Intercultural Education*, 1945, 47, box 76, folder 1, Curriculum Reports, SFUSD Records.

9. Tara Zahra, *The Lost Children: Reconstructing Europe's Families after World War II* (Cambridge, MA: Harvard University Press, 2011), 4, 6, 19.

10. John W. Dower, *Embracing Defeat: Japan in the Wake of World War II* (W. W. Norton, 1999), 45, 48, 62, 250, 263. For a discussion of the conditions that children faced in Japan, see L. Halliday Piel, "Food Rationing and Children's Self Reliance in Japan, 1942–1952," *Journal of the History of Childhood and Youth* 5, no. 3 (2012): 393–418.

11. The commission had been established by the American Council on Education to coordinate with the state department and armed service in sending school supplies and books to Japan, Korea, Austria, and Germany following World War II. See Commission on the Occupied Areas, American Council on Education, *Occupied Areas Handbook*, 2nd and completely rev. ed., (Washington, DC: American Council on Education, 1950), 14, 52, 68.

12. Fieldston, *Raising the World*, 56.

13. Fifteen dollars in 1948 is the equivalent of almost $149.00 in 2016 (CPI Inflation Calculator, http://www.bls.gov/data/inflation_calculator.htm).

14. Alva Bernheimer Gimbel, Report on United Nations Contacts, Minutes of the Executive Board of the Camp Fire Girls, ca. 1950, CFNH; and Camp Fire Girls, Field

Department, Report, 1948, 8, CFNH. In addition, girls in Oklahoma were writing to girls in China as late as 1948 (Clipping in Beverly Barry, Camp Fire Girls Scrapbook, c. 1930s–1940s, in collection of Phyllis Raines, Tulsa, OK).

15. Gimbel, Report on United Nations Contacts.

16. Girl Scouts of the USA, *Hands around the World: International Friendship for Girl Scouts* (New York: Girl Scouts of the USA, 1949), 53.

17. For an explanation of why *Seventeen* did not match pen pals, see Letters to the Editor, *Seventeen*, September 1947, 7.

18. The desire to send CARE packages was so high before the Thanksgiving holiday that CARE could not meet the demand before the holiday. See William R. Conklin, "3,000 CARE Parcels Undelivered; Sent Abroad as Christmas Gifts," *New York Times*, April 2, 1949, 17.

19. *People-to-People News* 2, no. 3 (1958): 2, JML Records, box 44, People-to-People Partnership 1958, EL; and Annual Survey of People-to-People Activities, January 1959, 26, DDEPAP, Administrative Series, box 2, George V. Allen—USIA, EL.

20. June Hammond, "News and Statistics on 'Meet the People,'" *Camp Fire Girl* 37, no. 5 (1958): 11; and *People-to-People News* 1, no. 10 (1957): 2–3, JML Records, box 38, People-to-People Partnership 1957, EL.

21. Penny M. Von Eschen, *Satchmo Blows Up the World: Jazz Ambassadors Play the Cold War* (Cambridge, MA: Harvard University Press, 2004); and Victoria Phillips Geduld, "Dancing Diplomacy: Martha Graham and the Strange Commodity of Cold-War Cultural Exchange in Asia, 1955 and 1974," *Dance Chronicle* 33 (2010): 44–81.

22. For an example of collaboration with the Office of Wartime Information, see "Friends in Camp Fire," *Camp Fire Girl* 27, no. 7 (1948): 9. Camp Fire Girls from Staten Island in New York City sent aid to the Philippines in cooperation with the Women's Committee for Postwar Europe and the Office of Wartime Information.

23. "A Family Council Meeting Discusses World Peace," *Bookshelf* 41, no. 3 (1958): 6–7. The YWCA resisted efforts by the federal government to interfere with private programs. Its World Emergency Committee voted in 1951 to recommend dissolution of the YWCA's relationship to CARE if it acted as an agency of the government. See Foreign Division Committee Minutes and Reports, February 3, 1951, Microfilm Reel 351, Microdex 5, YWCA Records, Smith.

24. Camp Fire Girls, *Book of the Camp Fire Girls*, new ed. (New York: Camp Fire Girls, 1946), 14, 20.

25. Roy A. Gallant, "The Voice of Billy Brown," *Boys' Life*, April 1954, 23; see also *Boys' Life*, November 1945, 50.

26. For a description of the World Brotherhood of Boys, see Boy Scouts of America, *The Boy Scouts' Year Book* (New York: D. Appleton, 1917), 221–224.

27. W. Arthur McKinney, "Youth and the World: A People-to-People Program Resource Book," n.d. [c. 1958/1959], 7–8, WHCOCY Records, box 183, Youth Activities Committee, People-to-People Program, EL.

28. Girl Scouts of the USA, *Girl Scout Handbook: Intermediate Program* (New York: Girl Scouts of the USA, 1947), 430–431; and Boy Scouts of America, *Handbook for Boys*, 5th ed. (New York: Boy Scouts of America, 1948), 493–494.

29. Leah Milkman Rich, "First Steps in Friendship," *Camp Fire Girl* 27, no. 5 (1948): 1, 4.

30. American Girl Scouts could be matched to correspondents in many localities, including Australia, Austria, Baltic countries (Lithuania, Latvia), Belgium, Brazil, Canada, Ceylon, Colombia, Costa Rica, Denmark, Ecuador, Egypt, England, Finland, France, Germany, Greece, Guam, Guatemala, Haiti, Iceland, India, Italy, Luxembourg, Mexico,

Morocco, the Netherlands, New Zealand, Newfoundland, Norway, Panama, the Philippines, Puerto Rico, Scotland, South Africa, Sweden, Switzerland, Ukraine (with those in camps for displaced persons), Wales, and Yugoslavia. See Girl Scouts of the USA, *Hands around the World*, 31–32.

31. Ibid., 54–55.

32. U.S. elementary and high schools placed little emphasis on foreign language training, and although World War II and the Cold War increased federal interest in language education in order to improve national security, only 21.9 percent of high school students in 1948 studied a language other than English, and most of them were in introductory classes. Less than 10 percent of high school students took more than two years of a foreign language. The training was to equip them to read great literature, and there was little expectation that they would be able to speak or write. Not until the 1958 National Defense Education Act did any federal dollars and research flow to foreign language programs in K–12 education. By 1963, still only 32.2 percent of high school students studied a foreign language. See John L. Watzke, *Lasting Change in Foreign Language Education: A Historical Case for Change in National Policy* (Westport, CT: Praeger, 2003), 44–50; and David Patrick Barnwell, *A History of Foreign Language Testing in the United States: From Its Beginnings to the Present* (Tempe, AZ: Bilingual Press, 1996), 89.

33. Girl Scouts of the USA, *Hands around the World*, 32–34.

34. Heihachiro Suzuki, Tokyo, to Maurine Simpson, Pasadena, California, October 11, 1951, CFNH; and Heihachiro Suzuki, Tokyo, to Ruth Teichmann, October 14, 1948, CFNH.

35. Mary Alice Sanguinetti, interview with author by telephone, June 7, 2011, Seattle.

36. For more on the Japanese in the San Gabriel Valley, see Leland T. Saito, *Race and Politics: Asian Americans, Latinos, and Whites in a Los Angeles Suburb* (Urbana: University of Illinois Press, 1998).

37. Maurine Simpson, San Gabriel Valley, California, to Heihachiro Suzuki, Tokyo, October 22, 1951, CFNH.

38. Annual Survey of People-to-People Activities, January 1959, 26, DDEPAP, Administrative Series, box 2, George V. Allen—USIA, EL.

39. Clipping, "Fatherless Family in Poland Gets Rialto Camp Fire Package," February 22, 1948, in Scrapbook 1947, San Andreas.

40. See Marci Shore, *Caviar and Ashes: A Warsaw Generation's Life and Death in Marxism, 1918–1968* (New Haven, CT: Yale University Press, 2006), 259; Michael Checinski, *Poland: Communism, Nationalism, Anti-Semitism*, trans. Tadeusz Szafar (New York: Karz-Cohl, 1982), 13, 39, 41, 55; and A. Kemp-Welch, *Poland under Communism: A Cold War History* (Cambridge, UK: Cambridge University Press, 2008), 26.

41. "A few continued clandestine Guiding" before its reemergence in the 1990s with the failure of communist governments. Young Poles and Hungarians who fled could become involved in a movement for Scouts and Guides in exile. In 1950, when an agreement between the church and the Polish government allowed for the reestablishment of Catholic agencies and permitted the continuation of religious education in schools, a structure opened in which the Scouts and Guides could exist surreptitiously, although imprisonment remained a real risk. Proctor, *Scouting for Girls*, 126, 136; and Kemp-Welch, *Poland under Communism*, 47–48.

42. Ruth Teichmann, New York, to Heihachiro Suzuki, Tokyo, March 8, 1951, CFNH; and Heihachiro Suzuki, Tokyo, to Ruth Teichmann, New York, March 17, 1951, CFNH. Several U.S. newspapers printed the Japan LPF Club's call for pen pals in 1951. See, for example, "Japanese Seek Pen Pals Here," *Arizona Republic*, December 22, 1951, 4. The organization may have been connected to the Japan LPF Club, which published a tract

in English on Japanese culture. It is surprising, however, if Suzuki, a staff member of the National Diet Library in Tokyo and businessman, would not know of it. The International Pen Friends described in the letter is not the same one that was founded in 1967 in Dublin, Ireland, and operates today. See International Pen Friends, "About IPF," usa.ipfpenfriends.com/about.htm.

43. Abbott Washburn to Eisenhower, December 20, 1955, Abbott Washburn Papers, box 18, People-to-People (7), EL.

44. Annual Survey of People-to-People Activities, January 1959, 25, DDEPAP, Administrative Series, box 2, George V. Allen—USIA, EL.

45. Ibid.; and Christian A. Herter to Alden B. Hoag, January 26, 1959, Christian A. Herter Papers, box 6, [Chronological File] January 1959 (1), EL.

46. For a similar argument about Soviet children's fan mail, see Catriona Kelly, "'Thank You for the Wonderful Book': Soviet Child Readers and the Management of Children's Reading, 1950–1975," in *The Global History of Childhood Reader*, ed. Heidi Morrison (New York: Routledge, 2012), 273.

47. SFUSD, *Building for World Understanding*, 36.

48. "Bulletin of Special News—Just for Blue Birds," February 7, 1948, CFEMC Records, carton 1, folder 44.

49. Girl Scouts of the USA, *Hands around the World*, 33. When Anne Frank wrote to her Iowa pen pal in 1942, her father probably helped her with translating (Rubin, *Searching for Anne Frank*, 11).

50. Girl Scouts of the USA, *Girl Scout Handbook*, 196.

51. Ibid., 196–197.

52. Camp Fire Girls, *Book of the Camp Fire Girls*, 20.

53. Girl Scouts of the USA, *Hands around the World*, 33–34.

54. Ibid., 34.

55. The Advertising Council, Radio-TV Bulletin, May–June 1956, JML Records, U.S. Information Agency Correspondence 1956, EL; and David M. Sanders, Press Release, Letters from America Week, 1956, JML Records, U.S. Information Agency Correspondence 1956, EL.

56. William J. Lederer and Eugene Burdick, *The Ugly American* (New York: W. W. Norton, 1958).

57. Victoria Langford, "I Made Friends in Other Lands," *Seventeen*, February 1953, 137.

58. McKinney, "Youth and the World," 15–16.

59. "Are Teen-Agers Responsible Citizens?" Survey, 1954, 1–3, YWCA of the USA Records, box 575, folder 1, Smith.

60. Ann Chenall, interview with author by telephone, July 12, 2011, Olympia, WA.

61. Dorothy Maddox, Roslindale, to Doris E. V. Foster, March 10, 1948, Doris E. V. Foster Scrapbook, CFEMC Records.

62. Proctor, *Scouting for Girls*, 125–126.

63. Barb Kubik, interview with author by telephone, August 11, 2011, Vancouver, Washington.

64. "What You Can Do in People-to-People," n.d. [probably 1958], JML Records, box 44, People-to-People Partnership 1958, EL.

65. Elizabeth Frank to Lore Petzka, May 10, 1958, copies of letters in author's possession.

66. Frank to Petzka, June 27, 1958.

67. Frank to Petzka, April 3, 1958.

68. Frank to Petzka, undated letter.

69. Frank to Petzka, May 10, 1958.

70. Frank to Petzka, July 24, 1958.

71. Frank to Petzka, July 24, 1958.

72. Frank to Petzka, July 24, 1958.

73. Frank to Petzka, July 23, 1961.

74. Frank to Petzka, November 21, 1961.

75. For U.S. government concerns about the image of the United States abroad, see "Suggestions on Methods of Answering Critics of the United States Abroad," 6, Mark Bortman Papers, box 3, Department of State Course on Ideological Conflict (2), EL.

76. Elaine Tyler May, *Homeward Bound: American Families in the Cold War Era*, rev. ed. (New York: Basic Books, 1999); and Kenneth Osgood, *Total Cold War: Eisenhower's Secret Propaganda Battle at Home and Abroad* (Lawrence: University Press of Kansas, 2006). Frank to Petzka, June 27, 1958.

77. Frank to Petzka, July 24, 1958; March 17, 1959; and May 10, 1960.

78. Frank to Petzka, July 24, 1958.

79. Kubik interview.

80. Frank to Petzka, September 8, 1958.

81. Frank to Petzka, September 18, 1958.

82. Mary L. Dudziak, *Cold War Civil Rights: Race and the Image of American Democracy* (Princeton, NJ: Princeton University Press, 2000).

83. Frank to Petzka, September 18, 1958.

84. "The Lost Class of 1959," *Life*, November 3, 1959, 25. See also Rebecca de Schweinitz, *If We Could Change the World: Young People and America's Long Struggle for Racial Equality* (Chapel Hill: University of North Carolina Press), 117, 124.

85. For the theme of rescue in women's missionary work, see Jane Hunter, *The Gospel of Gentility: American Women Missionaries in Turn-of-the-Century China* (New Haven, CT: Yale University Press, 1984). See also Peggy Pascoe, *Relations of Rescue: The Search for Female Moral Authority in the American West, 1874–1939* (New York: Oxford University Press, 1990). For a discussion of how the U.S. government and population use the perceived status of women to justify military intervention and imperial expansion, see Chandra Talpade Mohanty, Minnie Bruce Pratt, and Robin L. Riley, "Introduction: Feminism and US Wars—Mapping the Ground" and Shahnaz Khan, "Afghan Women: The Limits of Colonial Rescue," in *Feminism and War: Confronting US Imperialism*, ed. Robin L. Riley, Chandra Talpade Mohanty, and Minnie Bruce Pratt (New York: Zed Books, 2008), 4, 161. See also Emily S. Rosenberg, "Rescuing Women and Children," *Journal of American History* 89, no. 2 (2002): 456–465.

86. Paul A. Kramer, "Is the World Our Campus? International Students and U.S. Global Power in the Long Twentieth Century," *Diplomatic History* 33, no. 5 (2009): 779.

87. Watzke, *Lasting Change in Foreign Language Education*, 44–50.

88. Frank to Petzka, July 22, 1961.

89. "So Many Ways to Serve," *Camp Fire Girl* 35, no. 8 (1956): 8–9.

90. Philanthropist Irving Hart, a Spanish American War veteran, stayed in the Philippines and built Boy Scout and Camp Fire clubs. The sanatorium colonies had been devastated by the war, losing an estimated four thousand of fifty-eight hundred residents through starvation and neglect during the Japanese occupation. Camp Fire Girls Department of Public Relations, "Camp Fire Girls in the Philippines," report prepared for broadcast, 1946, copy at CFNH. Irving Hart, Manila, to Miss Obrien, New York, July 22, 1945, includes his raw description of the destruction of the colonies, copy at CFNH.

91. "Philippine Children to Receive Books," *Camp Fire Girl* 24, no. 6 (1945): 4; and "So Many Ways to Serve,"8–9; and R. H. Nichols, "Home Town Stuff," *Vernon (Texas) Daily Record*,

October 24, 1954, I. Government officials disinfected letters before they left the quarantine area (Irving Hart, Manila, to Jean Tanquary, Troy, January 1, 1947, in Irving Hart Correspondence, CFNH).

92. "So Many Ways to Serve," 9.

93. "From Paris, France," Letters to the Editor, *Seventeen*, July 1952, 4.

94. Commission on the Occupied Areas, *Occupied Areas Handbook*, 67.

95. Linda Lou Harris, Scrapbook, Oklahoma City, 1947–1949, OKC.

96. Clipping in Scrapbook of the San Diego Leaders' Association, 1948–1951, San Diego.

97. *Seventeen*, April 1953, 169.

98. Girl Scouts of the USA, *Hands around the World*, 28.

99. "Duffel Bag Party," *Girl Scout Leader* 30 (February 1953): 22.

100. Doris E. V. Foster, "Hello, World, Let's Get Together," 1948 Record Book, Greater Boston Council, CFEMC Records, carton 1, folder 44.

101. Gail Oblinger, interview with author by telephone, June 8, 2011, Bakersfield, CA.

102. Frank to Petzka, June 24, 1958.

103. SFUSD, *Building for World Understanding*, 35.

104. "This Is a New Kind of Babysitting," *Seventeen*, March 1948, 200.

105. For a useful discussion of how U.S. psychological discourse asserted the primacy of family relationships in the reconstruction of postwar Europe, see Fieldston, *Raising the World*.

106. "Chère Marraine," *Seventeen*, August 1950, 208.

CHAPTER 3   "FAMOUS FOR ITS CHERRY BLOSSOMS"

1. Masako Ina, Tokyo, to friend, enclosed with Heihachiro Suzuki, Tokyo, to Lucille Hein, New York, August 31, 1948, CFNH. Ironically, "cherry blossom" was also what kamikaze aircraft were called near the end of World War II. Thanks to George Yagi for pointing this out.

2. The memories of childhood attitudes are reported in William M. Tuttle Jr., *"Daddy's Gone to War": The Second World War in the Lives of America's Children* (New York: Oxford University Press, 1993), 171–172.

3. Marjorie Young, "Miss Moto Draws a Line," *Albuquerque Journal*, August 23, 1942, 19; and Max Hastings, *Retribution: The Battle for Japan, 1944–45* (New York: Alfred A. Knopf, 2008), 35, 46. On Japanese propaganda, see also John W. Dower, *War without Mercy: Race and Power in the Pacific War* (New York: Pantheon, 1986); David Desser, "From the Opium War to the Pacific War: Japanese Propaganda Films of World War II," *Film History* 7, no. 1 (1995): 32–48; and Nancy Brcak and John R. Pavia, "Racism in Japanese and U.S. Wartime Propaganda," *Historian* 56, no. 4 (1994): 671–684.

4. For a discussion of Japan, see Naoko Shibusawa, *America's Geisha Ally: Reimagining the Japanese Enemy* (Cambridge, MA: Harvard University Press, 2006). For Germany, see Petra Goedde, *GIs and Germans: Culture, Gender, and Foreign Relations, 1945–1949* (New Haven, CT: Yale University Press, 2003). For a discussion of reconciliation and women's importance to new understandings of enemies, see Erika Kuhlman, *Reconstructing Patriarchy after the Great War: Women, Gender, and Postwar Reconciliation between Nations* (New York: Palgrave Macmillan, 2008), 2–3. For a useful discussion of how military officials viewed military wives and children as having a role in reforming Japan and Germany and as promoting a positive image of America abroad, see Donna Alvah, *Unofficial Ambassadors: American Military Families Overseas and the Cold War, 1946–1965* (New York: New York University Press, 2007).

5. Girls' efforts, though not part of an explicit State Department program, reflected its policies. The public affairs office, for example, promoted awareness of State Department policy objectives, making them available through pamphlets that went out to civic organizations such as the YWCA. See Autumn Lass, "'To Promote Knowledge and Understanding': Teaching the American Public to Support a Global Cold War, 1947–1950" (paper presented at the 2014 Society for Historians of American Foreign Relations Conference [SHAFR], Lexington, KY, 2014). In a democracy, such offices operate discursively with civic agencies to form ideologies that bring policymakers and private citizens into cooperation. Policy converges with ideology when it reflects how Americans think about their nation and its role in the world. See Michael Holm, "Ideology, Rhetoric, and U.S. Foreign Aid Since 1945" (paper presented at the 2014 SHAFR Conference, Lexington, KY, 2014). On the overlap between ideology and policy in foreign diplomacy, see Elizabeth Borgwardt, *A New Deal for the World: America's Vision for Human Rights* (Cambridge, MA: Harvard University Press, 2007).

6. Shibusawa, *America's Geisha Ally*, 7, 33. On American occupation and Japanese reactions to it, see John W. Dower, *Embracing Defeat: Japan in the Wake of World War II* (New York: W. W. Norton, 1999). For further discussion of changing racial attitudes in the United States during World War II, see Gary Gerstle, *American Crucible: Race and Nation in the Twentieth Century* (Princeton, NJ: Princeton University Press, 2001), 187–237; and Takashi Fujitani, *Race for Empire: Koreans and Japanese as Americans during World War II* (Berkeley: University of California Press, 2011).

7. Goedde, *GIs and Germans*, xx, xix.

8. Walter LaFeber, *America, Russia, and the Cold War, 1945–2006*, 10th ed. (New York: McGraw Hill, 2008); and Mary Fulbrook, *The Divided Nation: A History of Germany, 1918–1990* (New York: Oxford University Press, 1991).

9. Mire Koikari, *Pedagogy of Democracy: Feminism and the Cold War in the U.S Occupation of Japan* (Philadelphia: Temple University Press, 2008), 18–20. For a discussion of how the World YWCA exposed a U.S.-dominated international arena as well as a gendered and racialized power structure in its reconstruction and reconciliation efforts, see Karen Garner, "Global Feminism and Postwar Reconstruction: The World YWCA Visitation to Occupied Japan, 1947," *Journal of World History* 15, no. 2 (2004): 191–227.

10. Shibusawa, *America's Geisha Ally*, 45–46. Ending sexism as a rationale for intervention is discussed by Alyson M. Cole, "The Other V-Word: The Politics of Victimhood Fueling George W. Bush's War Machine," 117–130; and Jennifer L. Fluri, "'Rallying Public Opinion' and Other Misuses of Feminism," 143–158, both in *Feminism and War: Confronting US Imperialism*, ed. Robin L. Riley, Chandra Talpade Mohanty, and Minnie Bruce Pratt (London and New York: Zed Books, 2008). The way nations are framed as childlike is akin to G. Stanley Hall's recapitulation theory, which viewed children as developing through racialized stages toward civilized maturity. For further discussion of the discourse on civilization and adolescent development, see Gail Bederman, *Manliness and Civilization: A Cultural History of Gender and Race in the United States, 1880–1917* (Chicago: University of Chicago Press, 1996). For a discussion of how the notion of separate spheres was equated with evolved gender roles, see Rosalind Rosenberg, *Beyond Separate Spheres: The Intellectual Roots of Modern Feminism* (New Haven, CT: Yale University Press, 1983). Historian Emily S. Rosenberg and others explain how Americans have historically used women's status abroad to gauge a culture's degree of civilization and to legitimize U.S. interference (often coercive and violent) in others' cultural and political practices. If a nation-state (coded masculine) has acted as an oppressive force rather than as a benevolent protector of women and children, then military

action has seemed justified in rescuing women and children. See Emily S. Rosenberg, "Rescuing Women and Children," *Journal of American History* 89, no. 2 (2002): 456–465; Ian R. Tyrrell, *Woman's World/Woman's Empire: The Woman's Christian Temperance Union in International Perspective, 1800–1930* (Chapel Hill: University of North Carolina Press, 1991); Jane Hunter, *The Gospel of Gentility: American Women Missionaries in Turn-of-the-Century China* (New Haven, CT: Yale University Press, 1984); Matthew Frye Jacobson, *Barbarian Virtues: The United States Encounters Foreign Peoples at Home and Abroad, 1876–1917* (New York: Hill and Wang, 2000); and Laura Wexler, *Tender Violence: Domestic Visions in an Age of U.S. Imperialism* (Chapel Hill: University of North Carolina Press, 2000). Despite the prominence of women and children in the gendered rescue discourse, it actually obscured women's and girls' roles as social and political agents.

11. Alice Barton, "It's Not an Easy Thing," *Seventeen*, July 1945, 16.

12. Homer Carey Hockett and Arthur Meier Schlesinger, *Land of the Free: A Short History of the American People* (New York: Macmillan, 1944), 466, 539–540, 663, 689. An exception is Fremont P. Wirth, *The Development of America* (Boston: American Book, 1944), which more regularly uses terms like "Japanese militarists" to describe Japan's expansion. Wirth also draws parallels between the Monroe Doctrine and what Japan was seeking in its Pacific Empire (640–641).

13. Henry W. Bragdon and Samuel P. McCutchen, *History of a Free People* (New York: Macmillan, 1954), 622. Oren Stephens, Director of Planning, Memorandum for Albert P. Toner, November 5, 1958, White House Office, Office of the Special Assistant for National Security Affairs: Records, box 21, United States Information Agency 351–525, EL.

14. Lewis Paul Todd and Merle Curti, *The Rise of the American Nation* (New York: Harcourt, Brace, 1961), 735.

15. Everett Augspurger and Richard Aubrey McLemore, *Our Nation's Story* (Chicago: Laidlaw Brothers, 1954), 716–717.

16. Bragdon and McCutchen, *History of a Free People*, 625, 631.

17. Augspurger and McLemore, *Our Nation's Story*, explained to high school students, "Perhaps you have been asked some time to lead a group in some school club or activity. Very likely you did not want the responsibility, but took it because there was no one else to take it. In a similar way, our country has been obliged to accept a leader's role in world affairs" (707). According to Eva Moskowitz, in "Lessons in Achievement in American History High School Textbooks of the 1950s and 1970s," *Pennsylvania Magazine of History and Biography* 112, no. 2 (1988): 249–271, publishing houses tried to "explain America's greatness to students" and to appease anticommunists who might question a textbook's pro-American credentials. On U.S. textbooks of this period, see also Frances FitzGerald, *America Revised: History Schoolbooks in the Twentieth Century* (Boston: Little, Brown, 1979).

18. Bragdon and McCutchen, *History of a Free People*, 661.

19. Ibid.

20. Ibid., 662.

21. Augspurger and McLemore, *Our Nation's Story*, 759–760. Gertrude Hartman's *America: Land of Freedom* (Sacramento: California State Department of Education, 1956) emphasizes MacArthur's "firm but just" dealings with Japan, which "won admiration and respect" along with the United States' crucial role in rebuilding Japan (684–685).

22. Todd and Curti, *The Rise of the American Nation*.

23. Bragdon and McCutchen's *History of a Free People* employs gendered discourse more than do other textbooks. See especially 305.

24. Latrobe Carroll, In Step with the Times, *American Girl* 28 (June 1945): 28.

25. Natalie Grace Merritt, "I Live on Okinawa," *American Girl* 30 (November 1947): 49.

26. Lloyd Weldon, In Step with the Times, *American Girl* 29 (January 1946): 10.

27. Michiko Sato, "The Japanese Family—Yesterday and Today," *Bookshelf* 36, no. 1 (1952): 6–7.

28. "Sisters in Uniform," *American Girl* 42, (March 1959): 50–51.

29. Betty Eikel, "An American in Japan," *Seventeen*, June 1948, 38.

30. See, for example, Richards Bennett, "Give It to Them," *Boys' Life*, January 1946, 10–11, 18.

31. Boy Scouts of America, *Handbook for Boys* (New York: Boy Scouts of America, 1948), 448; and Irving Crump, "World Brotherhood," *Boys' Life*, February 1946, 7, 24.

32. Koikari, *Pedagogy of Democracy*, 23.

33. "U.S. Woman Aids Girl Scouts Here," *Nippon Times*, February 6, 1950, clipping in Heihachiro Suzuki Correspondence, CFNH; "Camp Fire People Now in Japan," Memorandum, January 1951, CFNH; and Don Typer to Ruth Teichmann, Tokyo, March 10, 1951, CFNH. See also Shibusawa, *America's Geisha Ally*, 52.

34. "U.S. Woman Aids Girl Scouts Here"; and Rieko Kage, *Civic Engagement in Postwar Japan: The Revival of a Defeated Society* (Cambridge, UK: Cambridge University Press, 2011), 28, 47. The Boy Scouts also expanded in postwar Japan, though not as fast as did the Girl Scouts (Kage, *Civic Engagement*, 27–28).

35. "How Camp Fire Was Organized in Japan," unpublished information sheet, probably 1952, CFNH; and Helen Rowe to James Donovan, Washington, DC, September 3, 1952, CFNH.

36. For a discussion of gender controversy in the Girl Scouts and Girl Guides, see Mary Aicken Rothschild, "To Scout or to Guide? The Girl Scout-Boy Scout Controversy, 1912–1941," *Frontiers: A Journal of Women's Studies* 6, no. 3 (1981): 115–121; and Tammy M. Proctor, *Scouting for Girls: A Century of Girl Guides and Girl Scouts* (Santa Barbara, CA: Praeger, 2009), 53.

37. On the "good wife and wise mother," see Kathleen S. Uno, "The Death of 'Good Wife, Wise Mother'?" in *Postwar Japan as History*, ed. Andrew Gordon (Berkeley: University of California Press, 1993), 293–322. On women's role in crafting the constitution, see Ray A. Moore and Donald L. Robinson, *Partners for Democracy: Crafting the New Japanese State under MacArthur* (Oxford: Oxford University Press, 2002), 223–238.

38. Heihachiro Suzuki, Tokyo, to Lucille Hein, New York, November 19, 1949, CFNH.

39. Martha F. Allen to Heihachiro Suzuki, Tokyo, March 9, 1950, CFNH.

40. Ruth Teichmann to Heihachiro Suzuki, Tokyo, November 21, 1951, CFNH; and Yoshiko Suzuki, Soka, Japan, to Ruth Teichmann, February 14, 1951, CFNH.

41. Mitsue Chinone, Taga-gun Ibaraki-ken, Japan, to a friend, June 10, 1948, CFNH. (The typed letter is a transcription. In it, "Mitsue" is rendered "Mitue," probably incorrectly.)

42. Kage, *Civic Engagement*, 46; Dower, *Embracing Defeat*, 398.

43. Yoshiko Suzuki, Soka, Japan, to Ruth Teichmann, November 6, 1950, CFNH.

44. Shinichiro Ishida, Kyoto, Japan, to Susan Swarts, Elkhort, IN, September 4, 1949, in collection of author.

45. Edwin P. Hoyt, *Inferno: The Fire Bombing of Japan* (Lanham, MD: Madison Books, 2000), xi. Japanese air raids against Chinese cities were similarly destructive. See Stewart Halsey Ross, *Strategic Bombing by the United States in World War II* (Jefferson, NC: McFarland, 2003), 30–31.

46. M. Y., Tokyo, Letters to the Editor, *Seventeen*, December 1950, 4.

47. Ruth Morowitz, Detroit, to Elizabeth McStea, December 18, 1950, CFNH; and Chieko Suda to Carolyn Morowitz, December 26, 1950, CFNH.

48. Morowitz, Detroit, to McStea, July 8, 1953, CFNH.

49. Goedde, *GIs and Germans*, 140.

50. Ibid., 120–121.

51. "Toys for Germany Sent by Girl Scouts," *New York Times*, December 12, 1948, 73.

52. Goedde, *GIs and Germans*, 135. Notably, separate Girl Scout and Guide programs were started in the French, British, and American occupation zones. The girls' organizations were consolidated in 1948. See Madeleine Loeb, "Girl Scouts Starting Work in Germany, but Not in Russian Zone, Session Hears," *New York Times*, July 13, 1947, 13; and "Girl Scouts Planning Program in Germany," *New York Times*, August 20, 1948, 14.

53. "Reporting—on the Reconstruction Fund," *Bookshelf* 31, no. 5 (1948): 10.

54. Goedde, *GIs and Germans*, 149.

55. Ibid.,164, 205.

56. Augspurger and McLemore, *Our Nation's Story*, 732.

57. Ibid., 710.

58. Frank Abbott Magruder, *National Governments and International Relations* (Boston: Allyn and Bacon, 1955), 615.

59. Bragdon and McCutchen, *History of a Free People*, 565.

60. Elizabeth Frank to Lore Petzka, July 24, 1958, copies of letters in author's possession.

61. Shibusawa, *America's Geisha Ally*, 92–95; and Goedde, *GIs and Germans*, 8–9. For a discussion of how German scholars interpreted Nazism as a pathological aberration in German history, see Roderick Stackelberg, *The Routledge Companion to Nazi Germany* (New York: Routledge, 2007), 29, 33.

62. Ongoing anger toward Japan is revealed in other sources. Irving Hart, who started Camp Fire clubs in the Philippines, wrote letters to Camp Fire national headquarters that were raw with emotion and pain. He was captured by Imperial Japan and held at Manila Area Civilian Camp until 1945. He recounted Japanese atrocities such as the starvation that was allowed to occur through neglect at the Hansen's Disease quarantine centers. After the war he struggled to rebuild Camp Fire clubs in the quarantine centers. See Irving Hart, Manila, to Miss O'Brien, New York, July 22, 1947, Irving Hart Correspondence, CFNH.

63. "Transatlantic Broadcast by High School Students," *Seventeen*, July 1945, 24–25, 97.

64. Dickey Meyer, "How Could They Be Like You?" *Seventeen*, July 1947, 36. The article also details the work of the United Nations Relief and Rehabilitation Administration (UNRRA) as well as U.S. and Canadian relief organizations caring for displaced persons in Germany. Dickey Meyer Chapelle's parents were pacifists of German heritage who cited Prussian draft laws in the 1840s as reason for the family's exodus (John Garofolo, *Dickey Chapelle under Fire: Photographs by the First American Female War Correspondent Killed in Action* [Madison: Wisconsin Historical Society Press, 2015], 2). For more on the movement and care of displaced persons, see Tara Zahra, *The Lost Children: Reconstructing Europe's Families after World War II* (Cambridge, MA: Harvard University Press, 2011).

65. Meyer, "How Could They Be Like You?," 76–77.

66. P. L., Yankton, SD, and E. E., Spring Lake, MI, Letters to the Editor, *Seventeen*, September 1947, 7.

67. "What Do You Think?" *Seventeen*, October 1948, 116–117.

68. "We Asked You," *Seventeen*, February 1949, 104–105.

69. Ibid.

70. Richard Elliott, "With the Underground," *Boys' Life*, August 1946, 7, 46.

71. John B. Stanley, "A Matter of Spelling," *Boys' Life*, April 1946, 8, 32; and Jim Ray, "Supermen Junior," *Boys' Life*, February 1948, 49.

72. Irving Crump, "World Brotherhood," *Boys' Life*, February 1946, 7.

CHAPTER 4 "PLAYING FOREIGN SHOPPER"

1. Girl Scouts of the USA, *Hands around the World: International Friendship for Girl Scouts* (New York: Girl Scouts of the USA, 1949), 43.

2. YWCA, Program Packets, Fall 1950, 57–59, YWCA of the USA Records, box 353, folder 10, Smith.

3. For a discussion of how American women learned about the world, asserted cosmopolitan identities, and exercised an imperialistic collection of the world's fashions and flavors during the early twentieth century, see Kristin L. Hoganson, *Consumers' Imperium: The Global Production of American Domesticity, 1865–1920* (Chapel Hill: University of North Carolina Press, 2007).

4. Lizabeth A. Cohen, *Consumers' Republic: The Politics of Mass Consumption in Postwar America* (New York: Vintage Books, 2003), 7.

5. Ibid., 8–9, 292.

6. For a discussion of the presence of girls' images in media and advertising in the United States and the Soviet Union, see Margaret Peacock, *Innocent Weapons: The Soviet and American Politics of Childhood in the Cold War* (Chapel Hill: University of North Carolina Press, 2014), 38–39.

7. Dwight Macdonald, "Profiles: A Caste, a Culture, a Market," *New Yorker*, November 22, 1958, 87. On youth-oriented consumer culture, see also Rachel Devlin, *Relative Intimacy: Fathers, Adolescent Daughters, and Postwar American Culture* (Chapel Hill: University of North Carolina Press, 2005), 82; Grace Palladino, *Teenagers: An American History* (New York: Basic Books, 1996); Susan J. Douglas, *Where the Girls Are: Growing Up Female with the Mass Media* (New York: Random House, 1994); Lisa Jacobson, *Raising Consumers: Children and the American Mass Market in the Early Twentieth Century* (New York: Columbia University Press, 2004); and Kelly Schrum, *Some Wore Bobby Sox: The Emergence of Teenage Girls' Culture, 1920–1945* (New York: Palgrave Macmillan, 2004).

8. Irwin Porges, "Your Teenager Is Big Business," *American Mercury* (July 1958): 94–96.

9. Cohen, *Consumers' Republic*, 318–320, 330–331.

10. Kelley Massoni says that family sources indicate that Valentine wanted to include African American models but because publisher Annenberg refused models of color did not appear. Kelley Massoni, *Fashioning Teenagers: A Cultural History of Seventeen Magazine* (Walnut Creek, CA: Left Coast Press, 2010), 55.

11. Elizabeth Borgwardt, *A New Deal for the World: America's Vision for Human Rights* (Cambridge, MA: Belknap Press, 2005), 119. See also John Lewis Gaddis, *The Cold War: A New History* (New York: Penguin Books, 2005), 32, 95; and Michael J. Hogan, *The Marshall Plan: America, Britain, and the Reconstruction of Western Europe, 1947–1952* (New York: Cambridge University Press, 1987).

12. Harry S. Truman, Address on Foreign Economic Policy, Delivered at Baylor University, March 6, 1947, http://trumanlibrary.org/publicpapers/viewpapers.php?pid=2193.

13. Quoted in Elizabeth A. Fones-Wolf, *Selling Free Enterprise: The Business Assault on Labor and Liberalism, 1945–60* (Urbana: University of Illinois Press, 1994), 200.

14. "*Seventeen* Looks at the World," *Seventeen*, October 1953, 55, 142.

15. "Yankee Teens in Tokyo," *Seventeen*, July 1953, 29.

16. Eleanor Hoffman, "Teen-Ager . . . Colombian Style," *American Girl* 34 (October 1951): 15.

17. YWCA, "Week of Prayer and World Fellowship," 1951, 3, YWCA of the USA Records, box 320, folder 2, Smith.

18. Such practices resemble voyeuristic or appropriative tourist activities. See Regina Scheyvens, *Tourism and Poverty* (New York: Routledge, 2011), 106–107; Rodolfo Acuña, *Anything but Mexican: Chicanos in Contemporary Los Angeles* (New York: Verso, 1995), 23–30; and Mark Wild, *Street Meeting: Multiethnic Neighborhoods in Early Twentieth-Century Los Angeles* (Berkeley: University of California Press, 2005), 59.

19. *Seventeen*, May 1953, 97, 100–105.

20. "The Eastern Princess," *Seventeen*, December 1955, 66; and "Mexico," *Seventeen*, April 1962, 105–121.

21. Ray Josephs, "Good Neighbors," *Seventeen*, February 1945, 84.

22. Irma Phorylles Torem, "Francine Is Seventeen and Lives in Paris," *Seventeen*, September 1950, 162–163, 190–193.

23. Benson and Benson, Inc., *Life with Teena: A Seventeen Magazine Survey* (New York: Triangle, 1945), 45.

24. Torem, "Francine Is Seventeen," 162–163, 190–193.

25. J. McD., Liverpool, England, Letters to the Editor, *Seventeen*, August 1952, 6.

26. "Chinese Girls Are Fighters," *Seventeen*, October 1944, 74.

27. T. S., Tokyo, Letters to the Editor, *Seventeen*, April 1950, 4.

28. YWCA, Program Packets, Fall 1949, 17, YWCA of the USA Records, box 353, folder 8, Smith.

29. YWCA, Program Packets, Fall 1948, YWCA of the USA Records, box 353, folder 6, Smith.

30. Diana Selig, *Americans All: The Cultural Gifts Movement* (Cambridge, MA: Harvard University Press, 2008), 1. Selig also writes that there was overlap with the interwar peace movement among exponents of cultural gifts. See also Hoganson, *Consumers' Imperium*, 232. Immigrants and their children created some of the interwar as well as the postwar multicultural images. The Madame Alexander line featured international dolls from Egypt, Spain, China, France, and other countries in the 1930s. During the 1960s, there was an International Dolls of the United Nations series with dolls in traditional or folk costumes. The Jewish daughter of Russian immigrants and founder, Beatrice Alexander, believed, "Dolls should contribute to a child's understanding of people, other times and other places." See Marjorie Ingall, "The Woman Behind the Dolls," *Tablet Magazine*, May 7, 2013, http://www.tabletmag.com/jewish-life-and-religion/131508/the-woman-behind-the-dolls.

31. YWCA, Program Packets, Fall 1948.

32. YWCA, Program Packets, Fall 1948. On Michigan's diversity, see Jack Glazier and Arthur W. Helweg, *Ethnicity in Michigan: Issues and People* (East Lansing: Michigan State University Press, 2001), 26–36.

33. Luther Halsey Gulick, *The Healthful Art of Dancing* (New York: Doubleday, Page, 1910), 25–26, 38–40, 133–134; Thomas Winter, "'The Healthful Art of Dancing': Luther Halsey Gulick, Gender, the Body, and the Performativity of National Identity," *Journal of American Culture* 22 (Summer 1999): 33–38; and Daniel J. Walkowitz, *City Folk: English Country Dance and the Politics of the Folk in Modern America* (New York: New York University Press, 2010), 3–4.

34. Walter Terry, "Join Hands and Dance," *Camp Fire Girl* 25, no. 10 (June 1996): 7; Walkowitz, *City Folk*, 9, 172.

35. Ibid., 153, 170–176. See also Mirjana Laušević, *Balkan Fascination: Creating an Alternative Music Culture in America* (New York: Oxford University Press, 2007).

36. W. Arthur McKinney, About Stamps, *Boys' Life*, January 1951, 45; W. Arthur McKinney, About Stamps, *Boys' Life*, April 1951, 55; "Pot 'o Gold Hobbies," *Boys' Life*, January 1947, 32; Elizabeth O. Colton, About Stamps, *Boys' Life*, May 1959, 58; and *Camp Fire Girl* 25, no. 10 (1946): 8–9.

37. In the interwar period, too, paper dolls with international costumes were said to increase goodwill. See Selig, *Americans All*, 57.

38. Girl Scouts of the USA, "Report for the National Program Committee by the 1959 Girls' Advisory Committee on International Friendship Activities," WHCOCY Records, box 166, Girl Scouts of the USA (2), EL; Girl Scouts of the USA, *Hands around the World*, 34, 47.

39. Camp Fire, San Andreas Council, Scrapbook, 1947–1948, August 10, 1948, and September 3, 1948, San Andreas.

40. Rumer Godden, *Miss Happiness and Miss Flower* (London: Macmillan Children's Books, 1961), 36. Thank you to Catherine Rymph for telling me about Godden's wonderful stories.

41. "All over the Map," *American Girl* 36 (July 1953): 41.

42. "A Seventeen Doll," *Seventeen*, September 1954, 60, 63.

43. "Your Tiny Ambassadors," *Seventeen*, January 1955, 15.

44. M. E., Berlin-Zehlendorf, Germany, *Seventeen*, February 1955, 4.

45. *People-to-People News* 2, no. 6 (1958): 3, JML Records, box 44, People-to-People Partnership 1958, EL.

46. A more famous example of corporate and UN-agency cooperation was the Pepsi sponsorship of Walt Disney's ride It's a Small World, which debuted at the 1964 World Fair as a fund-raiser and "salute" to UNICEF. Pulling together folk dance and costume with display and cosmopolitan internationalism, Walt Disney had envisioned children singing their own national anthems, but the cacophony resulted in the commissioning of the Sherman brothers' now-famous song of that same name. When the ride debuted at Disneyland in Anaheim in 1966, international dignitaries were in attendance and local folk dance groups and the International Children's Choir of Long Beach performed. Wade Sampson, "The History of 'It's a Small World,'" MousePlanet, May 7, 2008, http://www.mouseplanet.com/8343/The_History_of_its_a_small_world.

47. YWCA, Program Packets, Winter 1948, YWCA of the USA Records, box 353, folder 6, Smith.

48. Katherine J. Parkin, *Food Is Love: Food Advertising and Gender Roles in Modern America* (Philadelphia: University of Pennsylvania Press, 2006), 1, 80; and Donna R. Gabbaccia, *We Are What We Eat: Ethnic Food and the Making of Americans* (Cambridge, MA: Harvard University Press, 1998), 6–8.

49. "Festival Program Do's and Don'ts," YWCA, Program Packets, Fall 1948.

50. *Seventeen*, May 1953, 128; Camp Fire, San Andreas Council, Scrapbook, 1947–1948, "Progressive Dinner Held by Tawaci Campfire Girls," June 1948, San Andreas.

51. I. W. Klein and Nettie Stevens, "A Taste-Teasing Party," *Seventeen*, May 1950, 37.

52. Judith Miller, "Internationally Flavored," *American Girl* 32 (February 1949): 18.

53. "Chow Mein, But . . ." *Seventeen*, August 1950, 56, 68.

54. Dorothea Love, "Blueprint for Birthday Week," *Camp Fire Girl* 27, no. 6 (1948): 3.

55. M. F., no address, Letters to the Editor, *Seventeen*, December 1951, 4.

56. Eleni Kalfoglou, "Introducing a Teen-Ager of Greece," *Bookshelf* 39, no. 5 (1946): 1–2.

57. Michiko Sato, "Youth of Modern Japan," *Bookshelf* 39, no. 1 (1955): 4; Marta Erazo, "A Typical Chilean Schoolgirl," *Bookshelf* 38, no. 3 (1956): 5; Elizabeth Binaisa, "A Young Girl of Uganda," *Bookshelf* 39, no. 4 (1956): 8; and Torem, "Francine Is Seventeen," 163.

58. "Girls of India," *Seventeen*, December 1944, 117.

59. "This Is Russia," *Seventeen*, November 1944, 91. The Russians in the *Seventeen* article dance and smile. HUAC (House Un-American Activities Committee) witnesses later used happy portrayals of Russians as evidence of communist propaganda. In 1947, Ayn Rand famously criticized *Song of Russia* (1943) for its smiling peasants.

60. Padmini Sengupta, "Teen-Ager . . . Hindu Style," *American Girl* 34 (June 1951): 13.

61. Harriet Rasooli Sa'eed, "Off with the Chaddar and Veil," *Seventeen*, March 1948, 128–129, 224–225.

62. Torem, "Francine Is Seventeen," 190–191.

63. Corinne Frazier Gillett, "International Date Line," *American Girl* 34 (February 1951): 18–19, 36–37. For further discussion of women marrying before or right after college graduation, see Elaine Tyler May, *Homeward Bound: American Families in the Cold War Era* (New York: Basic Books, 2008), 81.

64. J. W., Airdrie, Scotland, Letters to the Editor, *Seventeen*, August 1950, 271; and B. D. Nymegen, Holland and M. E. Bodö, Norway, Letters to the Editor, *Seventeen*, July 1947, 4.

65. Penny for Your Thoughts, *American Girl* 34 (August 1951): 60.

66. Gillian Carlyle-Datta, London, Letters to the Editor, *Seventeen*, July 1951, 4.

67. L. S., Prague, Letters to the Editor, *Seventeen*, April 1949, 6.

68. M. M., Lahore, Pakistan, Letters to the Editor, *Seventeen*, February 1951, 4.

69. See C. J. Van W., Laren, Holland, Letters to the Editor, *Seventeen*, August 1952, 6; and H. P., Nuremburg, Germany, July 1954, 4.

70. E. W., Buffalo, NY, Letters to the Editor, *Seventeen*, August 1951, 4.

71. "Magazines for Friendship," Flier, c. 1955, C. D. Jackson Papers, box 82, People-to-People (2), EL. Magazines for Friendship was organized by Albert Croissant, a professor at Occidental College.

72. People-to-People, Review of Activities, November 1957, 10, JML Records, box 38, People-to-People Partnership 1957, EL.

73. "The People-to-People Program—What the Average American Can Do to Help Get Across the American Story Abroad," *Congressional Record*, July 24, 1958.

74. USIA, Project No. E6—Catalogues, JML Records, box 30, Overseas Propaganda (Questions of the Advertising Community's Role) 1956, EL. The government worked with advertisers throughout the Cold War. This meant getting business on board with Cold War policy. The Ad Council developed a program to convince American businesses that the Marshall Plan benefited American business, since "totalitarian infiltration . . . endangers world markets everywhere," and to persuade corporate advertisers to appeal to Europeans through overseas advertising explaining the American way of life. Quoted in Daniel L. Lykins, *From Total War to Total Diplomacy: The Advertising Council and the Construction of the Cold War Consensus* (Westport, CT: Praeger, 2003), 91. Although Lykins says business interest quickly waned when Europeans accepted the Marshall Plan (91–95), corporate leaders continued to work closely with the Eisenhower government. The Business Council for International Understanding, modeled on the Ad Council, was composed of business leaders and carried out public relations projects abroad using USIA themes. Corporate leaders also headed many of Eisenhower's People-to-People committees, answering the president's pleas that they supplement the information apparatus of the United States with their resources and expertise. See Kenneth Osgood, *Total Cold War: Eisenhower's Secret Propaganda Battle at Home and Abroad* (Lawrence: University Press of Kansas, 2006), 232–234, 237. In these collaborations, government information experts urged business and advertisers to show and not tell the significance of free enterprise. Public relations staff were wary of offending Europeans, who did not

necessarily connect political freedom with free enterprise, with the idea that Americans were trying to push their system on everyone.

75. Memorandum of Discussion at the 136th Meeting of the National Security Council, No. 566, March 11, 1953, Whitman File, EL, https://history.state.gov/historicaldocuments/frus1952-54v08/d566; and House of Representatives, Subcommittee to Study H.R. 3342, Committee on Foreign Affairs, May 20, 1947, Pre-Presidential Papers, box 145, Hearings vol. 4 (1), EL.

76. Girl Scouts of the USA, *Hands around the World*, 33–34.

77. Girl Scouts of the USA, *Girl Scout Handbook: Intermediate Program* (New York: Girl Scouts of the USA, 1953), 413. Both the first imprint and the revised fifth imprint of the 1953 new edition carried this recommendation. The fifth imprint used more careful language, however, asking girls to think about the emotional content of the ads but not directing them to consider how advertising played on fears, as the first imprint had. The change was caused by criticisms that Girl Scouts mocked "free enterprise." George W. Robnett, advertising executive and founder of the superpatriot group Church League of America, criticized the Girl Scout handbook as evincing dangerous attitudes by suggesting girls examine "free enterprise" along with stereotype and prejudice (Lucile Cannon to Gertrude Simpson, September 7, 1954, ALC, box 3, Handbook Criticism/Revision—August 1954–December 1954, GSUSA). Ross Roy, a Girl Scouts Detroit Area Council adviser, argued that the small bit getting girls to analyze the emotional appeal of advertising was evidence of "prejudice on the part of the author against advertising" (Ross Roy to Olivia Layton, September 10, 1954, ALC, box 3, Handbook Criticism/Revision—August 1954–December 1954, GSUSA).

78. Martha Shaeffer, "You Are an American Ambassador," *Seventeen*, May 1953, 94–95.

79. Ruth Teichmann, "Your Leadership Counts," *Camp Fire Girl* 30, no. 8 (1951): 1.

80. Martha F. Allen, "Imperishable Values" (address delivered to the Golden Jubilee, New York, November 1, 1960), 6–7, Transcript, CFEMC, carton 1, folder 7.

81. Landon R. Y. Storrs, *The Second Red Scare and the Unmaking of the New Deal Left* (Princeton, NJ: Princeton University Press, 2013), 10.

82. Storrs, *The Second Red Scare*, 67.

83. Ibid., 116; and Cohen, *Consumers' Republic*, 106. Storrs, *The Second Red Scare*, demonstrates that support for a liberal consumer outlook was more mainstream than previously thought before right-wing attacks devastated the movement.

84. YWCA, Program Packets, Fall 1947, YWCA of the USA Records, box 353, folder 3, Smith.

85. Dorothy T. Groeling, "Economics and Race Relations Are World Questions," in YWCA Program Packets, Winter 1947, YWCA of the USA Records, in box 353, folder 3, Smith.

86. YWCA, Program Packets, Winter 1948.

87. YWCA, "Meet the People through Material Aid," in Program Packets, Fall 1948.

88. "The Time Is Now," *Camp Fire Girl* 30, no. 5 (1951): 3.

89. Virginia Weyman, excerpt of essay in *Seventeen*, January 1953, 112.

CHAPTER 5 "WE HAND THE COMMUNISTS POWERFUL PROPAGANDA WEAPONS TO USE AGAINST US"

1. Ruth Kenny to Gertrude Campbell, January 11, 1952, ALC, box 2, Communism and Un-American Activities Correspondence, GSUSA; Rosemarie Edwards, Santa Ana, to Dorothy Stratton, New York, January 21, 1953, ALC, box 2, Criticism of the Girl Scouts, GSUSA; Mrs. T. G. Graham, Santa Ana, to Dorothy C. Stratton, New York, January 21, 1953, ALC, box 2, Communism and Un-American Activities—Publications, GSUSA;

Ruth Kenny to Leonard Lathrop, Memo on Mr. LeFevre's Article, April 19, 1954, ALC, box 3, Human Events, GSUSA; and Besse S. Kranz, Memo, May 23, 1952, ALC, box 2, Criticism File, GSUSA.

2. Alice Carney, Memo on Houston, October 1953, ALC, box 2, Criticism File, GSUSA. See, for example, Dorothy C. Stratton, New York, to Carolyn Moseley, Bay City, MI, November 6, 1953, ALC, box 1, General—1953–1954, GSUSA.

3. Martha F. Allen, "The Future of Camp Fire," *Camp Fire Girl* 30, no. 7 (1951): 1–2.

4. On grassroots conservatism and women's involvement in anticommunist networks, see June Melby Benowitz, *Challenge and Change: Right-Wing Women, Grassroots Activism, and the Baby Boom Generation* (Gainesville: University Press of Florida, 2015), 25, 178–179; Catherine E. Rymph, *Republican Women: Feminism and Conservatism from Suffrage through the Rise of the New Right* (Chapel Hill: University of North Carolina Press, 2006), 106; Helen Laville, *Cold War Women: The International Activities of American Women's Organisations* (New York: Manchester University Press, 2002), 132; Lisa McGirr, *Suburban Warriors: The Origins of the New American Right* (Princeton, NJ: Princeton University Press, 2001); and Donald T. Critchlow, *Phyllis Schlafly and Grassroots Conservatism: A Woman's Crusade* (Princeton, NJ: Princeton University Press, 2005).

5. The story of the Girl Scouts' response to charges of communist infiltration was first told by Mary Logan Rothschild, "Girl Scouting, Internationalism, and the Communist Menace" (paper presented at the Berkshire Conference on the History of Women, Claremont, CA, 2005). See also Ann Robertson, "The Girl Scout Red Scare," Girl Scout History Project, 2014, gshistory.com/2014/08/07/the-girl-scout-red-scare-part-three/; and Sara Fieldston, *Raising the World: Child Welfare in the American Century* (Cambridge, MA: Harvard University Press, 2015), 87–88. For a discussion of the YWCA accusations, see Amanda Lee Izzo, "The Commandment of Love: Liberal Christianity and Global Activism in the Young Women's Christian Association of the USA and the Maryknoll Sisters, 1907–80" (PhD diss., Yale University, 2010). For a discussion of the broad-based anticommunist sentiment in the United States, see Richard M. Fried, *Nightmare in Red: The McCarthy Era in Perspective* (New York: Oxford University Press, 1990). For a discussion of the effects of anticommunism, see Landon R. Y. Storrs, *The Second Red Scare and the Unmaking of the New Deal Left* (Princeton, NJ: Princeton University Press, 2013).

6. John Beck, "It's Your Country," *Pampa Daily News*, April 24, 1955, 16. For a discussion of anticommunist suppression of leftist educators, see Julia L. Mickenberg, *Learning from the Left: Children's' Literature, the Cold War, and Radical Politics in the United States* (New York: Oxford University Press, 2006), 125–144. See also Marjorie Murphy, *Blackboard Unions: The AFT and the NEA, 1900–1980* (Ithaca, NY: Cornell University Press, 1992), 175–208; Clarence Taylor, *Reds at the Blackboard: Communism, Civil Rights, and the New York City Teachers Union* (New York: Columbia University Press, 2013), 130–177; and Stuart J. Foster, *Red Alert! Educators Confront the Red Scare in American Public Schools, 1947–1954* (New York: Peter Lang, 2000).

7. Allen A. Zoll, *They Want Your Child!* (New York: National Council for American Education, 1949), 11–12, George H. Wilson Collection, Series 1, box 6, folder 3, Carl Albert Center, Congressional Archives, University of Oklahoma.

8. *Educational News Service* 1, no. 4 (1954), ALC, box 2, Criticism, GSUSA.

9. Storrs, *The Second Red Scare*, 219.

10. Mrs. James V. Zeder, Mrs. Anson N. Holcomb, and Mrs. Virgil T. Frantz, to Carolyn Moseley, c. May 1954, and enclosure of Frances B. Lucas, Statement on UNESCO, Book IV, ALC, box 4, Outside Organizations, GSUSA.

11. Associated Farmers of Orange County, *Bulletin* 1, no. 4 (n.d.): 1, ALC, box 2, Communism and Un-American Activities Correspondence, GSUSA.

12. T. G. Graham, Santa Ana, to Dorothy C. Stratton, New York, January 21, 1953, ALC, box 2, Criticism, GSUSA.

13. See Ruth Bloomer, "Let's Get Together and Dance," *Camp Fire Girl* 27, no. 7 (1948): 7; Dorothea Love, "Blueprint for Birthday Week," *Camp Fire Girl* 27, no. 6 (1948): 3; Elizabeth Rowe, "From the Editor," *Camp Fire Girl* 31, no. 1 (1951): 1; and "The Time Is Now," *Camp Fire Girl* 30, no. 5 (1951): 3. Girl Scouts' national office did not endorse trick or treat for UNICEF because organization policy said the Girl Scouts would not raise money for another organization, but local groups participated in the fund raising. For a discussion of how UN support brought greater legitimacy to Canadian women's organizations, in contrast to the American Girl Scout experience, see Tarah Brookfield, *Cold War Comforts: Canadian Women, Child Safety, and Global Insecurity* (Waterloo, ONT: Wilfrid Laurier University Press, 2012), 76. Karen Paget also argues that the National Student Association found anticommunist legitimacy in its early UN affiliations, though its connections to the CIA and to anticommunist liberals make it a distinct case (Karen M. Paget, *Patriotic Betrayal: The Inside Story of the CIA's Secret Campaign to Enroll American Students in the Crusade Against Communism* [New Haven, CT: Yale University Press, 2015], 57).

14. Storrs, *The Second Red Scare*, 64, 97, 98.

15. Phyllis Schlafly, "What's Happened to the C in YWCA?" 1952, 13, 14, YWCA of the U.S.A. Records, box 130, folder 5, Phyllis Schlafly and the Alton Assoc., 1951–1953, Smith.

16. Storrs, *The Second Red Scare*, 89, 105; and Mary Aickin Rothschild, "To Scout or to Guide? The Girl Scout-Boy Scout Controversy, 1912–1941," *Frontiers: A Journal of Women Studies* 6, no. 3 (1981): 115–121.

17. Camp Fire officials checked the background of foreign correspondence societies and avoided relationships with those that they could not confirm were anticommunist. Still, outsiders would not have been aware of this diligence. The Girl Scouts and the YWCA monitored their affiliations more closely after the anticommunist attacks, but I found no evidence that they did so beforehand. For an example of such scrutiny of foreign agencies, see Ruth Teichmann, New York, to Heihachiro Suzuki, Tokyo, March 9, 1951, CFNH; and Heihachiro Suzuki, Tokyo, to Ruth Teichmann, New York, March 17, 1951, CFNH.

18. Jay Mechling, *On My Honor: Boy Scouts and the Making of American Youth* (Chicago: University of Chicago Press, 2001), 43.

19. The Camp Fire Girls and the Boy Scouts of America, despite their internationalist programs, never faced scrutiny like YWCA and the Girl Scouts. Although Geoffrey Stone says the Camp Fire Girls and the Boy Scouts of America appear in the first volume of the Dies Committee hearings, this was not due to suspicions of communist affiliation (Geoffrey R. Stone, *Perilous Times: Free Speech in Wartime from the Sedition Act of 1798 to the War on Terrorism* [New York: W. W. Norton, 2004], 246). Isolated Boy Scout troops were named as being under control of the American Bund (17) and a letter on Girl Scout stationery showing interest in German folk dance was submitted to the committee to show interest in German Bund activity within the United States (35), but these groups were not named as communists. Listed among groups "whose activities increase international understanding or which support peace organizations through affiliation" were the Boy Scouts of America, Camp Fire Girls, Girl Scouts, International Friendship League, Junior Red Cross, and Pan-American Union, but they were not identified as suspect (672). The Girls' Friendly Society and the Girl Scouts, however,

were listed among organizations planning to participate in the 1938 World Youth Congress, a "red jubilee," alleged to be communist dominated (615–616). See U.S. Congress, House, *Investigation of Un-American Propaganda Activities in the United States: Hearings before a Special Committee on Un-American Activities*, vol. 1 (Washington, DC: Government Printing Office, 1938), https://archive.org/stream/investigationofu19380runit #page/n3/mode/2up.

20. Margaret Peacock, *Innocent Weapons: The Soviet and American Politics of Childhood in the Cold War* (Chapel Hill: University of North Carolina Press, 2014), 113–115.

21. Boy Scouts of America, "Constitution and By-Laws of the Boy Scouts of America" (New York: Boy Scouts of America, 1946), 8, 56. See also David I. Macleod, *Building Character in the American Boy: The Boy Scouts, YMCA, and Their Forerunners, 1870–1920* (Madison: University of Wisconsin Press, 1983), 181.

22. Eduard Vallory, "Status Quo Keeper or Social Change Promoter? The Double Side of World Scouting's Citizenship Education," in *Scouting Frontiers: Youth and the Scout Movement's First Century*, ed. Nelson R. Block and Tammy M. Proctor (Newcastle, UK: Cambridge Scholars, 2009), 207–222.

23. David I. Macleod, "Original Intent: Establishing the Creed and Control of Boy Scouting in the United States," in *Scouting Frontiers*, 16, 17.

24. *Investigation of Un-American Propaganda Activities in the United States*, vol. 1 (1938), 582, 607.

25. Ibid., 667.

26. U.S. Congress, House, *Investigation of Un-American Propaganda Activities in the United States: Hearings before a Special Committee on Un-American Activities*, vol. 15 (Washington, DC: Government Printing Office, 1943), 9215, 9574, 9750, https://archive.org/ details/investigationofu194315unit.

27. Constance M. Anderson to Mrs. A. A. Richards, Mobile, AL, October 20, 1948, YWCA of the U.S.A. Records, National Administrative Office, box 129, folder 14, General—1948–1973, Smith.

28. Elizabeth Kirkpatrick Dilling, *The Red Network: A "Who's Who" and Handbook of Radicalism for Patriots* (Kenilworth. IL: pub. by author, 1934), 250; and Communist Party quoted in YWCA National Board, "Information Regarding an Article in the Sunday School Times Entitled 'The Red Streak in the Y.W.C.A.,'" April 19, 1949, YWCA of the U.S.A. Records, National Administrative Office, box 129, folder 14, General—1948–1973, Smith.

29. Letter to Presidents of Local Association, December 27, 1934, YWCA of the U.S.A. Records, box 129, folder 13, General—1934–1947, Smith. The American Youth Congress (AYC), founded by Viola Ilma, invited a variety of organizations, from the Boy Scouts to the Young Communist League (YCL). According to the director of research for the Special Committee on Un-American Activities of the U.S. House of Representatives, J. B. Matthews, the YCL took over Ilma's program and threw her out (*Investigation of Un-American Propaganda Activities in the United States*, vol.1 [1938], 873). See also Eugene G. Schwartz and the United States National Student Association, ed., *American Students Organize: Founding the National Student Association after World War II; An Anthology and Source Book* (Westport, CT: American Council on Education/Praeger, 2006), 30. For a discussion of the YWCA affiliation, see Izzo, "The Commandment of Love," 128–129, 134–135. For a discussion of the 1930s student movement and communist and socialist participation within the two major student activist groups—the American Student Union and the AYC—see Robert Cohen, *When the Old Left Was Young: Student Radicals and America's First Mass Student Movement, 1929–1941* (New York: Oxford University Press, 1993), xvi.

30. "Summary of Principles Suggested in Discussion of Place of Communists in Our Organization," December 18, 1944, YWCA of the U.S.A. Records, box 129, folder 13, General—1934–1947, Smith. For a discussion of the purging of communist-led unions from the Congress of Industrial Organizations, see Ellen Schrecker, *Many Are the Crimes: McCarthyism in America* (Princeton, NJ: Princeton University Press, 1998), 338–340.

31. Memo from the Young Communists League of the United States of America, July 8, 1943, and Grace H. Stuff, Executive Division of Community YWCA to Grace Loucke Elliott, General Secretary of the National Board, October 13, 1943, both in YWCA of the U.S.A. Records, box 129, folder 13, General—1934–1947, Smith. Naomi Ellison, a Tacoma Association member and chair of the National YWCA Industrial Council, was elected an American Youth for Democracy (AYD) national officer. YWCA officials did not censure her but made clear she went to the convention as an individual and not a YWCA representative (Eleanor Anderson, Industrial Secretary Division of the Community YWCA, to Naomi Ellison, October 8, 1943, YWCA of the U.S.A. Records, box 129, folder 13, General—1934–1947, Smith). J. Edgar Hoover characterized the name change as an effort to disguise the Communist Party affiliation of the organization and HUAC labeled AYD a front group (U.S. Congress, House, *Investigation of Un-American Propaganda Activities in the United States: Report on American Youth for Democracy*, [Washington, DC: Government Printing Office, 1947], 17).

32. Constance M. Anderson to Mrs. Henry Rau, June 29, 1949, YWCA of the U.S.A. Records, box 130, folder 2, Williams Intelligence Summary and Queens Charges, Smith.

33. Statement by Constance M. Anderson as President of the National Board, YWCA, January 13, 1949, YWCA of the U.S.A. Records, box 129, folder 14, General—1948–1973, Smith.

34. "D.A.R. Speaker Sees YWCA and PTA as Red Dupes," YWCA of the U.S.A. Records, box 130, folder 6, YWCA, Marian M. Strack, 1947, Smith. For further discussion of women's consumer advocacy and social justice activism, see Lizabeth Cohen, *Consumers' Republic: The Politics of Mass Consumption in Postwar America* (New York: Vintage Books, 2003), 102–109; and Storrs, *The Second Red Scare*, 78–79.

35. J. Parnell Thomas, U.S. Congress, *100 Things You Should Know about Communism and Religion* (Washington, DC: Government Printing Office, 1949), 48; and "Red Infiltration Found in Religion," YWCA Clipping from *New York Times*, November 23, 1948, YWCA of the U.S.A. Records, box 129, folder 15, Newspaper Clippings, 1948–1956, Smith.

36. Grace Loucks Elliott to All National Board and Staff Members, March 17, 1948, YWCA of the U.S.A. Records, box 129, folder 14, General—1948–1973, Smith; and Howard Rushmore, "House Gets Data on YWCA Reds," YWCA Newspaper Clipping from *New York Journal American*, January 20, 1948, YWCA of the U.S.A. Records, box 129, folder 15, Newspaper Clippings, 1948–1956, Smith. The establishment of self-appointed committees by right-wing conservatives was a typical strategy of anticommunists. For details of a similar committee appointed to investigate a librarian, see Louise S. Robbins, *The Dismissal of Miss Ruth Brown: Civil Rights, Censorship, and the American Library* (Norman: University of Oklahoma Press, 2000), 56.

37. For Y-Teen membership, see Leta H. Galpin, "Conference Program Is Club Program," *Bookshelf* 33, no. 2 (1949): 2. For the international membership, see Mary French Rockefeller, "YWCA International Success Story," *National Geographic*, December 1963, 905; Rushmore, "House Gets Data"; and "Reds Charged with Using YWCA to Communize Girls," YWCA of the U.S.A. Records, box 130, folder 4, Williams Intelligence Summary and Queens Charges, Newspaper Clippings, 1947–1948, Smith.

38. "Notes on Meeting Held in Brooklyn," February 2, 1948, YWCA of the U.S.A. Records, box 130, folder 2, YWCA, Williams Intelligence Summary and Queens Charges, General—1947–1950, Smith; "Reds Trying to Propagandize Teen-Aged Girls," YWCA Newspaper Clipping from Columbus, Nebraska, *Telegram*, March 12, 1948, YWCA of the U.S.A. Records, box 130, folder 4, Williams Intelligence Summary and Queens Charges, Newspaper Clippings, 1947–1948, Smith. The *Forest Hills Post* article also noted that neither CPUSA nor the YWCA had an "official songbook" ("Local Women's Argument that YWCA Is Fed Up Leads to One Conclusion," YWCA of the U.S.A. Records, box 130, folder 2, Williams Intelligence Summary and Queens Charges, General—1947–1952, Smith). A popular YWCA songbook was *Sing Along the Way* (1940). Anticommunist critics probably referred to songbooks with folk songs, which the Socialist Party, CPUSA, and individual unions published in the 1930s to create union consciousness and solidarity. See Ronald D. Cohen, *Folk Music: The Basics* (New York: Routledge, 2012), 68. These included the *Workers Songbook* by the 1932 Composers' Collective; the *Red Song Book* by the Worker's Library in 1932; and *Songs for America*, a 1939 work from the Worker's Library, which the *New York Times* called a "communist collection" of "marching songs." See Benjamin Bierman, "Solidarity Forever: Music and the Labor Movement in the United States," in *The Routledge History of Social Protest in Popular Music*, ed. Jonathan C. Friedman (New York: Routledge, 2013), 31–43; and "To Fit the Times," *New York Times*, May 15, 1940, 23.

39. Royal Riley, "Reds Behind Skirts of YW, 3 Quitting Say," YWCA Newspaper Clipping from *New York News*, October 16, 1947, YWCA of the U.S.A. Records, box 130, folder 4, Williams Intelligence Summary and Queens Charges, Newspaper Clippings, 1947–1948, Smith. See also copy of Lucille Hunt's report of complaints, YWCA of the U.S.A. Records, box 129, folder 13, General—1934–1947, Smith.

40. See the heading "Pledge," in "History," World Federation of Democratic Youth, [1945], http://www.wfdy.org/history/.

41. The Office of Private Cooperation, USIA, "Summary Report: World Communism's Propaganda in 1956," October 31, 1956, Mark Bortman Papers, box 3, Department of State Course on Ideological Conflict (3), EL. For a detailed discussion of the controversy that surrounded the American delegates at the World Youth Conference and the affiliates to the WFDY, see Wayne Arnason and Rebecca Scott, *We Would Be One: A History of Unitarian Universalist Youth Movements* (Boston: Skinner House Books, 2005), 61–72.

42. Lempi Matthews, "Report on the World Youth Conference," March 2, 1946, YWCA of the U.S.A. Records, box 131, folder 9, World Federation for Democratic Youth, 1945–June 1946, Smith.

43. Joseph P. Kamp, *Behind the Lace Curtains of the YWCA* (New York: Constitutional Education League, 1948), 18. In Graves's defense, the YWCA national office also noted that she resigned from the WFDY in 1948 when its undemocratic and unchristian methods were clear to her (YWCA National Board, "Information Regarding an Article in the Sunday School Times"). A HUAC report on WFDY, however, had already named Graves as affiliated with the YWCA industrial council and as having been elected as a council member and vice chairman of WFDY (*Investigation of Un-American Propaganda Activities in the United States: Report on American Youth for Democracy*, 13). Right-wing anticommunists repeated such evidence, which circulated through their publications without regard for updates or changes in status of the individuals involved.

44. For the YWCA creating distance from the WFDY, see Mollie E. Sullivan to Victor Lasky, September 11, 1952, YWCA of the U.S.A. Records, box 131, folder 13, World Federation for Democratic Youth, 1950–1967, Smith. The State Department had considered providing

C-R Troop transport ships to Europe for the 1947 conference but ultimately denied the YWCA request on the grounds that only academic passengers were permitted to make use of the ships. See Marlvene Lawrence to Eric C. Bellquist, June 21, 1947, and Eric C. Bellquist, n.d., YWCA of the U.S.A. Records, box 131, folder 9, World Federation for Democratic Youth, 1950–1967, Smith. For a discussion of State Department policy, see Frank A. Ninkovich, *The Diplomacy of Ideas: U.S. Foreign Policy and Cultural Relations, 1938–1950* (Cambridge, UK: Cambridge University Press, 1981), 158. For mainstream newspapers, see "3 Officers Quit Y.W.C.A. in Queens," *New York Times*, October 16, 1947, 29.

45. "Counterattack's Ten-Point Program to Solve the Nation's No. 1 Security Problem," New York, c. 1947, YWCA of the U.S.A. Records, box 129, folder 16, Counterattack: Newsletter of Facts about Communism, 1947–1959, Smith.

46. "Notes on Meeting Held in Brooklyn," February 2, 1948; and excerpts from *Counterattack*, October 24, 1947, YWCA of the U.S.A. Records, box 129, folder 13, General—1934–1947, Smith. Regarding the Dies Committee testimony naming Terlin, she submitted an affidavit testifying that her passport showed she was out of the country and must have been fairly satisfied that she was in the clear. The accusations reappeared after the war, however. See Constance M. Anderson to Members of the National Board and Professional Staff, December 19, 1947, with enclosure, box 129, folder 14, YWCA, General—1948–1973, Smith. In 1946, Congressman George A. Dondero entered Terlin's name into the *Congressional Record* as a faculty advisor to the School of Political Action Techniques, a workshop on the science of political campaigns and organizing whose organizers on the National Citizens' Political Action Committee had ties to the Congress of Industrial Organizations Political Action Committee and were accused of communist influence. Dondero noted she had previously been incriminated for being an adviser to the AYC and to their publication, the *Champion*, and the charges began to circulate again. See George A. Dondero, "Americans, Take Notice," *Congressional Record*, June 11, 1946, 1. For facts concerning specific charges contained in *Counterattack*, October 24, 2947, see YWCA of the U.S.A. Records on Rose Terlin, box 130, folders 7, YWCA, 1939, 1946–1947, Smith.

47. Izzo, "The Commandment of Love," 141.

48. Barbara S. Giberson, Alton, IL, to Constance M. Anderson, New York, April 7, 1952, YWCA of the U.S.A. Records, box 130, folder 5, YWCA, Phyllis Schlafly and the Alton Assoc., 1951–1953, Smith.

49. On the loyalty oath, see confidential internal memoranda, November 19, 1951, in YWCA of the U.S.A. Records, box 130, folder 5, Phyllis Schlafly and the Alton Assoc., 1951–1953, Smith. For Schlafly's criticisms, see Josephine Ainsworth, Special Purpose Visit to Alton, May 11, 1953, in YWCA of the U.S.A. Records, box 130, folder 5, Phyllis Schlafly and the Alton Assoc., 1951–1953, Smith.

50. Schlafly, "What's Happened to the C in YWCA?" 12.

51. Ibid., 1.

52. *Counterattack* 6, no. 49 (1952): 2, in YWCA of the U.S.A. Records, box 129, folder 16, Counterattack: Newsletter of Facts about Communism, 1947–1959, Smith; On the YWCA China affiliation, see Kay Barrington, "Report on Red China Objective Masterpiece," October 9, 1955, YWCA newspaper clipping from St. Paul, Minnesota, *Pioneer Press*, YWCA of the U.S.A. Records, box 129, folder 15, Newspaper Clippings, 1948–1956, Smith; Grace Loucks Elliott, New York, to Harry L. Luerich, Gloversville, NY, April 1, 1948; and National Committee of the YWCA's of China, Excerpts of Letters, 1948, in YWCA of the U.S.A. Records, box 130, folder 17, Community Assoc. Eastern Region, April 1949–1958, Smith.

53. Schlafly, "What's Happened to the C in YWCA?" 3, 4.

54. Izzo, "The Commandment of Love," 143–144. In 1949, the Atlantic City YWCA severed its ties with national, citing "left-wing 'infiltration'" of the national board and staff. See Nancy Marie Robertson, *Christian Sisterhood, Race Relations, and the YWCA, 1906–1946* (Urbana: University of Illinois Press, 2007), 170–171.

55. National Board, "Policy with Respect to Communism," September 28, 1953, YWCA of the U.S.A. Records, box 129, folder 14, General—1948–1973, Smith.

56. The USIA had a list of words and phrases they would not use because officials said communists had "appropriated" them. These included exchanging experience (comparing notes), imperialism, and militarism (The Reminiscences of Theodore Streibert, the Columbia University Oral History Research Office Collection, December 10, 1970, 24). In 1948, the Advertising Council and State Department avoided *democracy* in favor of *individual liberty*, since communists used *democracy* to refer to one-party dictatorship (Advertising Council, "European Anti-Communist Campaign," 12, HST Papers, Staff Member and Office Files: Charles W. Jackson Files, box, 11, Overseas Information Meeting, April 1, 1948, TL). For the YWCA quote, see YWCA National Board, "Information Regarding an Article in the Sunday School Times," April 19, 1949, YWCA of the U.S.A. Records, box 129, folder 14, YWCA General—1948–1973, Smith.

57. Dorothy Groeling, "Citizenship Programs in Y-Teen Clubs," *Bookshelf* 37, no. 3 (1954): 9.

58. Girl Scouts of the USA, *Hands around the World: International Friendship for Girl Scouts* (New York: Girl Scouts of the USA, 1949), 12.

59. Ibid., 50–51.

60. Elizabeth Burns, Memo on Current International Developments in Our Work with the United Nations, February 19, 1954, Outside Organizations, International Groups, United Nations, General, 1946–1983, GSUSA.

61. For a statement of the multiple origins of criticism, see Mary J. Shelly to National Staff at Convention, October 1955, ALC, box 3, Handbook Criticism/Revision—August 1954–December 1954, GSUSA.

62. Quoted in Leonard Lathrop, "Developments on 'Human Events' Article Region VII," May 3, 1954, ALC, box 3, Handbook Criticism/Revision—August 1954–December 1954, GSUSA.

63. See, for example, Leamamae F. Stribling, Atlanta, to Dorothy Stratton, New York, June 18, 1954, ALC, box 4, Outside Organizations Cooperation with Girl Scouts —Correspondence—4/54–8/54, GSUSA.

64. Leonard Lathrop, "Human Events in Region VII," April 16, 1954, ALC, box 3, Human Events, GSUSA.

65. Corliss Lamont, *Freedom Is as Freedom Does: Civil Liberties Today* (New York: Horizon Press, 1956), 204.

66. Girl Scouts of the USA, Statement Concerning Allegations of Communist Affiliation, March 18, 1949, box 4, Procedures for Handling Criticism, GSUSA.

67. Elizabeth J. Mundie, Memo on Recent Accusation of Communism in 11, December 10, 1951, ALC, box 2, Communism and Un-American Activities Correspondence, GSUSA.

68. Elizabeth J. Mundie, Memo on Leader Involved with Civil Liberties Union, November 7, 1951, ALC, box 2, Communism and Un-American Activities Correspondence, GSUSA; and Elizabeth J. Mundie, Memo on Brownie Leader—Civil Liberties Union Situation in Mamaroneck, December 14, 1951, ALC, box 2, Communism and Un-American Activities Correspondence, GSUSA.

69. Alice Wagener, "Report on a Communist Situation in Seattle," June 20, 1954, ALC, box 2, Communism and Un-American Activities Correspondence, GSUSA; and Dorothy J.

Petron, "Seattle's Problems Concerning Communism," July 9, 1954, ALC, box 2, Communism and Un-American Activities Correspondence, GSUSA.

70. Alice Wagener, Memo on Investigation of Un-American Committee in Dayton, Ohio, September 17, 1954, ALC, box 2, Communism and Un-American Activities Correspondence, GSUSA; and Alice Carney to Ann New, October 28, 1952, ALC, box 2, Communism and Un-American Activities—Communist Organizations, GSUSA.

71. Alice C. Carney to Ruby Simpson, c. February 1951, ALC, box 2, Communism and Un-American Activities Correspondence, GSUSA.

72. Lenore Amerman, Memo on TASS Reporter's Daughter, December 24, 1952, ALC, box 2, Communism and Un-American Activities Correspondence, GSUSA; and American Legion, Resolution, National Convention Assembly, St. Louis, Missouri, August 31–September 3, 1953, YWCA of the U.S.A. Records, box 129, folder 14, General—1948–1973, Smith.

73. Alice Carney to Alice Wagener, March 6, 1953, ALC, box 2, Communism and Un-American Activities Correspondence, GSUSA. For a discussion of the production of *Salt of the Earth* and the protests, see Schrecker, *Many Are the Crimes*, 316, 331–336.

74. For a defense of Alpenfels, see Olivia Layton, New York, to Mrs. Irvin F. Fox, Wheeling, WV, February 2, 1954, ALC, box 1, General—1953–1954, GSUSA; and Ethel J. Alpenfels, Address at Girl Scouts of the USA National Convention, Cincinnati, Ohio, October 19, 1953, 7, ALC, box 1, General—1953–1954, GSUSA. Alpenfels's speech called for leaders to make progress toward inclusion by diversifying organization leadership and breaking down barriers between neighborhoods, races, religions, and socioeconomic groups.

75. Older girls are Senior Scouts and younger ones are Brownies, and although their guidebooks had similar material, they were never the centers of controversy. *The Blue Book of Policies* contains the Girl Scouts' official policies and values, but it was never the center of controversy, either.

76. Girl Scouts of the USA, "Facts about the Girl Scout Handbook," Distributed to Regional Directors, August 17, 1954, ALC, box 1, American Legion Attack File, GSUSA.

77. Margarite Hall, Memo on Answers to Mrs. Eldridge Smith, May 10, 1954, ALC, box 3, Handbook Criticism/Revision—April 1954–July 1954, GSUSA.

78. Robert LeFevre, "Even the Girl Scouts," *Human Events,* March 31, 1954, 2. LeFevre reported that the Fort Lauderdale Girl Scouts withdrew their invitation. The Girl Scouts claimed LeFevre backed out of the event. See Leonard Lathrop to Mrs. John Kraus, April 27, 1954, ALC, box 1, General—1953–1954, GSUSA. LeFevre was a libertarian who in addition to denouncing the United Nations "condemned the Right's statist defense posture" even though most on the right championed a strong militarized foreign policy (McGirr, *Suburban Warriors*, 174–175).

79. LeFevre, "Even the Girl Scouts," 1–4.

80. Frances Faeth to Gertrude Simpson, November 29, 1954, ALC, box 1, General—1953–1954, GSUSA.

81. Anne L. New, Memo to Dorothy C. Stratton and Virginia Blunt, June 9, 1954, ALC, box 1, General—1953–1954, GSUSA.

82. Mrs. John Kraus, Racine, to Florence Otto, May 13, 1954, and Claire S. Davidow to Mrs. John Kraus, May 25, 1954, in ALC, box 1, General—1953–1954, GSUSA. The Girl Scouts also cited the Winnetka Girl Scout Council Board of Directors for offering suggestions that were incorporated into the revised handbook. Olivia Layton to Mrs. Guilford R. Windes, June 23, 1954, ALC, box 1, General—1953–1954, GSUSA.

83. Muriel D. Lickel, Memo on Vulnerability of Girl Scout Publications and Report, July 30, 1954, ALC, box 3, Handbook Criticism/Revision—April 1954–July 1954, GSUSA.

84. World Association of Girl Guides and Girl Scouts, *Trefoil around the World: Girl Guiding and Girl Scouting in Many Lands* (London: WAGGGS, 1958).

85. Congressional Record Appendices, 1954 assorted dates, ALC, box 2, Congressional Record, GSUSA. On Lillian Gilbreth, see Jane Lancaster, *Making Time: Lillian Moller Gilbreth; A Life Beyond "Cheaper by the Dozen"* (Lebanon, NH: Northeastern University Press), 72.

86. American Legion Department of Illinois, Resolution 33, Chicago Illinois, August 1954, in ALC, box 1, American Legion Attack, GSUSA.

87. Marguerite Twohy, Memo to Dorothy C. Stratton and Mary Jo Shelly, August 11, 1954, ALC, box 1, American Legion Attack, GSUSA.

88. Girl Scouts of the USA, Summary of the Week, August 16–21, 1954, ALC, box 1, American Legion Attack, GSUSA.

89. "How Screwy Can the Legion Get?" Clipping from *Chicago Daily Sun-Times*, August 9, 1954; "Yes, Even the Girl Scouts," Clipping from *Charlotte News*, August 10, 1954; "As We See It—" Clipping from *Chicago Daily News*, August 9, 1954; and Eleanor Roosevelt, "Legionnaires Frown on Girl Scouts," Clipping from *San Francisco News*, August 12, 1954. (Clippings in ALC, box 1, American Legion Attack, GSUSA.) A 1954 Herblock cartoon, published August 11, 1954, The Herb Block Foundation.

90. Special Community Report from Mattoon, Illinois, Girl Scout Council, received September 8, 1954, ALC, box 1, American Legion Attack, GSUSA; Summary of Reports from National Branch Offices and of Headquarters Correspondence in Connection with Action of Illinois American Legion, August 9—September 3, 1954, ALC, box 1, American Legion Attack, GSUSA; and Vaal Stark to Revel Robertson, August 10, 1954, ALC, box 1, American Legion Attack, GSUSA. The heaviest correspondence came from the Great Lakes Region, which included Illinois, and from the West Coast.

91. Olivia Layton to Fellow Presidents, September 14, 1954, ALC, box 1, American Legion Attack, GSUSA.

92. Layton's press release is described in "Girl Scout Official Angrily Protests New Attack by Legion," *Washington Star*, September 3, 1954, ALC, box 1, American Legion Attack, GSUSA.

93. Girl Scouts of the USA, *Girl Scout Handbook: Intermediate Program*, 1st impression (New York: Girl Scouts of the USA, 1953, 1st imprint), 9, 10.

94. Lois Fisher, *You and the United Nations*, rev. ed. (Chicago: Children's Press, 1951). Compare to Lois Fisher, *You and the United Nations*, rev. ed. (Chicago: Children's Press, 1958). The first edition (1947) was revised in 1951 to include the Universal Declaration of Human Rights.

95. Olivia Layton to Girl Scout community, included with insert, August 9, 1954; and Girl Scouts of the USA, "Editorial Changes in the Fifth Impression of the Girl Scout Handbook," August 1954, in ALC, box 1, American Legion Attack, GSUSA.

96. Harriet D. Vernon to Mrs. Richard Beckhard, August 24, 1954, ALC, box 1, General—1953–1954, GSUSA.

97. Girl Scouts of the USA, Press Release by Olivia Layton, August 9, 1954, ALC, box 1, American Legion Attack, GSUSA.

98. Alice Wagener, Memo on Some Suggestions for Interpretation to Our Membership re Legion Attack, August 12, 1954; and "Bulletin to Board of Directors," August 8–13, 1954, in ALC, box 1, American Legion Attack, GSUSA.

99. Girl Scouts of the USA, "Editorial Changes in the Fifth Impression."

100. Ibid.

101. Ibid.

102. Ibid.

103. Lathrop, "Developments on 'Human Events' Article Region VII."

104. Girl Scouts of the USA, "Editorial Changes in the Fifth Impression."

105. Mrs. Walters, Richmond Area Girl Scout Council, to Olivia Layton, New York, September 24, 1954, ALC, box 3, Handbook Criticism/Revision—August 1954–December 1954, GSUSA.

106. Girl Scouts of the USA, *Girl Scout Handbook: Intermediate Program*, 5th impression (New York: Girl Scouts of the USA, 1954), 207.

107. Summary of Reports from National Branch Offices and of Headquarters Correspondence.

108. Janice Emory, Berkeley, CA, to Girl Scouts of [the USA], January 28, 1955, ALC, box 3, Handbook Criticism/Revision—1955, GSUSA.

109. Caroline Beatty, Claremont, CA, to National Board, Girl Scouts of the USA, October 24, 1955, ALC, box 3, Handbook Criticism/Revision—1955, GSUSA.

110. Girl Scouts of the USA, News Notes, August 16, 1954, ALC, box 1, American Legion Attack, GSUSA.

111. Mildred Llewellyn, "Girl Scout Handbook for '53 & '54," Unpublished report to Girl Scouts, 1954, ALC, box 1, American Legion Attack, GSUSA. On the CFRW's review, see Mary Howard Ellison to Eleanor B. Garfield, August 20, 1954, ALC, box 1, American Legion Attack, GSUSA.

112. Llewellyn, "Girl Scout Handbook for '53 & '54."

113. Lucile Cannon to Florence "Jo" Otto, May 17, 1954, ALC, box 1, General—1953–1954, GSUSA.

114. Mark M. Jones, "Girl Scouts, Inc.," August 5, 1954, ALC, box 2, Criticism, GSUSA.

115. Ross Roy to Olivia Layton, September 10, 1954, 2, ALC, box 3, Handbook Criticism/Revision—August 1954–December 1954, GSUSA.

116. Ross Roy to Mrs. Warren Cooksey, September 30, 1954, ALC, box 2, Criticism, GSUSA.

117. The fifth edition of the Boy Scouts of America's *Handbook for Boys* went through multiple printings between 1948 and 1959. The first through fourth printings include a drawing of the UN General Assembly (115).

118. Constance Rittenhouse to Dorothy Stratton, November 4, 1954, ALC, box 2, Criticism, GSUSA.

119. Ross Roy to Mrs. Warren Cooksey, September 30, 1954.

120. Ross Roy to Dorothy Stratton, August 10, 1954, 8, ALC, box 3, Handbook Criticism/Revision—August 1954–July 1954, GSUSA.

121. Ibid., 12.

122. Ibid., 8, 12.

123. Ross Roy to Olivia Layton, September 10, 1954, 3; Roy preferred that the Girl Scouts "explain how advertising and freedom of choice of consumers go hand in hand" (Ross Roy to Dorothy Stratton, August 10, 1954, 11).

124. Edith W. Conant, Memo on Handbook Analysis, October 1954, ALC, box 3, Handbook Criticism/Revision—August 1954–December 1954, GSUSA. See Boy Scouts of America, *Citizenship: Merit Badge Series* (New Brunswick, NJ: Boy Scouts of America, 1953), 64.

125. Conant, Handbook Analysis, October 1954.

126. Ibid.

127. Ben H. Bagdikian, "Girl Scouts in Retreat," 11–12, and Louis M. Lyons, "The New Handbook: A Close Look," in *Christian Register* (February 1955): 13, ALC, Atlantic Monthly

File, GSUSA. See full broadcast at Louis M. Lyons, from WGBH Broadcast, November 26, 1954, ALC, box 4, Radio Reports, GSUSA. See also Ben H. Bagdikian, "Retreat," *Atlantic Monthly*, May 1955, 63–64.

128. Mary B. Meyer, Memo to Gertrude Simpson, March 2, 1955, ALC, box 1, American Legion Attack, GSUSA.

129. Jane E. Romeyn, East Hartford, CT, to Girl Scouts of America, January 3, 1955, Handbook Criticism/Revision—1955, GSUSA.

130. Peggy Staples Morrow, West Barrington, RI, to Girl Scouts, January 17, 1955, ALC, box 1, General—1955–1956, GSUSA.

131. Alice C. Carney, Memo on the American Legion, April 14, 1955, ALC, box 1, American Legion Attack, GSUSA.

132. Mrs. Leicester Williams, Berkeley, CA, to Mrs. Marshall Simpson, New York, April 26, 1955, ALC, box 1, General—1955–1956, GSUSA.

133. Dorothy C. Stratton, New York, to Mrs. Joseph F. Stehlik, Philadelphia, July 26, 1956, ALC, box 1, Atlantic Monthly File, GSUSA.

134. Gertrude W. Simpson, Memo to Nora G. Springfield, May 1964, ALC, box 2, Communism and Un-American Activities Correspondence, GSUSA.

135. Maurice S. Rice, Washington, DC, to Marjorie M. Culmer, New York, September 12, 1959, ALC, box 2, Communism and Un-American Activities—Communist Organizations, GSUSA.

136. J. Edgar Hoover, *Communist Target-Youth: Communist Infiltration and Agitation Tactics* (Washington, DC: House Committee on Un-American Activities, May 12–14, 1960), 1.

137. Girl Scouts of the USA, Minutes, All Executive Staff Meeting, September 17, 1954, ALC, box 1, General—1955–1956, GSUSA.

138. Mrs. Gordon C. Hunger, Statement for "News-of-the-Day," December 28, 1954, ALC, box 3, Handbook Criticism/Revision—August 1954–December1954, GSUSA; and Olivia Layton to Ross Roy, November 9, 1954, ALC, box 1, General—1953–1954, GSUSA.

139. Dorothy C. Stratton to Mrs. Gridley Dawe, August 26, 1954, ALC, box 1, General—1953–1954, GSUSA.

140. Iris Chekenian, "People-to-People," *American Girl* 42, no. 7 (1959): 28, 49. The Camp Fire Girls and Y-Teens likewise adopted the title "Meet the People," for their international exchanges.

141. Dorothy C. Stratton, New York, to Sherman Adams, Washington, DC, November 3, 1956, Dwight D. Eisenhower, Records as President, White House Central Files, box 767, OF 325-U Youth Committee, EL.

142. Among youth leaders connected to People-to-People in its earliest stages were Arthur Schuck, chief Boy Scout executive and chair of the People-to-People Youth Activities Committee until 1959; Martha Allen, national executive director of the Camp Fire Girls and subsequent chair of the People-to-People Youth Activities Committee; 4-H leaders Guy Lee Noble, T. A. Erickson, and Norman Mindrum; Dorothy Stratton, national executive director of the Girl Scouts of the USA; and Lilace Reid Barnes, president of the Chicago YWCA and former world president of the international YWCA. See *People-to-People News* 3, no. 8 (1959): 2, JML Records, People-to-People Partnerships 1959, EL; Unnamed author, "Current Biography," October 1959, 3–4, CFNH; and "Semi-annual People-to-People Survey Shows Outstanding Progress," *Congressional Record*, August 12, 1958, White House Office, Office of the Special Assistant for National Security Affairs: Records, OCB Series (Subject), box 5, People-to-People (3) [May–August 1958], EL; Abbott Washburn, Memorandum to James C. Hagerty, May 29, 1956, Dwight D. Eisenhower, Records as President, White House Central Files, box 764,

OF 325 People-to-People Program (2), EL; and Short Course on World Ideological Conflict, People-to-People Committees and Representatives, Mark Bortman Papers, box 3, Department of State Course on Ideological Conflict (2), EL.

143. W. Arthur McKinney, "Youth and the World: A People-to-People Program Resource Book," 1960, WHCOCY Records, box 183, Youth Activities Committee, People-to-People Program, EL. Committee members who worked with McKinney included Boy Scout staffer Joseph Brunton Jr.; Gwendolyn Elsemore, national advisor for the senior Girl Scout program; Rabbi Philip Goodman of the National Jewish Welfare Board; June Hammond, national program advisor for the Camp Fire Girls; Wayne McDonald of the International Committee of the YMCA; and Walter MacPeek of the Boy Scouts. Edward Richards of the American Junior Red Cross, William C. Rogers of the Minnesota World Affairs Center, Louise S. Kjellstrom of the Girl Scouts of the USA, Joan Blair of the Camp Fire Girls, Benjamin Schmoker of the Committee on Friendly Relations among Foreign Students, Barbara Putscher of the *Crawford Chronicle*, and Rebel Robertson, Jean Bader, Donald Ross, and William Hoffmann of the Boy Scouts of America also contributed to the Resource Guide (McKinney, "Youth and the World," v).

144. McKinney, "Youth and the World," 6, 10–13, 20, 25, 37, 51.

145. Girl Scouts of the USA, International Program, 1958–1959, WHCOCY Records, box 166, Girl Scouts of the USA (2), EL. For "Say It," see also McKinney, "Youth and the World," 58; and Girl Scouts of the USA, "Report of the Triennium," October 1963, 9, WHCOCY Records, 1930–1970, box 291, Girl Scouts of the USA (2), EL.

146. Girl Scouts of the USA, "Girl Scout Roundup: A Mile High—a World Wide," 1959, WHCOCY Records, box 166, Girl Scouts of the USA (4), EL.

147. Girl Scouts of the USA, "National News Bureau Fact Sheet and Highlights," 1959, WHCOCY Records, box 166, Girl Scouts of the USA (4), EL.

148. Girl Scouts of the USA, "Evaluation Report Prepared for the 1960 White House Conference on Children and Youth," 1959, WHCOCY Records, 1930–1970, box 188, Evaluative Report Girl Scouts of the USA, EL.

149. Girl Scouts of the USA, *Around the World with Girl Scouts of the U.S.A.,* 1963–1964, WHCOCY, 1930–1970, box 291, Girl Scouts of the USA (2), EL.

150. Vaal Stark to Kathryn Kendrick, San Francisco, August 12, 1954, ALC, box 1, General—1953–1954, GSUSA.

151. Hunger, Statement for "News-of-the-Day."

152. Lyons, "The New Handbook," 13.

EPILOGUE

1. "I Belong to the Y-Teens," *Bookshelf* 33, no. 2 (1949): 9–11.

2. Ibid.

3. Elizabeth Cobbs Hoffman, *All You Need Is Love: The Peace Corps and the Spirit of the 1960s* (Cambridge, MA: Harvard University Press, 1998), 41. For a discussion of how Peace Corps volunteers on the ground came to challenge liberal international development practices to create more sophisticated understandings of third world cultures and peoples, see Fritz Fischer, *Making Them Like Us: Peace Corps Volunteers in the 1960s* (Washington, DC: Smithsonian Institution Press, 1998).

4. Fischer, *Making Them Like Us*, 91.

5. Ibid., 94, 98.

6. Camp Fire Girls, "Horizon Club Conference Afloat," *Camp Fire Girl* 46, no. 3 (1966): 7–10.

7. Tammy M. Proctor, *Scouting for Girls: A Century of Girl Guides and Girl Scouts* (Santa Barbara, CA: Praeger, 2009), 134; Girl Scouts of the USA, "World Centers," http://www .girlscouts.org/en/about-girl-scouts/global/world-centers.html.

8. Marcia Chatelain, "International Sisterhood: Cold War Girl Scouts Encounter the World," *Diplomatic History* 38, no. 2 (2014): 261–270.

9. For youth participation figures, see Edward Wynne, "Adolescent Alienation and Youth Policy," *Teachers College Record* 78, no. 1 (1976): 23–40. For Peace Corps numbers, see Hoffman, *All You Need Is Love*, 189.

10. Camp Fire Girls, *Annual Report of the Camp Fire Girls*, 1965, CFNH; Martha C. Burk, "Directions for the Future" (address delivered to the National Council Meeting of the Camp Fire Girls, Houston, November 21–22, 1975), Annual Meeting Minutes, 3, CFNH; and Ad Hoc Planning Committee of the National Board of Directors of the Camp Fire Girls, "It's a New Day," 1974, 8, CFNH. Mary Logan Rothschild, "Girl Scouts," in *Girl Culture: An Encyclopedia*, ed. Claudia A. Mitchell and Jacqueline Reid-Walsh (Westport, CT: Greenwood Press, 2008), 316. For a representative story of the demise of the Y-Teens in one locale, see Kathleen L. Endres, "History of YWCA in Summit County," 9–14, http://blogs.uakron .edu/womenshistory/files/2013/02/YWCA-of-Summit-County-History.pdf.

11. Proctor, *Scouting for Girls*, 150.

12. Ibid., 158–159, 162.

13. Camp Fire, Inc., *Adventure* (Kansas City, MO: Camp Fire, 1978), 139–140, 215; and Camp Fire, Inc., *Adventure Trails* (Kansas City, MO: Camp Fire, 1983), 129, 138.

14. Girl Scouts of the USA, *You Make the Difference: The Handbook for Cadette and Senior Girl Scouts* (New York: Girl Scouts of the USA, 1980), 46, 48–49.

15. Nicholas D. Kristof and Sheryl WuDunn, *Half the Sky: Turning Oppression into Opportunity for Women Worldwide* (New York: Vintage Books, 2010), 230–232.

16. Girl Scouts of the USA, "Global Girl Scouts," http://www.girlscouts.org/en/about-girl -scouts/global.html.

17. Michelle Acker Perez, "Things No One Tells You about Going on Short-Term Mission Trips," *Relevant*, May 9, 2016, http://www.relevantmagazine.com/reject-apathy/things -no-one-tells-you-about-going-short-term-mission-trips.

18. Andrew Root, "The Youth Ministry Mission Trip as Global Tourism: Are We OK with This?" *Dialog: A Journal of Theology* 47, no. 4 (2008): 315.

19. Joerg Rieger, "Theology and Mission between Neocolonialism and Postcolonialism," *Mission Studies: Journal of the International Association for Mission Studies* 21, no. 2 (2004): 202.

20. Pippa Biddle, "The Problem with Little White Girls (and Boys): Why I Stopped Being a Voluntourist," February 18, 2014, http://pippabiddle.com/2014/02/18/the-problem -with-little-white-girls-and-boys/.

21. For further discussion of the Cheetah Girls, see Elizabeth Marshall and Özlem Sensoy, "One World: Understanding the Discourse of Benevolent Girlhood through Critical Media Literacy," in *Adolescent Literacies and the Gendered Self: (Re)Constructing Identities through Multimodal Literary Practices*, ed. Barbara J. Guzzetti and Thomas W. Bean (New York: Routledge, 2013), 34–36.

22. Lesley J. Pruitt, who studies peace building, calls for peace-building efforts that involve adoelscents and educate children on human rights to "alter common cultural norms of managing violence" (Lesley Pruitt, *Youth Peacebuilding: Music, Gender, and Change* [Albany: State University of New York Press, 2013], xvi).

23. Girl Scouts, "Social Issues," http://www.girlscouts.org/en/faq/faq/social-issues.html. See, for example, Hannah Orenstein, "This Teen Can't Open a Bank Account Because

They Don't Identify as Male or Female," *Seventeen*, May 2, 2016, http://www.seventeen .com/life/real-girl-stories/news/a40130/this-teen-cant-open-a-bank-account-because -they-dont-have-a-gender/; Camp Fire, "History," http://campfire.org/about/history; and YWCA, Mission Statement, adopted in 2009, http://www.ywca.org/site/c.cuIRJ 7NTKrLaG/b.7515887/k.9633/Mission__Vision.htm.

24. Boy Scouts of America, Messenger of Peace Information Sheet, http://www.scouting .org/sitecore/content/Home/International/messengersofpeace/FactSheet.aspx.

INDEX

ABOUT THE AUTHOR

JENNIFER HELGREN is an associate professor of history at the University of the Pacific in Stockton, California. She is coeditor of *Girlhood: A Global History* and is the author of several articles on U.S. girlhood, among them "Native American and White Camp Fire Girls Enact Modern Girlhood, 1910–39," *American Quarterly* 66, no. 2 (2014): 333–360; and "A 'Very Innocent Time': Oral History Narratives, Nostalgia, and Girls' Safety in the 1950s and 1960s," *Oral History Review* 42, no. 1 (2015): 50–69.